FOR THE LOVE OF THE GAME...

Britain's Sporting Achilles Heel

CHRIS SHEPPARDSON

FOR THE LOVE OF THE GAME...
Britain's Sporting Achilles Heel

First Publishied in Great Britain in 2016 by DB Publishing, an imprint of JMD Media Ltd

ISBN 978-1-78091-537-1

Printed and bound in the UK by Copytech (UK) Ltd Peterborough

"The reason why Englishmen are the best husbands in the world is because they want to be faithful. A Frenchman or an Italian will wake up in the morning and wonder what girl he will meet. An Englishman wakes up and wonders what the cricket score is."

Barbara Cartland [1]

To my girls. Thank you for being mine.

They have laughed at my love of sport and wondered how I can be so emotional about what is essentially just a game. Just a game? If only it was just a game. They have giggled at my emotional outbursts, jumps for joy and cries of despair. They have been patient and tolerated me for many years and have even tried to watch matches with me to try and understand my love for sport

Thank you

In the 1800s, the Victorian Public Schools refreshed and created a strong amateur ethos for sport with the aim of teaching good character and discipline to young men. As the British Empire grew so sports spread to new countries across the globe including Australia, India, the Caribbean, South America, Africa and to North America.

However the ethos itself became a barrier to progress as the adopting nations developed their own ideology in sport, which allowed sport to evolve to a different tune from the British. For many of the "new" nations, sport was an important part of their national identity and acted as a motivator and influence in society and culture. Britain though stayed true to the old school ethos and government did not appear to recognize the real social value of sport, but British teams still competed almost against the odds.

It took many generations – until the governments of John Major and Tony Blair – to truly understand that sport sits centrally within British culture and society and has an important role to play.

Sports needs political support to flourish, but even when governments have not taken sport seriously, it has been supported by the British supporter and business for one simple reason…a real love for games. Sport has thrived in Britain, at times, in spite of the national structure. One has to wonder how so few governments have understood how important sport has been to the national wellbeing and the psychology of the nation.

One can argue that many governments were blind to the importance of sport. One only has to look at how many column inches and pages over the decades have been dedicated to sport in the national newspapers and the hours of coverage on television to understand that sport engages both readers, viewers and advertisers. It wouldn't have taken much for governments to have had a clearer perspective on the nation they led. The NHS has sat at the heart of national debate for four decades. Does one not think that health and fitness is linked to this debate, but again it has only been since the 90s that this has become more central? In the US, both Eisenhower and Kennedy recognised sports importance back in the 50s and 60s.

Sport, in many countries, has been a catalyst for social change, for the breakdown of prejudice, for gender and racial equality and for providing an opportunity for rare talent to shine. Britain invented not just a series of great sports that spread the world but also something that had far deeper and greater meaning than anyone would have envisaged at the start of the journey.

The author, John Carlin Wrote that: "Sport was a powerful mobilizer and shaper of political perceptions"[2].

Carlin was writing not about Britain but about South Africa and the importance of Mandela's relationship with Francois Pienaar and the South African Springboks. He argues that the relative smooth transition of political power from the whites to Mandela's ANC was partly down to Mandela's seduction of the South African whites by his support and relationship with the Springboks in the 1995 Rugby World Cup. Sport is one of the world's greatest influences.

Nelson Mandela noted that: "Sport has the power to change the world. It has the power to inspire, the power to unite people that little else has…It is more powerful than governments in breaking down racial barriers"[3].

This is the story of the journey from the Victorian ethos for sport to its modern day position and role. It has been a long journey with many heroes and villains along the way.

Contents

CAPTAIN PROFILES

"The Captain of England? Why, he should be blond and swashbuckling and arrogant"[4]

The captains of the sporting teams have always held a unique position within British history and folklore. The national captains are often reflective of the era in which they played and the leading values and principles of the day.

The British have always warmed to visible, clear leaders and the captains carry an unique responsibility in sport. They are seen to be almost solely responsible for the performance of the team – sometimes fairly so; sometimes less fairly so. Captaincy will not define a career, but it will determine how the captain goes down in history.

Chris Robshaw's tenure as England Rugby Captain will always be remembered for his decision in the 2015 Rugby World Cup match against Wales to go for a line-out on the Welsh try line rather than allow Owen Farrell to kick a penalty that would have potentially drawn the scores level. Bobby Moore and Martin Johnson will always hold elevated positions as the captains of World Cup winning teams. David Gower will be best known as a great batsman and a good commentator rather than for his captaincy achievements. Between each chapter, we profile selected captains. Not all have been the greatest captains but all have played important roles and represent the story of British sport's evolution.

1. Finlay Calder – Captain of Scotland the British Lions, 1989
2. David Gower – Captain of England Cricket Team, 1983–86 and 1989
3. David Beckham – England Football captain, 2001–06
4. Michael Vaughan – Captain of England Cricket Team, 2002–07
5. Bobby Moore – Captain of England Football Team, 1965–72
6. Tony Grieg and Mike Brearley – England Cricket Captains from 1975–81
7. Martin Peters – England Football Captain, 1972–74
8. Gareth Edwards – Wales Rugby Captain on 13 occasions between 1967–78
9. Gavin Hastings – Scotland Ruby captain, 1993–95 and British Lions Captain, 1993
10. Martin Johnson – England Rugby Captain, 1999–2003
11. Lawrence Dallaglio – England Rugby Captain, 1997–99 and 2004–05

INTRODUCTION

The Road to Change

Sport has played a central and important role in British culture and society for many centuries. The British have, over the years, invented many leading sports such as cricket, rugby, football, golf, as well as badminton, snooker, netball, lawn tennis (although this was adapted from the French game of real tennis), table tennis, squash, darts, rounders and even baseball. The game of cricket can be dated back to the Tudor period, as can darts with Anne Boleyn giving Henry VIII a dartboard as a gift. Football can be dated back to the 1300s, whilst the creation of badminton and snooker can be linked to British recreation in India in the 18th and 19th centuries.

It was the Victorians though that both brought organization to sport and gave it new meaning in the 1800s. They exported football, cricket and rugby to the four corners of the world.

British success in international competition was commonplace until World War Two, but since that time, it has been a harder journey. It has not always been understood as to why the journey became harder, but it was for good and fair reasons. For too long sport was almost left to its own devices whilst other countries developed a close alliance between government, funding and sport; understanding that success on the international sports fields had a major role to play, in the modern world, developing national prestige and respect. Arguably Margaret Thatcher did more than most to alienate sport with her desire for a boycott of the 1980 Olympics in Moscow; the open criticism of the rebel cricket tour to South Africa in 1982 and her advocating of National Identity Cards for football supporters. Sport moved on without adhering to Thatcher's desires. There had long been a blindness from government to understand the importance of sport. Harold Wilson understood its electoral importance, but still relatively little was put in place. He was not alone. Harold MacMillan, Ted Heath and James Callaghan created little change to policy to help sport during the 60s and 70s. It was a political generation out of step with how important sports had become on the International stage.

It was not until the Major and Blair governments that the UK finally understood that this link was important and that sport should not be left outside of the central arenas.

It seems strange to understand the thinking of both politicians and administrators over the years as there has been such a hunger for success but there was gulf in understanding, by the establishment, of what sporting success could mean to the national psyche. It always meant more than just entertainment and recreation.

There have been many false dawns, moments of failure and disappointments along the road. It has not been all bad, as there have been equally many highlights and successes but there was a decline in the ability of Britain to compete effectively at the top table from the 1950s though to the late 90s and gradually there has been a return to strength across many sports.

Throughout the highs and lows, there have been some very special players that have captured the imagination and represented the nation at International level. *For the Love of the Game* aims to provide a historical perspective on Britain's love for sport. Over the last 150 year period, Britain had been world leading in many sports and has produced some of the greatest ever players to grace games with the likes of Bobby Moore, Bobby Charlton, Harry Vardon, Nick Faldo, Gareth Edwards, Jonny Wilkinson, Kenny Dalglish, Martin Johnson, Lawrence Dallaglio, Kevin Keegan, Len Hutton, Gavin Hastings, Alastair Cook, Seb Coe, Chris Hoy, Jackie Stewart, Steve Redgrave, Matthew Pinsent, and many more. Many of these names are historical figures that may mean little to some readers but they played their own roles in building Britain's sporting legacy.

The argument during the 70s and 80s was that British players lacked the technical skills of those from other countries. The real story is that Britain had the talent but, until the late 90s, neither the funding nor professional structures to ensure the expert development of the nation's talent. Sports administration was often amateurish in approach. It is no coincidence that as sport became closer to politics so funding and structure has improved and the performance of the international sports teams has improved.

In fairness, it was never about bad intent; more about how the importance of sport was perceived. Government policy had always been to see sport as separate from culture and society until the sports-loving John Major started to change this and was followed by the Blair Government, which did embrace sport far more and understood its importance within society. Maybe it was just a result of a new generation of political leadership coming through, but there is no doubt that the Victorian ethos that sport was a recreation to teach youth character and discipline remained as a driving influence for far longer than it should have. The world moved on far faster than the British view of sport. In the Victorian era, the great national triumphs were often more military and political. After the two world wars, national prestige was often won on the sports fields.

In today's world, sport has become both a business and also a key part of the national psyche. Great sporting triumphs generate strong national celebrations and a deep sense of pride. It has just taken time for the British to adapt the mind-set from one created by the Victorian amateur players to the needs of the modern professional era. For too many years, sports administration and structure was managed by those with an interest in sport rather than it being their main focus. It is no surprise that British sport struggled to compete at the highest of international level, as sport itself was not seen to have an important enough role in society. The view could not have been more wrong.

In 2005, a BBC report noted that:

> The government is estimated to spend £2.2bn a year on sport and physical activity in England alone.
>
> But when David Moffett resigned as chief executive of Sport England in 2002 he was hugely critical of the manner in which sport in this country is organised. 'Many sports are still run in an amateurish way and there is a huge need for modernisation,' he said. 'Unless this happens, this country will never have any meaningful success.'
>
> There are currently over 500 different organisations involved in running sport in this country – with 13 in golf alone.
>
> Recent reorganisations have streamlined the unwieldy structure of sport in the United Kingdom, but doubts remain over its effectiveness and efficiency...All in all it is a tangled web which has failed to provide a streamlined system which enables sport to thrive at either the grass roots or elite level in the UK [5].

The following is a story of beliefs, passion, change and evolution. The speed of change increased as politics woke up to the importance of sport in society and this has been supported by new funding structures, television, sponsorship and the rise of new generations that has viewed sport through different eyes.

Change is today in the air. The Premiership season of 2015–16 maybe illustrates this more than anything else, as the two dominant teams have been unlikely teams with good English players in the lead led by Leicester and Tottenham Hotspur. The future looks promising with the likes of Harry Kane, Dele Alli, Eric Dier, James Vardy, Danny Rose, John Stones and Ross Barkley. The foreign players in the premiership have not been the dominant figures for the first time in many years.

The young English talent may still fall short, but they represent a new generation and new hope. It is not just in football. In Rugby there are some exceptional young players breaking through with Watson, Ford, Farrell, Itjo, Vunipola, Daley, and Launchbury. Cricket too and England's twenty-twenty team played some bold, exciting, innovative cricket. The test team possesses great young talent too in Stokes,

Butler, Bairstow, Root and Broad. There is a new generation of sports stars who are emerging that suggest that British sport may lie in good hands.

In 2013, Tim Adams wrote a feature entitled *British sport: we are the champions* (21 July):

> *It is hard to say precisely when the great shift – the national conversion from doubt to faith – occurred. As with all quasi-religious experiences it was probably a different, singular moment for each of us.*
>
> *...It was that enduring sense of amateur grit or dogged grace that made watching the British lose at sport such a formative and masochistic pleasure. Somewhere deep down, like many of us, I held on to the generally unsustainable belief that we only lost because the rest of the world, with particular reference to Eastern Europeans and Americans (and of course Australians) took it all a bit more seriously than we cared to. The games we had invented and codified were still – this sentimental theory went – not to be planned too meticulously, or coached too scientifically, or played too single-mindedly. Those Victorians and Edwardians who gave these sports to the world (lumping them in with 'pastimes', as enemies of boredom) were also in thrall to the myth of the heroically failing explorers, of Scott and Shackleton, and the idea that losing dramatically and well was always more compelling than any simple victory. That conviction proved hard to shift. Sport was the arena in which Britain proved those famous lines from Kipling's If – even if failure was the imposter that tended to turn up far more frequently than his elusive twin, success...If you were to look back for the moment when the current shift in British sporting fortunes – and collective faith – began, when the habit of winning began to catch up with that of losing, you would probably start with the first occasion I had the chance to send one of those texts in the opposite direction.*
>
> *Almost exactly a decade ago, when Jonny Wilkinson kicked his famous drop goal to win the 2003 Rugby World Cup against the Australians on their home turf, it was a vindication not only of the fly-half's nerve, but also, apparently, of the scientific approach to preparation that had got him there. Sir Clive Woodward, England coach, had been planning for that winning moment in painstaking rigorous and determinedly non-British detail for the previous six years. If Wilkinson had missed, and Australia had won, Woodward's entirely earnest and dedicated approach to 'improving not one thing by 100% but 100 things by 1%', to finally giving British sport a professional culture, would perhaps have been dismissed by sportswriters*

with a romantic hankering for the supremely gifted Welsh sides of the 1970s – for Barry John's legendary 'you just throw it OK and I'll catch it' approach – as trying too hard...Instead Wilkinson, perhaps himself the most obsessively dedicated player England has ever produced, got that kicking detail right when it mattered, and Woodward's managerial ideas, which owed as much to the boardroom as the coaching manual, appeared proven. The British swimming and cycling and rowing and athletics teams, cowed by failure in successive Olympics in the 1990s and now enthusiastically targeted by lottery funding, pursued a version of England rugby's winning approach ever more rigorously (led by Sir Dave Brailsford in the velodrome) once the London Olympics were secured; England cricket, undermined for decades by inconsistency and politics in selection, embraced a culture of centrally funded contracts that ensured the one factor that makes success most likely in team sports: continuity.[6]

It is a fascinating tale as the British, with the fifth largest economy in the world and one of the strongest education systems, have taken longer than many others to learn about the importance of structure, diet and rest in sport. There has never a lack of interest or passion in sport. Even when there were just three television channels, Saturday afternoons would be dominated by *Grandstand* (on BBC1) and *World of Sport* (on ITV) but there was a blindness to what was needed to make Britain consistently competitive on the international stage.

It is a story of change created by a new generation born outside of the influence of the world wars and old school thinking. It is a story of a natural evolution that has seen sport become increasingly part of our culture and heritage.

Chapter One

THE BRITISH STRUGGLE

Have you ever wondered why a country that invented football, cricket and rugby has struggled to be consistently successful in international competition since the end of World War Two? There have certainly been many theories put forward to those willing to listen.

Of course, no country ever has the right to be able to compete at the highest levels of international competition. Success needs to be earned but it is true that British teams have often underachieved. As Tim Allen stated in the Introduction:

"It was that enduring sense of amateur grit or dogged grace that made watching the British lose at sport such a formative and masochistic pleasure. Somewhere deep down, like many of us, I held on to the generally unsustainable belief that we only lost because the rest of the world, with particular reference to Eastern Europeans and Americans (and of course Australians) took it all a bit more seriously than we cared to. The games we had invented and codified were still – this sentimental theory went – not to be planned too meticulously, or coached too scientifically, or played too single-mindedly" (21 July 2013, *The Guardian*)[7].

There is greater truth in the above words than may initially appear. The Victorians created an ethos that sport was about building character and that one should play sport for fun and not money. Even in the late years of the Victorian era, Amateur cricketers would play alongside professionals, but the latter were seen to be of lower status. It became part of culture – love sport and competition but one did not need to take it too seriously as it was, after all, "just a game". This was certainly a prevalent view but there was a view that sport was for recreation in society rather than playing a wider and more important role. Of course, this is a great ideal but it was not in tune with real life, as sport was important to many generations and carried more meaning than just being a game. Also the Victorian ethos was soon outdated as the world changed with the world wars and sport came to play an important role in social change and breaking down barriers. It is strange that the Victorian ethos retained its importance as the world moved on – but it did and it generated a barrier to success. Sport, culture and society are close allies in modern day life and sport's evolution is representative of our social and cultural development. How this evolution has taken place in Britain is a fascinating tale of contradictions, disappointments, successes, glory and learning.

Chariots of Fire (1981) is Britain's best known sports film. At the heart of the film lies the story of prejudice and changing perceptions in society. It tells the true story of two athletes in the 1924 Olympics in Paris. At the centre of the film stands Eric Liddell, a devout Scottish Christian who runs for the glory of God, and Harold Abrahams, an English Jew who runs to prove himself. He is portrayed as an intense young man with a real talent who needs to win to feel his worth. He also retains Sam Mussabini, a professional trainer to improve his technique. This was an approach criticised by his Cambridge college masters who alleged that it was not gentlemanly conduct for an amateur to employ a professional coach. It is reflective of how life and sports were moving on, even in the 1920s, against an establishment that did not see the need for change. Abrahams understood that sport was not just a recreation but a discipline that would define as a man – hence the intensity of his emotion throughout the film and story as he felt hat that by not maximising his potential he was letting himself down and not being the best that he could be – and Abrahams stove to be the very best that he could be. Liddell was not that much different. He believed that God gave him a talent and that his talent and achievements reflected God's gift. Both strove to be the best that they could be against a backdrop that believed that sport was first and foremost a recreation for the young.

Next to Liddell and Abrahams stands the establishment and society figures Lord Andrew Lindsay, and Aubrey Montague. Lindsay is a flamboyant aristocratic figure who saves the day by giving up his place to Liddell, so he does not to have to race on a Sunday.

The film is important as it shows how sport was seen to be important for national pride, but not at the expense of a dedicated professional ethos which is "mistrusted". Abrahams and Liddell are portrayed as the intense figures out of step with the likes of Lindsay but the truth was the opposite. In the 1920's, the establishment was already out of step with the young and sport. It is the paradox that lies at the heart of the book – a desire to succeed but almost via an amateur ethos and a refusal, for many years, to change.

Looking from today's perspective, it can be hard to understand why the establishment did not seek to change with the times and a world that was changing at speed, but one has to remember that this was an age dominated by other issues – two world wars, a depression in the 30s and austerity, rationing and rebuilding after World War Two and recessions in the 70s and early 80s. There were greater problems to focus on and the thinking became almost blinkered towards sport. One can argue that it was an example of the British island mentality, but more likely sport was simply seen as a recreation and a good distraction rather than possessing real importance when placed against the ills of recession, austerity and war.

The truth was that sport had great meaning. It was just not seen as it should have been, but it was a false understanding as Britain has, for a long time had one of the largest sporting infrastructures in the world with clubs and players. Arguably, until maybe the sports loving Prime Minister John Major, there has been no relationship in Britain between sport and politics and this has been illustrative in how sports has been viewed by the establishment. Interestingly, it was Major's predecessor, Margaret Thatcher, who never saw sport as being a method for building relationships and breaking down barriers. In fact, Thatcherism and sports stood in almost opposite corners. Thatcherism was about the freeing of individuals whilst sports can often be about the community.

In 2012, Britain was inspired by the London Olympics. This was far less the case by the 1948 London Olympics. Between 1945–64, as before the war, there was no government "sport policy" as such. The Attlee administration's extension of welfare principles did not extend to the sporting arena. Ministerial backing for the 1948 Olympics was designed primarily to bolster post-war economic recovery.

One would have hoped that the 1948 Olympics would have created an impetus for change but for several years thereafter, it was left to a small number of MPs and peers, working through a newly created Parliamentary Sports Committee, to argue for the sports agenda. They spoke of the fact that Britain's sporting infrastructure remained deeply inadequate compared with other advanced industrialised nations but few in power listened.

During the 1950s and 60s, Britain's unpaid amateurs found it increasingly difficult to compete on the international stage against the likes of state-sponsored Soviet athletes. In the 1950s, one British Olympic diver living in London had to fund regular travel to Cardiff to access the nearest indoor high-board training facility.

The Conservative governments of the 1950s maintained a minimalist approach, leaving sport to run its own affairs. This stance largely prevailed despite the publication in 1960 of the influential Wolfenden Report, which called for a range of state initiatives to enhance "sport in the community". However, there was no action on the central recommendation to introduce a "Sports Development Council" as a focal point for the building of a new generation of athletic tracks and multi-purpose sport centres.

It was during the years spanning the Wilson-Heath-Callaghan administrations of 1964–79 that an initial government sport policy began to emerge. Labour's Harold Wilson was an astute politician who became aware of the importance of sport as a potential vote winner and believed that he would do his party no harm to be linked closely with sport. He was therefore supportive of providing Treasury funds to help ensure the success of the 1966 Football World Cup and he made sure that he was personally associated with the success of the English team.

Wilson was the first Prime Minister to appoint a Minister for Sport in 1964, and within months he had established a Sports Council, initially as an advisory body with the Minister as Chairman. This was, fair to say, a step forward as at least there was recognition but compared to the support being provided by other international governments to their own countries sporting structures, it was just a drop in the ocean.

Again in fairness, between 1973 and 1977 the number of facilities for indoor sport in Britain almost trebled, and there were notable advances in the construction of multi-purpose leisure centres, up from just 12 in 1971 to 449 in 1981[8].

History is of course easy in retrospect but the idea of a country as advanced as Britain only having 12 leisure centres in 1971 and even only 449 in 1981 is mildly ridiculous and it is easy to understand why sporting success on the international stage was limited. Success in sport is all about structure, access to facilities and coaching. Britain's approach was poor in comparison to other leading nations. One could argue that Britain's approach was in fact regressive and a barrier to any opportunity for consistent success. Success on the international stage lay in the hands of the talent itself to find the road forward.

With the only sporting infrastructure that existed in the 70s and 80s, Britain continued to punch above its weight and off the back of support from supporters and businesses rather through government and structural investment. If one looks at the great Lions tours of 1971 and 1974 (to victory over New Zealand and South Africa respectively) the players did so only with the blessing and support of their employers and communities. The same would have been true for those that competed in the Olympics.

The counter argument is that the 1970s was a particularly difficult economic decade for the government with the days of the three-day week (under the Heath Government), soaring inflation (under Wilson) and the humiliation of the IMF bailout (under Callaghan's government). This was all true, but it is interesting that the 1970s are a decade that many look back on with affection with good reason. It was a great sporting decade, as British sport did compete in some exciting series whether the Lions series (stated above), The Cricket Test Series of 1974, 75 and 77 against Australia and the World Cup in 70, 74 and 78. The England football team may have failed to qualify for the 74 and 78 World Cups but Scotland's did qualify for both tournaments and they were even one of the pre-tournament favourites for the Argentina World Cup.

Admittedly, Scotland's team did not perform as well as hoped in the 78 tournament but they still played one of the most exciting games of the tournament in the 3–2 win over Holland (one of the eventual finalists). The 1978 Scotland team could have been one of Britain's greatest even teams with the likes of Kenny Dalglish, and Graeme Souness, Archie Gemmill, Joe Jordan, Asa Hartford, Alan Rough, Sandy Jardine, John Robertson and Kenny Burns but the truth was that were not quite good enough at the top level. Many will say Scotland's 1967 team with the likes of Dennis Law, and the core of Celtic's Lisbon Lions (European Cup Champions in 1967) – but again the truth is that Scotland team underachieved when it had so much talent in the team. Was it the team that was the barrier to success? Or the structure, psychology or administration?

In 1974, Scotland left the West Germany hosted World Cup unbeaten having beaten Zaire and drawn 0–0 with the might of Brazil and 1–1 with the then Yugoslavia. It was a very creditable performance and the 1970s marked arguably Scotland's finest international era in football, although some will argue that the 60s team was better.

The 1970s was also the decade of Abba winning the 74 Eurovision Song Contest, *Grease* and *Star Wars*. *Grease* and *Star Wars* dominated at the box office so the recessions still clearly allowed for people to enjoy entertainment. Abba may have led the "pop" era but they were not alone. This was the era of the Bee Gees, Rolling Stones, Rod Stewart, David Bowie, Queen, Wings, Donna Summer, Billy Joel, Stevie Wonder, The Bay City Rollers, the Osmonds, the Jackson Five, Neil Diamond and Carly Simon. Pop was in a golden era and record sales were at record high levels.

The underlying point is that the UK may have been suffering economically,but spend was high on sport, film and music. There was love for the creatives and mavericks in all areas as they were a step apart from the establishment and daily economics – so in sport, football saw a new breed of hero step forward in the likes of George Best (Manchester United), Charlie George (Arsenal), Frank Worthington (Leicester), Alan Hudson (Chelsea and Stoke), Kevin Keegan (Liverpool), Tony Currie (Sheffield United), Stan Bowles (QPR), Rodney Marsh (Manchester City) and Martin Chivers (Spurs). They too were out of step with the old establishment ways and represented brave new possibilities. They were flair players seeking to be creative rather than be restrained by a system. However, the 70s were known as a cynical age too and the counter to these players were the no nonsense, tough tackling defenders of the age such as Ron "Chopper" Harris (Chelsea), Tommy Smith (Liverpool), Larry Lloyd (Liverpool and Nottingham Forest), Peter Storey (Arsenal), Frank McLintock (Arsenal), Willie Young (Spurs and Arsenal) and

Norman Hunter (Leeds United) and each week these two sets did battle together. It was almost like a battle between the old school versus the new school on the fields of play.

Britain's performance in the Munich Olympics was average (four gold medals) and the Montreal Olympics of 76 (three gold medals) were a disappointment certainly for athletics – however British sport was still working to compete almost against the odds. Maybe Government, in the 1970s, had begun to realise that sport was not just a minor cultural and social issue, but could be of real importance but there still a long road to travel.

If it was hoped that Thatcherism would create an impetus for improvement then this was a false hope. Thatcher's period of time was often controversial and in fairness, her politics changed much for the better in Britain, but sadly not in sports. Early on in her first term was the 1980 Olympic boycott in support of the USA in the Cold War hostilities after the Soviet Union invaded Afghanistan. Her Government sought for the Olympic team to boycott the games, but the British Olympic Committee voted to go citing that: "We believe that sport should be a bridge and not a destroyer"[9].

It was always a slightly difficult argument for the government to make as Britain has always stated that sport stood beyond the political arena, so it was hard to change position and bring influence. However, this did not deter Thatcher involving herself in sports. In 1982, she criticised the rebel South African tour for political reasons, and the organiser Geoffrey Boycott was banned for three years as a result. In football, she was an open advocate for a football identity membership scheme in 1989 and throughout the 1980s there was a belief that British sports was simply not supported by government. The friction heightened with the human loss stories of Heysel and Hillsborough where many felt that the government did not do enough to be of support.

It was John Major who brought a softer approach with his visual and clear love for cricket. It was Major's government that saw the introduction of the lottery that began the process of real change. Tony Blair's Labour Government, elected in 1997, was far more enlightened and they seemed to really understand the importance of sport in a strong society.

In 1995, Blair had indicated his support for sport when he had famously played head tennis with the then successful manager of Newcastle United Kevin Keegan – at the time Keegan's Newcastle was perceived as the most exciting team in the Premiership and everyone's second favourite team. An interest in sport was a populist venture and was all part of his "Cool Britannia" approach. At the time,

Blair's new government brought fresh hope for real change. Blair is today an often disliked figure but his support for sport did create a lasting legacy and one which has given the platform for change in sports.

The Major and Blair's governments did mark – after 1993 – both the start of a long period of prosperity for the UK and also a move towards an often kinder society that also enjoyed an improved way of life. There is little doubt that the modern generations – even taking into account of the problems of the financial crisis of 2008/9–13 – enjoy a far better quality of life than those that lived in the 60s and 70s who in turn felt that their quality of life was far better than in the 40s and 50s. As the quality of life has improved so it is natural that an interest in health has developed and with this, sport has taken on a new central position in society.

If there is an example of Blair's genuine commitment to sport, it lies not just with his support in 2003 for the Olympic bid, but his long term involvement in sports-based charities such as a foundation for north-east English sport launched in 2007 and Beyond Sport which supports international development through sport. Blair believed in the power of sport, an idea that is easy to be cynical about, but there are many examples where sport has helped people from all walks of life improve their circumstances.

It was John Major and Tony Blair that allowed sport to become politically important and supported arguments for resources in return for clear benefits. The expertise that has been developed and the subsequent successes have been remarkable.

So much has changed and one can make an argument that more has changed in the last twenty years, since Blair's Government came to power, than in the previous one hundred and fifty years. This can be illustrated by the change in performance levels in the Olympics from the low of Atlanta in 1996 to consistently high performances at Sydney in 2000, Beijing 2008 and London 2012 and in how much more competitive GB is in international sports across many disciplines. One gold medal was won in Atlanta. Nine were won in Sydney, nineteen in Beijing and twenty-nine in London. Over sixteen years, this marks a real change in expectation and performance.

Since the Post War era, the British sporting culture has quietly, even reluctantly, been forced to evolve from an almost amateur ethos to a level of high professionalism that operates within the leading clubs today. In recent years, sport has become increasingly central to everyday life and also big business in its own right as major brands such as Nike, and Adidas have become household names and brands. Commercialism in sport sits centrally for all activities from local sponsorship deals of village and town football clubs to Virgin Money's sponsorship of the London

Marathon, RBS's of the Six Nations or Barclays of Football's Premiership. Each week one can easily witness both the relationship between players and supporters in stadia across the country and also the increased commercialism and wealth in sport. They are such strange bedfellows; the directors of clubs across the land trying to ensure that their stadiums and clubs are commercially viable, paying high wages to their star players and courting sponsors whilst the average fan looks forward to attending matches so that they can "let go", relax and be part of the tribe that follows the team. Often these bedfellows will be at odds but sometimes they are one in moments of joy and despair – the moments that build histories.

The momentum for change has been supported by a social revolution, which has seen personal fitness grow in importance with each passing decade. As of the 2016, London Marathon one person in every 100 has run the Marathon. Over one million runners have passed the finish line since its founding in 1981.

Amateur sport in this country is impressively large but sport is, in today's world, a business and no longer just a recreation and of course the pressures of both will create challenges, tensions and change.

In past eras, sport used to be a recreation and a simple source of entertainment. In 2016, it is a far more than just a pastime. 7.7m people in the UK play sports more than three times per week and this has grown by 17% in the last decade. 9.5m people are involved in sports clubs in the UK and six million play competitive sport. In terms of sports at amateur level, it is important to understand that the traditional perception of football dominating the English sports scene is not as clear as many would predict. In fact, football, cricket and rugby – the three leading national sports are not as dominant as one may initially suspect. 1.8m play football and this actually lags behind other sporting activities. The leading sports in terms of participation are swimming, at 2.5m, athletics at 2.3m and cycling at 2m.

One of the great features of life in Britain is the breadth of sporting activity as this list can go on with 431,000 playing Badminton; 163,000 play Basketball. 114,000 – Boxing; 180,000 – Cricket; 36,000 – Canoeing; 88,000 – Hockey; 192,000 – Rugby Union; 49,000 – Rugby League; 39,000 – Rowing; 54,000 – Netball; 445,000 –Tennis 14,000 – Judo; 93,000 Table Tennis; 212,000 Squash; 85,000 mountaineering; 12,000 fencing and 51,000 Gymnastics. The list can go on[10].

Given the above, one could argue that cricket and rugby punch above their weight on the international stage whilst swimming, athletics and tennis may underachieve. In the UK, there are 1,477 registered clubs in Athletics, 1,800 registered clubs in Cycling and 1,151 registered clubs in Swimming. These three key groups alone represent a market of nearly 4,500 clubs[11].

A *Telegraph* article (23 June 2015) – "UK triathlons set investors' pulses racing" by Professor Gregg Whyte – noted:

> British Triathlon says that the number of people who are participating in UK triathlon events has risen from 120,000 in 2009 to 196,000 last year, at more than 850 registered events. The sport now has TV coverage in 160 countries with an estimated global viewer audience of 207 million and serious prize money available. The Abu Dhabi triathlon is worth $230,000 (about £151,000) to the winner.
>
> The growth opportunity has been spotted by Dalian Wanda, the property company that is controlled by China's richest man, Wang Jianlin. It recently paid $650m for World Triathlon Corporation, the owner of Ironman, which organises more than 200 races a year from Tenby to Buenos Aires and this year expects revenues of more than $180m.
>
> Triathlon's growing appeal is a global trend being led by the US, where the Triathlon Industry Association (TIA) says participation in the sport is growing by 20pc a year.
>
> At the sport's elite level, International Triathlon Union events now take place in an increasing number of cities, in a similar model to Formula One racing. Former F1 world champion Jenson Button competes in triathlons when he can fit them around his race schedule. And while the wealth on show is not the same as in motorsport's top tier, amateur triathlon has an appeal skewed towards affluent demographic groups. In the UK, a TIA survey in 2013 reported an average salary of £45,000 and a household size of 2.6 people. British respondents averaged 40 years of age, with 83pc having completed a degree or college education
>
> The London triathlon in August – the world's largest event with 13,000 entrants – attracted sponsors and partners such as AJ Bell, the stockbroker, and the Bose audio products group. The Chicago triathlon has 20 sponsors, including Panasonic, while last month's Los Angeles triathlon was backed by sports nutrition group Herbalife.
>
> Panasonic is the headline sponsor of next year's New York Triathlon, and says its global sporting partnership programme is based on events and activities that resonate with its philosophy of "contributing to society by providing cutting edge technology"[12].

The natural thought to occur is whether Britain is not as successful in its three lead national sports on a consistent basis for the simple reason that the country's talent is clearly divided between so many sports. Would this be the case in another country or would talent development in sports have a more focused approach on key disciplines?

Should sport be about the easy enjoyment of the pleasures it brings or should be played to a greater goal? The following tale explores this as the British arguably do tend to play sport for more than the importance that success in play can bring to Britain's standing in the world, whilst other nations do see their sporting teams and national identities as being closely aligned. Where does sport stop just being a sport and become more than a game?

The following story is one of a real love affair between the British and sport – any sport. The British love sports genius and have always struggled with those that take it too seriously. The result has been that cultural and social pressures have made the road to professionalism a long path and at times one that has seen the international teams create their own barriers to success. So many of the disappointments and failures have been self-inflicted and misunderstood; a natural consequence of the evolution in thinking about sports within our society.

The Struggle for Consistency

The teams may have struggled on the international stage but sport, itself, has always been king. The country is fortunate to play host to some of the world's greatest sporting contests from the Six Nations to British Golf's Open Championship; from the Premier League to Test Match Cricket to Wimbledon; The Cambridge and Oxford Boat Race to Royal Ascot, Aintree, and Henley Regatta. There is a very special love affair that exists between the British and sports.

It is just that when one of the home nations has become world leading in its discipline, the decline from the pinnacle has been swift. It is as though the country just do not know how to play as champions.

Consider England's football team that won the World Cup in 1966, only to go into a gradual decline after 1968 and not even qualify for the World Cup Finals from 1970 until 1982. English Cricket became the Number one ranked team in 2011, only to again lose its position in 2012 and be thrashed 5–0 in the Ashes series of 2014. The England Rugby Team won the World Cup 2003 and yet by 2006 was playing some of the worst Rugby, under Andy Robinson, that had been seen from England since the mid eighties.

The legendary Welsh rugby team of Gareth Edwards, Barry John, J.P.R. Williams, and Phil Bennett, – arguably one of the greatest sides in the history of the game – dominated all between 1970–76 and were the backbone of the great Lion's wins in New Zealand (1971) and South Africa (1974) but then decline set in as the greats, one by one, retired. In fairness, rugby was amateur in those days and players had to find a balance between playing, fame and their working lives, which was never easy. Barry John arguably was lost too early – he retired from playing from Wales at the age of 27 – and he was one of the most naturally gifted of talents. He retired when his celebrity began to detract from his love of the game. He is quoted as saying:

"I have always been someone who would rather sit in the corner of a room, listening and observing, than holding court in the middle of it." He said. "I just wanted to play rugby and I felt that all the attention was affecting my form. I did not want to stop playing; I just felt I had to, if only to be fair to myself. The regret, which I still have, was not ending my career, but having no option. I felt I had at least a couple more years at the top, but only if I could be me and the celebrity thing was getting in the way of that."[13] (Paul Rees, The Guardian, April 2012)

John was a loss to the game. He played the game in a way that was free, brave and inspired the crowds of the day:

"There is nothing to be gained in comparing the game then with today. It is different in so many ways, but all I would say is that rugby has become a science: players wear tracking devices and have to tick certain boxes, but it is a pity that magic is not one of them. I see rugby as an art form, a battle of wits."[14] (Paul Rees, The Guardian)

British Golf has often threatened to really breakthrough. British Golf was dominant in the latter nineteenth and early twentieth century, but only a few players really played at the top level until the 80s and 90s saw a resurgence in the major Championships. This was led by Nick Faldo, and Sandy Lyle and more recently with the likes of Lee Westwood, Rory McIlroy and Danny Willets (Masters Champion 2016) but – bar performances in the Ryder Cup – competing for the majors has been inconsistent. It is as though, for the British, reaching the pinnacle is enough.

It is not through lack of talent. There have been many great sportsmen that have lit up the imagination but few teams have prevailed. If one accepts that the talent exists, one has to ask where does the problem lie?

Is it through a lack of competitive spirit and desire? This is hard to accept as the British are highly competitive. One only needs to read the sports pages in the broadsheets or see the coverage across all the media outlets to witness the passion for sports. One can feel the buzz and passion around Britain's stadia as the field of play is in action. It is one of the great draws for international sportsman to play in this country. The British teams are admired across the world for their spirit and attitude.

There is no doubt that, for many sports, funding has been an issue and as funding improved so did the performance levels of the sports. However, this has not been true in football – and other games – when success on the pitch has not matched the increase in wealth, pay and support structures. The increase in success has been more noticeable in individual sports rather than in team sports.

The introduction of lottery funding changed the manner in which many sports were able to compete on the global stage. There has been a steady improvement in the infrastructure of sport across the country, which has allowed the raw talent to be developed. In the following story, we look at how the United States, Australia and Germany have invested in their sporting infrastructures as sporting success has been viewed as key to their national identity. In the United States, especially, sport is taught to be crucial to a child's development from an early age and is both a family/ community event. In the UK, sport has for a long time been the escape for men and there has been a clear gender gap – although increasing numbers of women are now embracing sports and of course, the results are beginning to be seen with increasing success.

Over the last twenty years, sport has become more central to everyday life and it is taken more seriously as a method for personal development and health than in previous times when health was not taken as seriously. Today there are even league tables for companies with the healthiest employees. This would have been laughed at thirty years ago.

Culture has changed. In the 1950s, 60s and 70s, private education especially was often structured and motivated to develop young men and women to be rounded characters as well academically able. Academic results were not the be-all and end-all. This came from a Victorian ethos that stated that the importance of sport lay in how it taught character to the youth and how a team was only as strong as its weakest link. The result was that the system produced real personalities and characters with a confidence and independence to go out into the world. In those decades, young men and women would leave home at 18 and be independent by their early twenties. This is arguably less the case today. In today's society where schools are judged by league tables, all the focus in on academic results and achievement. The pressure on children is that much greater and there is less room for allowing rounded personalities to evolve. However, there does appear to be a greater focus on self-achievement. Everything is of a higher standard. Is it a coincidence that there has been a rise in sports participation since the introduction of league tables and a change in the achievement is perceived in school? Today's youth strive for greater and greater achievement as a means in itself whilst one of the strength and weaknesses of the 1960s, 70s and 80s was sport was just a sport. Play hard both on the field and off was the old maxim and many players did. The modern professional era is more play hard, train hard but rest and be nutritional. Neither are wrong but it does highlight the change in mentality.

The United States have arguably always been 20 years ahead of the British thinking. But the truth is that the US has always viewed sport differently to the British. In the United States, the Summer School has been an accepted holiday model for children and teenagers to encourage their development for many years. In the UK this model has never really taken off, as families prefer to stay together during the summer. The British family comes together over the summer to enjoy the delights of both holidays and family life. Neither is right or wrong; it is just different, but it is natural that a structure which has sports and learning at the heart of the community will excel over the structure which views it as a recreation.

The counter is that, for the British, sport is not just about the field of play but the comradeship, the club ethos and the supporters. There is a belief in qualities that are almost more important than winning – the tribe, friendship, teamwork, and the pure love of the game.

As much as the British loved sport, it faced three huge hurdles to overcome if it wished to compete on the highest stages – one was structural, one was mind-set and one was cultural. The following is the story of why this was the case and how the British sporting culture has evolved and developed through to the success of the modern age.

So much has changed over the years and most especially since the mid 90s when sport really awakened to the commercial possibilities. For long periods of time, the British game was simply not adequately prepared to compete on the highest stages. At times, the pressures of professionalism has seemed to hinder the freedom of players to express themselves and play their natural game. They were just not as mentally and maybe physically as prepared as the leading nations who invested more into their sporting prowess. Just talent alone was never enough.

The result was that often British teams have been conservative and almost negative in their approach. Jack Nicklaus, the great American golfer, once stated his belief that American players possessed a more "go for it" aggressive approach whilst playing golf. The American player would shoot for the round-changing shots that build a momentum in the game whilst the British would play a more conservative game. The British player aims to play a steady game over the course whilst the American will seek to build a momentum that changes the nature of the round. Nicklaus himself was renown for his "charges", as was Woods in later years, on the final nine holes whereby he would seek to score a series of birdies between holes 10–16 which would pressurise his opponents into submission. If one looks at the great Major wins by British players – Nick Faldo, Sandy Lyle, Paul Lawrie, David Willets – often another player loses the championship as much as the steady play of the British players has prevailed.

One would think that the opposite would almost be true, as the British believe there is more to sport than just winning and the Americans play a very competitive game. It is an interesting debate in Golf as so often a conservative approach can be viewed as sensible and pragmatic and brave play can win and lose championships. In 1996, Greg Norman played the brave golf only to collapse on the final day and let Nick Faldo in. In 2016, Jordan Spieth arguably should have easily won the Masters after holding a three shot lead as he turned for the final nine holes. However after a disastrous 12th hole he lost his lead and Danny Willets who played a very composed, calm game won the Championship by three shots. Spieth was the reigning champion and had played superb golf up to the moment of the 12th hole so what happened?

After the end of play, Spieth was quoted as saying: "*I knew that par (on the back nine) is good enough (to win) by at least a shot. You go away from your natural game plan and play conservatively. I told (caddie) Mike 'Buddy, it seems like we are collapsing'.*"[15] (*Metro* 12 April 2016)

It is very difficult to change one's approach during a match as it can change the whole psychology. The key underlying point though is that brave game play in Golf will often triumph over conservative play but the latter can win too. It holds true for all sports. England lost the 1970 World Cup quarter-final against Germany after leading 2–0. They withdrew Bobby Charlton, a player that concerned the Germans and tried to secure their defence. It was logical but lost the balance of the team and the psychology of the match changed. England fell to a 3–2 defeat and lost their crown as World Champions. In the 1991 Rugby World Cup Final, Will Carling's England team played different tactics to those that had been used to lead them to the Final as the management felt that Australia could easily contain a forward dominated game plan. England had lost the previous summer in Australia by close to thirty points and they still carried the scars. England had improved their fitness and had won some tough matches and arguably should have stayed true to the game that had brought them success. Twickenham in November is very different to Australia in June. The reasoning was sound, but it is so difficult for a team to be skilled in an expansive running game when they had played the opposite for the past twelve months. They could have been world champions but instead Australia triumphed – and in fairness they were the more complete team. One could argue that had England won the 1990 Grand Slam match against Scotland, they would have developed into a more complete team than the 1991 team came to be. The same players but a different psychology lay at the heart between 1990 and 1991 and all because of one single defeat that scared the players. The 1990 team did not keep its nerve and stay true to a philosophy that it was trying to develop but instead reverted to play a safe conservative game where it could overpower weaker opponents. This was effective until they played the likes of David Campese, Nick Farr-Jones and Michael Lynagh (Australia's playmakers in 91). So much of sport's success lies in the psychology of the game.

Over the years, it can be seen that the greatest teams play a hard, positively aggressive game that seeks to dominate the opposition. This creates a team that can intimidate the opposition even before they have entered the field of play. The England Rugby team had this in 2002–03. The Australian Cricket team between 1996–2004; The West Indies in the early 1980s and the New Zealand All Blacks from 2011–15.

What made the England 2003 stand apart was that Clive Woodward understood that excellence in sport required real investment into structure, coaching and facilities. The argument, at times, was that Woodward would frustrate the RFU in the way that he refused to cut corners and penny pinch. This may have been true but the result was the finest team to represent England with a list of world class players such as Jonny Wilkinson, Lawrence Dallaglio, Martin Johnson, Will Greenwood, and Jason Robinson. One could be provocative and argue that the 1991 team was a more naturally talented team with Brian Moore, Will Carling, Jeremy Guscott, Rory Underwood. Mike Teague, Peter Winterbottom and Jason Leonard, but they could not match the 2003 team in terms of preparation, professionalism and mentality.

Before the 2003 Grand Slam decider in Ireland, Martin Johnson famously refused to move his team on request prior to meeting the Irish President. The England team felt that a few of the Irish administrators were trying to unsettle the team through petty behaviours. The tensions had started earlier behind the scenes when the England team had been asked to take the field earlier than was the norm. They refused. Once on the pitch, they were being asked to move from the position they took in readiness for the Anthems. Johnson refused and made a stand in front of the Irish President and crowd. At the time they were outraged by Johnson's apparent rudeness to the Ireland team and President. The perception though that moment of stubbornness told everyone that Johnson and his team were not going to be intimidated and that they were in Dublin to win – which they then proceeded to do with relative ease. Would Carling have been so stubborn? Unlikely. In the 1990 Grand Slam decider against Scotland in Edinburgh, it was always perceived that England could not handle the occasion as the Scots did raise the temperature. England won the Grand Slam the following two years and Carling's team claimed they learnt from 1990 – but the truth was they played a more controlled restricted game. The 90 team was fluent and positive in its play and after the Scottish defeat, they withdrew into themselves although they dominated European Rugby.

Did Johnson's behaviours really have any impact on the sporting contest? In truth probably not, but the 2003 team was prepared to compete on the greatest stages.

It is sometimes easy to say that the British are full of contradictions. They are but this comes from a long historical legacy that some of the leading sporting nations do not possess. Is it a coincidence that America, Australia and even Germany are relatively new countries? It may sound strange to say this about Germany but it was only reunited after 1990 and has been building a new society after the divisions of 60 years ago. India too, one of the oldest civilisations in the world, possesses huge issues in developing a truly competitive sporting culture due to historical, social and cultural reasons.

Brazil, in contrast, has become the spiritual home of football based off a belief that every class of Brazilian will play an adventurous game whether on the beach in Rio, in the backstreets, parks and beyond. In Brazil, football is the pride of a nation against a political and economic structure that has been often unstable.

A Nation of Contradictions

As one would expect, the contradictions evident within the British is not just confined to the sports players but the supporters too. Arguably, this is a quintessential characteristic of the British sports fan. They can be highly tribal, competitively minded, often immersed in sentiment, preoccupied with personality and yearn less for cold, efficient victory than for the dramatic romance of defeat. It has often been commented on that the British love the brave loser rather than the cold, arrogant winner. They also possess an impressive capacity to forgive their sports stars their weaknesses. Many continued to believe in George Best even after many transgressions and episodes of poor behaviour. They are forgiven as the supporter dreams of just more moment of magic from their idol.

Every British sports fan is forever waiting for a moment of brilliance from a maverick figure, rendered great by instinctive talent not methodical coaching, and driven by volatile emotion, not a clear-eyed will to win. David Gower split opinions in the late 80s and early 90s as his talent was not of the modern professionalism being introduced under Graham Gooch's captaincy. It all came to a head when Gower flew a Tiger Moth over an on-going Tour game in Australia to bring some humour to the occasion and was seriously censored by the tour's management who reportedly even considered sending Gower home. Of course, this would have made a minor story into a major story and Gower's behaviour was just an attempt to lift morale rather than doing anything particularly seriously wrong. However the leadership team wanted a hard work ethic and to move away from the relaxed, humour that maybe Gower represented. Of course, great teams possess a balance of both and this was the point missed. The management should have just laughed with Gower and moved on without comment and the fact they didn't showed their weakness and vulnerability. It was no coincidence that the fortunes of the England team in the 90s would decline far lower than they were in the 1980s – the tone of which the management were trying to move away from.

Paul Gascoigne made a nation fall in love with him at Italia 90 and still by 1996 his career was on the wane and opinions were split. By 1998, he was not even in the squad. Ian Botham was often a controversial character but the public loved him.

The British love natural genius and the maverick player. They create a sporting narrative that the British public love. The British love their sport but not at all costs. Many will say it is all about winning but only on their rules. "For the love of the sport" charts the reluctant journey to professionalism

Why is this even important?

Sport has changed dramatically over the last 70 years since World War Two. It has emerged as a global phenomenon over the last forty years and today is as much big business as it is about the sport. This is one of the contradictions that many real lovers of sport have struggled with, but as sport becomes ever bigger, drawing record audiences and attracting TV income then the dynamics and expectations naturally change. This change is not just in terms of money but also in what makes sport sit at our core – emotion and aspiration.

Sport, traditionally, was escapism from daily life. One will see even the most mild-mannered accountant become animated and emotional when watching sport. Sport allows the British to be free of their daily persona and let go. One hopes that this will never change.

It may be escapism, but its popularity has made it all become a very serious business. Should sport be so serious? Well in today's world, the rewards are huge so there is no choice. Sport brings rewards that could never have been imagined even thirty years ago. In 2015, Floyd Mayweather earned an estimated $300m, of which only $15m was through endorsements. Christiano Ronaldo earned a base salary of $52m and $27m in endorsements. The top British players were Rory McIlroy who earned $48m of which $32m were in endorsements and Lewis Hamilton who $39m of which $36m was salary and only $3m in endorsements. Wayne Rooney was the highest British player in the Premiership with earnings of $26.9m.[16]

In 1990, the highest paid athlete was Mike Tyson with earnings of $28.6m. Only four athletes earned more than $10m in a year.[17]

A top England footballer from the 1970 team would have earned an average £12–15,000 per year (£75-95,000 in today's money) The 1966 World Cup winning team were rewarded with a £1,000 bonus.

The rewards have changed with each passing decade.

One can argue that David Beckham, at his height, was as influential as almost any UK politician. One can argue over the rights and wrongs but the growth in media resources has helped the rise in popularity of sport across the globe and sport is now at a point where it is seen as an important part of modern society. In 2006, the United Nations Secretary-General Kofi Annan wondered about; *"if only world politics could be as well organized as the World Cup Games".*[18]

Of course, FIFA have since been ridiculed and humbled within corruption scandals but the point is still valid. Both activities were universal: the UN had then 191 members; while football's governing body FIFA had 207. There are more people across the world that would rather talk about sport than about politics. National governments were making migration difficult – but soccer teams had players drawn from the best across the world.

Sports brings peoples together whilst politics creates divisions. Football teams have international supporters that transcend national borders. Manchester United, Real Madrid and Barcelona are global teams with supporters across the world. In fact some have more supporters in other countries than at home. It used to be said in the 1980s that Manchester United had more supporters in London than in Manchester and, in 2010, it was more in China than the UK. Whether true of not, the point is valid in that football is global. The four major European leagues – Premier League, La Liga, Serie A and Bundesliga – are major global businesses, which attract large revenues from outside their own countries.

The Olympics are now the biggest peacetime event in modern history. The Modern Olympics is not a political activity but it is a patriotic activity. A country's wellbeing can be judged by its athletes. Athletes are the peacetime warriors, bringing respect and glory to their country. This may all sound a touch extreme but for countries such as America, Australia and Germany, sport has been a key part of their national identity. They compete harder as it means more. In 2012, London created a genuine feel good factor that really buoyed the nation. This created pride in the athletes competing and also pride in the organization of the event. For weeks, Londoners walked with a spring in their step.

There are many studies that talk of how sport players have become the heroes of society along with leading movie actors but this has been the case since the dawn of the media age. In the 1930s and 40s, there was Clark Gable, John Wayne, Cary Grant, Stanley Matthews, Dennis Compton and the list can go on. It is easy to explain; it is aspiration, hope and something above the day to day. The two often understood the value of each other. It is no coincidence that both Bing Crosby and Bob Hope were such avid golf players and both had their own tournaments. They understood sport and status linked together.

In Britain, though, sport holds a different place in life compared to other countries. The real importance is that it is where the British show the world their love for something deeper than just winning. It has taken a long time for the British to have a truly professional outlook on how they treat their bodies. Often the diets have been poor. It is interesting to note that countries with long histories and strong class structures have struggled more in this regard than the new countries such as Australia and America where sport has also become a major part of the national identity and indeed the history of their country.

There is little doubt that Britain's sporting ethos, developed in the leading Public Schools in the Victorian Age has had a major cultural hold on how the British viewed sport and created a barrier to progress. This perception was in need of changing but there was a process and journey that needed to take place first before it could find the right balance.

THE CAPTAINS

Through good days and bad

"I had rather have a plain, russet-coated Captain, that knows what he fights for, and loves what he knows, than that which you call a Gentle-man and is nothing else."[19]
Oliver Cromwell

Leadership is such factor in British sporting culture. The British need a visible lead and captain to be their representative on the field of play. The captains are held responsible – personally so – for the fortunes of the team and the well being of the supporting community. Some captains hold positions as leaders that almost match the greatest political leaders. They have become legends. Others have been seen worse moments.

So between each chapter, we carry a profile on some of the great captains of the past.

Finlay Calder - (1)
Captain of Scotland and the British Lions 1989

Many will be surprised that Calder is profiled as an important captaincy figure. Finlay Calder was a player's player and is rarely mentioned as one of the great players of the 1980s and early 90s but this is to under rate the man and player. He may not have been the most naturally gifted of players but he was a fierce competitor and made of the most of his talents.

In some ways, Calder represents the paradox of British Sport. He was determined, steely and would never give an inch to an opponent. He was a man that his team-mates could trust as both a friend and as a player. He was honest and true and he made the most of his talents. He possessed all the traits that are admired in a sportsman bar the fact that he was not a world-class player. He was an excellent player but not as good as Michael Jones (New Zealand) or Peter Winterbottom (England) but he was a man his comrades would turn to in a moment of need. He would not be daunted or intimidated and his players knew he would meet fire with fire.

If any single moment symbolized the Scottish team spirit and gritty determination in 1990s Grand Slam decider it was surely the sight of Finlay Calder, early on in the match, collecting a loose ball and driving hard into the English forwards.

Calder, as a captain, was a no nonsense leader who would lead by example. He would put his body on the line and he was a rugby warrior that was almost old school. He was no egotist and never sought attention. He was not at ease as a communicator. He just loved the sport and winning was everything.

Calder was seen to be latecomer to international rugby. His twin brother Jim's international career was already over when Finlay broke into the international team in 1986, alongside David Sole and the Hastings brothers. Jim was viewed to be the more talented and arguably better player, but there is a reason why Finlay will be the more remembered. It illustrates the point that captaincy elevates a player over talent.

Calder, alongside Derek White and John Jeffrey, formed a back-row partnership which is possibly the best Scotland have ever produced. Calder was a devastating attacking flanker and a ruthless tackler – he was a full-backs' worst nightmare, charging after a high, hoisted Garry Owen and arriving simultaneous with the ball.

Despite his late start Calder went on to win 34 caps between 1986 and his retirement after the 1991 World Cup, and this after taking an early season sabbatical following the 1989 British Lions tour of Australia. Calder was the first Scottish player to captain the Lions since Michael Campbell-Lamerton in 1966 and the first winning captain since Willie John McBride in 1974.

His greatest achievement was as captain of the Lions in Australia. The Lions underperformed in the first Test and were well beaten. In the TV interviews afterwards, one can see that he was hurting and that he was determined to make amends. If one watches the footage, it was as though he resented having to answer the questions but knew it was his duty so as politely as he could he worked his way through the process. He has commented since that he just felt that the team had been complacent and almost naive and lost a game that they should have won. For a man of Calder's character, this would create deep frustration and it is no surprise that he told the team after that no place was secure, including his own and that the shirt would need to be earnt.

For the nest Test they made a number of changes including replacing the young Craig Chambers with the experienced Rob Andrew and bringing in the young talent of Jeremy Guscott to play alongside a fellow Scot in Scott Hastings (brother of Gavin); a man Calder knew he could trust. He also brought in Wade Dooley to play with Ackford and be an enforcer in the scrum.

The Australians will argue that the Lions used intimidating tactics to get back into the series and certainly the Lions played the game on the boundaries of legality. They played as their captain would play – uncompromising, physical and put their bodies on the line. The Lions won the series throughout a combination of winning the physical battle and through a poor error by Australia's star player, David Campese who gifted the Lions a try. The argument is that the error happened as the Lions strangled the natural flair of the Australians.

Were the Lions the better team? No. The Australians were the more talented complete team as they would show in the 1991 World Cup but the Lions played a tough, uncompromising game that unsettled the more talented Australians. The Lions were a team that really played for each other and led at the front by their skipper.

There is danger that Calder does become a forgotten leader bar for those that played with him. This will not worry Calder for as far he would be unconcerned for he achieved as much as he set out to do but he is an important leader to fairly recognise.

Chapter Two

SPORT IS FOR THE BRAVE

Top level sport is not only the home for those that are technically gifted in their craft but for those able to play with inhibition, fluidity and the ability to keep a cool mind as all those around – especially in the watching audiences – raise the temperature.

International sport is about moments and whether a player – or a team – can seize an opportunity. John McEnroe, the great American tennis player, once commented the difference in skill between the world's top 20 players was less than one percent. The difference between the players lay in the mind – the desire to win, the dedication, and the ability to seize the day. Jonny Wilkinson and Clive Woodward have often spoken about how one percent margins make the difference and how the line between winning and losing can be so very thin on the international stage.

In 1999, the England Rugby Union team were defeated in the quarter-final of the Rugby World Cup to South Africa. The teams were finely matched, but South Africa triumphed due to a game of drop-kicking brilliance in open play by their fly-half that neutralised any threat from the English. However, the nucleus of the 99 team stayed together, learnt their lessons and became the dominant force in World Ruby within three years. In 2003, one just know that Johnson, Dallaglio, Wilkinson, Hill, Dawson and Greenwood were as mentally prepared and able as any opponent could be. This was proved in those crucial moments in the 2003 Final that led to the Wilkinson dropped goal that sent the nation into celebration.

I think it's the mark of a great player to be confident in tough situations. (John McEnroe) [20]

Most top sportsmen would echo these words. Confidence is the major factor that lies between success and "what might have been". It is about the inner confidence that allows one to win against the best opponents even when the game is not going to plan. Alex Ferguson, the legendary Manchester United manager, stated that it is the 1–0 victories in a campaign that really show the mark of a championship winning team. The great Liverpool teams of the early 80s were often gifted at scoring goals in the dying minutes of a game as players began to think of the showers but those goals won titles. Ferguson's Manchester United team would score late goals too and injury time at the end of a match was nicknamed "Fergie time". The great teams play to the final moment.

Top sportsmen will often talk about the importance of building a winning mentality when they have the inner belief that they will win whatever the situation. Both the great Manchester United and Liverpool teams would possess this belief, as would the great Australian and All Black rugby teams. In the 1991 Rugby World Cup, Ireland scored a try to take the lead with just a few minutes remaining. Many believed, even in those moments, that Australia would come back and sure enough Michael Lynagh engineered a try in the final moments of the match to snatch victory for Australia. In 2014, Ireland were leading the All Blacks as they entered added on time at the end of the match. It would have marked a famous victory but the All Blacks ran the ball back from their own 22 to score a winning try and break Irish hearts. Some possess a belief that they will overcome adversity whatever the circumstances.

Over the history of sport, there have been many players that just intimidate the opposition by their very presence – Viv Richards, Dennis Lillee, Jeff Thomson, Richie McCaw, Gareth Edwards, Barry John, Seb Coe, Lawrence Dallaglio, Martin Johnson, Shane Warne, Dan Carter, and the list can go on. Jonny Wilkinson raised Toulon's game with his presence to become European champions. Carter is doing the same with Racing Metro who reached the European Final with his presence and drive. Wilkinson and Carter will possess very special places in rugby history as their country's greatest fly-halves and for moving to a foreign country (France) and creating new rugby dynasties (Toulon and Racing Metro respectively).

The above list does name a few of British greats but most sports fans will know that few British players have inspired the confidence that they will intimidate the opposition by their very presence. Maybe the great Welsh Rugby team of the 70s; the England World Cup teams of 2003 (Rugby) and 1966 (football); Redgrave and Pinsent (1992–2004); Nick Faldo (1987–92); Harry Vardon (1896–1914): Dennis Compton (1946–48), Ian Botham (1981), Seb Coe and Steve Ovett (1978–84): Daley Thompson (1980–84):Chris Hoy and Bradley Wiggins (2008–12; James Hunt (1976), Jackie Stewart (late 60s and early 70s), Nigel Mansell (1990–94) and Lewis Hamilton (2008–present) but few beyond. Given this covers a 100 years of sport, it is the greatest of lists.

History is littered by moments of underachievement or moments when the team just did not live up to its billing. The England football team disappointed a nation in 1950, 1958, 1970, 1973, 1978, 1992, 2006 and 2008. The England Rugby team in 2011 and 2015. The England Cricket team in 2006 and 2014. The Olympic team in 1996. There have been times of greatness but more moments of disappointment.

British sport has seemingly too often played on the extremes of pure courage and passion or stifled belief and negativity. The argument has always been that British teams are not as technically skilled as other nations but the truth is more complex. Britain has possessed the gifted players as will be illustrated through the ensuing story but the real difference has been in the mind-set.

The school of thought that argues over a lack of technical ability amongst the British is an easy, almost simplistic, argument to make. It is partially true but it is also designed to explain why so many hopes have been dashed over the generations. It also apportions blame – to the coaching structure, to the clubs and to the administrators. There is no doubt that there have been serious flaws in structure and management but the talent has always existed.

Where this school is right is that there has been a lack of devotion to the hardest work ethic and real professionalism required to develop the players for the highest levels, but it has been on the mental side rather than the technical side. Many will point to the success of British rowers, cyclists and athletes since the advent of lottery money in sport and there is no doubt that lottery funding has allowed British athletes to be far more competitive but the major team sports had the money in the game, so why has it been such a struggle to compete on a consistent basis. After all Britain does possess more clubs and teams than in any other country in football, cricket and rugby. The most clubs must mean the most players so the problem must lie either with the preparation and development of the players or within a cultural attitude towards sport in the UK.

If the problem lies in the mental preparation – how can this be the case? After all, the British sides have always been known for their passion, commitment, never say die attitude. This is very true but this is different to professionalism.

Commitment and passion has never been an area of concern and will become apparent. The issue has been a deeper cultural one in that sport has traditionally been viewed as a recreation and a source of entertainment rather than there being a real need for physical sport and development to be viewed as the equal of academia as can be argued does take place in the United States and in Australia. In the USA, sports sits at the heart of the community and the major events are family occasions. From an early age, children are taught that exercise and sport are important in the overall development of a person.

That is sadly not been the case in Europe. In fact an EU report in 2011, with the catchy title: "Improving Leisure-Time Physical Activity in the Local Arena towards social equity, inter-sectoral collaboration and participation".

The report stated that:
> In the EU, two thirds of the adult population do not reach recommended levels of activity and a social gradient exists. Although poorer people are more likely

to walk or they are less likely to be active in their leisure time. Lack of nearby sports facilities, transport or sufficient money may act as a barrier to engaging in leisure time physical activities. A range of policy documents published by both the European Union and the World Health Organisation highlight the importance of equalising opportunities to engage in physical activity through inclusive and participatory approaches, stakeholder networks and multi-sectoral action. A central theme to all of these strategies is the strong emphasis placed on policy – and environmental interventions, which appear to show most promise for increasing physical activity levels of the population. Key features of such interventions are highlighted as: strong government intervention and leadership, community based action and the potential of a societal role for organised sports to improve PA behaviour and public health.[21]

The vision and targets set were to achieve the following:

- A general improvement in public health through increased physical activity in the population
- An increase in the number of children and youth who are physically active for at least 60 minutes per day
- An increase in the number of adults and elderly people who are moderately physically active for at least 30 minutes per day.

One has to wonder why this was written in 2011 rather than in 1980. Compare the above with debate and policies undertaken in the United States during the 1950s and 60s which has a completely different dynamic to its thinking. In 2006, Thomas M. Hunt from the University of Texas wrote a paper on American Sports Policy under Eisenhower and Kennedy and stated:

During the mid 1950s, President Eisenhower, concerned at the declining fitness levels of American children and military draftees, established the President's Council on Youth Fitness. Conceived by the president as a central coordinating body rather than an extensive federal undertaking, the Council reflected the administration's belief, in Eisenhower's words, that "the fitness of our young people is essentially a home and local community problem." Nevertheless, the Council leadership advocated improved fitness on the part of the entire population as the federal government's central goal. As articulated by Dr. Shane MacCarthy, its executive director, "Perhaps as we consider the next Olympics, the theme should be not so much 'Win in [the 1960 games in] Rome' as 'Win at home."' In terms of benefits for elite international athletics, MacCarthy continued, "If we succeed in getting our country off its seat and on its feet, the victories in the field of international competition will inevitably follow." Eisenhower's successor in the White House, John F. Kennedy, took a broader view toward the relationship between sport and the Cold War. As part of his campaign for a "New Frontier" in American life, Kennedy authored a 1960 article for Sports Illustrated magazine titled "The Soft American" that gave voice to his apprehension of the in fragility of the populace. "We face in the Soviet Union," he asserted, "a powerful and implacable adversary determined to show the world that only the Communist system possesses the vigor and determination necessary to satisfy awakening aspirations for progress."[22]

American fitness was consequently perceived as crucial to the waging of the Cold War and might even, according to the president-elect, "determine the future of freedom in the years to come."

Such wording and comments certainly escalate the importance of fitness and sport and certainly beyond how any British politician would have declared at the time. In fact, given such comments being made by American Presidents over the importance of fitness within a nation's youth, one would have thought that the British Government many have followed suit with some depth but it did not seem to register.

Kennedy later published his thoughts in what amounted to nothing less than a sports manifesto for the American people. Part of a nation's prestige in the cold war is won in the Olympic Games.

"In this day of international stalemates nations use the scoreboard of sports as a visible measuring stick to prove their superiority over the 'soft and decadent' democratic way of life." The "success of Red-bloc countries in the Olympics and other international competitions" in comparison to the United States was intolerable in that it, "has given these nations an appearance of strength. It was, according to the attorney general, "thus in our national interest that we regain our Olympic superiority; that we once again give the world visible proof of our inner strength and vitality."[23]

In view of this environment, Kennedy accordingly argued that there must be "encouragement – with action as well as words – by government at all levels.

This does raise a number of thoughts:

1. The Americans were arguably forty years ahead of Europe in the need for its people's to be physical fit. Why?

2. The Government policies towards sport in the US seem to view sport as an important feature in the overall identity of the country. Again did the major European countries not view its importance in the same way?
3. America was clearly motivated by the Cold War and the contest with the USSR. But still why did this not impact on European thinking?
4. Did it matter?

As one reads the following story it is clear that the link between sport and national identity is a very strong motivational force. The argument is that sport was never an important feature of the British overall identity and yet it was so important to the culture of the country. However the real disconnect between the UK and US seems to be that as much as there is a love for sport it is seen as being different to the nation embracing physical fitness as an objective in itself.

There is a school of thought that will argue that as the US grew in economic strength along with the USSR after World War Two so it sought to compete on all political, social and sporting fronts. Britain was not as motivated by the Cold War and after the war, it needed to spend its time and resources on rebuilding the infrastructure of the country and sport was not viewed as a priority. In fact, sport was seen to be an escape from day to day life and almost independent of the political arena.

Maybe there is truth to this argument. It is easy to criticise government for not investing in sport but did sport want the support and involvement of government or did it seek to run its own path?

Or maybe as the problem was clearly pan European, maybe long established societies have always viewed sport as a pastime and recreation rather than possessing a greater importance?

The truth lies between all the answers to the questions. Britain like many other European countries took a long time to recover from the ravages of war and the money just did not exist until arguably the late 1980s for investment into the infrastructure of sports. Recessions were a common colleague on the path to recovery from war until the early 80s. When the money did exist, arguably sport was a controversial area for investment as hooliganism was at its height across Europe and this continued until the late 1980s. It was in the nineties that the importance of sport became seen in a clear light and there is no coincidence that the new generation of politics that arrived in the mid 90s under Prime Ministers, John Major and Tony Blair, saw sport rise up the scale in terms of priority. One can almost visibly see that after 1997, British sport once again became to become more competitive on the International stage.

Strangely enough – and maybe only strange as we understand the importance of sporting infrastructure far better today – there was no angst about the lack of investment in sports. It was just a fact of life and many sportsmen would happily tell tales of how they learnt how to play sport in the backstreets of post war Britain. Although other countries were pressing ahead in terms of sports innovation and development programmes, the UK was almost blissfully unaware and the debates simply raged over why our international teams were not as competitive as they should be. Was it down to technical skills of the players? Were the players not as hungry? After all, British club sides were still the envy of many across Europe and England's football teams ruled over the premier competition in Europe from 1977 to 1985. Surely this proved that British sports were still competitive?

On certain levels the answer was yes but other countries were overtaking the old country in professionalism and ability. There was certainly a lack amongst professionals of real understanding and knowledge on how to care for their bodies.

In 2001, the BBC published the following report on England's leading footballers and their "watering" behaviours[24]:

> Alcoholism and binge-drinking are problems which continue to dog football. Revelations in Hull Crown Court showed that, despite all the talk of increased professionalism in the English game, there are players who continue to hit the bottle in a big way. Leeds defender Jonathan Woodgate testified in court that he drank seven or eight pints of a vodka and rum cocktail on the night Sarfraz Najeib was attacked. And team-mate Lee Bowyer was described by a witness as being 'absolutely hammered' in Leeds' Majestyk nightclub.
>
> They are not the first – and undoubtedly will not be the last – footballers to paint the town red. Tony Adams, Paul Gascoigne and Paul Merson have all been guilty of overdoing it, often with serious consequences.
>
> Alcohol, among other things, nearly wrecked the careers of all three players and certainly had a major effect on their lives. Adams' battle was well-publicised and even cost him his freedom at one stage. The former England defender served 56 days of a three-month sentence at Chelmsford Open Prison in 1990 for drink-driving. But it was not until 1996 that he admitted he had a problem and cleaned himself up. Gascoigne's boozing cost him his international career. After one drinking session too many, the former Lazio star was dropped on the eve of the 1998 World Cup finals by then England manager Glenn Hoddle. The midfielder vowed to bounce back but has so far been unable to force his way back into the

international reckoning. Despite Gazza's well-publicised problems, it was not until last September that he actually admitted he was a recovering alcoholic.

"If I wasn't playing, I would drink Saturdays, then Sunday, then Monday," he told The Observer. "Then I would try and train and it was no good, then have another drink just to pass the day away.

Gascoigne was at the centre of another infamous incident involving the England team. Prior to Euro 96, several players – among them Gascoigne and Teddy Sheringham – partied to excess in Hong Kong.

At one point, revellers took turns to sit in the "dentist's chair" while comrades poured drinks into their mouths.

It came as no surprise when pictures from the bash appeared in national newspapers a few days later. The photographs seemed to undermine attempts within the England camp to keep drinking to a minimum. The Football Association stepped up random breath testing to combat alcohol abuse in the game, but not all the warnings were heeded. Sheringham found himself embroiled in controversy again when, just before the start of France 98, he was seen drinking and smoking in a Portuguese bar. There were calls for him to be booted out of the squad, but the striker escaped with a stern ticking-off.

Footballers were in the headlines again last year when the Leicester City team were expelled from a hotel in Spain. The squad were on a four-day break as part of their preparations for the Worthington Cup Final against Tranmere.

But when players got well-oiled on the first night – and troubled striker Stan Collymore let off a fire extinguisher – they were soon on the plane back home.

There are signs that things may be improving, however. And leadership from the top will no doubt have a big impact.

Following his appointment as England coach, Sven Goran Eriksson announced his intention to ban alcohol in the build-up to big games.

"If you play for England, you don't need to drink wine or beers with your meals," said the Swede. "We are together to play football, not for anything else."

Aston Villa boss John Gregory has also banned alcohol from the players' bar at Villa Park while a number of other managers are keen to promote healthy living. Unfortunately, not everyone has come round to

*their way of thinking. As Woodgate has proved, there is still a long way
to go before all footballers can be rightly called "the model professional".*[24]

Should people have been more shocked than they were? The answer is that, of course, such reports should have more of a shock factor but in truth the concept of footballers drinking too much had been an accepted norm since the 1960s.

One of the ever-enduring traits that mark out the British love affair with sports is the relationship between the players and the supporters. There are hundreds of examples of the constant forgiveness of players' excess behaviour and one can visibly see how players and fans interact so effectively in stadia every week up and down the country.

The British character loves the warrior spirit of fighting till the end, never giving in until it is over. It is one of the core traits of the nation and many, as an example, will quote Churchill's great wartime speech on 9 June 1940:

> *Even though large tracts of Europe and many old and famous states have fallen or may fall into the grip of the Gestapo and all the odious apparatus of Nazi rule, we shall not flag or fail.*
>
> *We shall go on to the end, we shall fight in France, we shall fight on the seas and oceans, we shall fight with growing confidence and growing strength in the air, we shall defend our Island, whatever the cost may be, we shall fight on the beaches, we shall fight on the landing grounds, we shall fight in the fields and in the streets, we shall fight in the hills; we shall never surrender, and even if, which I do not for a moment believe, this island or a large part of it were subjugated and starving, then our Empire beyond the seas, armed and guarded by the British Fleet, would carry on the struggle, until, in God's good time, the New World, with all its power and might, steps forth to the rescue and the liberation of the old.*[25]

It was a speech that inspired and gave heart to a nation and has come to symbolise British spirit.

In sport, Brian Close, the England cricketer, may be one of the finest examples of this famed spirit and especially during his bravery in facing Michael Holding and Andy Roberts, the leaders of the West Indies fast bowling attack, at Old Trafford in 1976. Close faced one of the most brutal spells of fast bowling ever witnessed in Test match cricket and on no few occasions Close just let the ball hit him rather than succumb. The West Indies smelt victory and they ruthlessly targeted the English batsmen. Close and John Edrich, his fellow batsman, faced the battery with genuine raw courage. In those days, the players did not wear helmets to protect them; there were no rules on the number of bouncers that could be bowled in an over and it was a moment in time that shocked many and led to change in the game. Barry Wood, the England cricketer, later remarked that he thought that he was watching the highlights of the game rather than the game live, as each ball seemed to be a drama in itself. The hard truth though is that England were not prepared for the ruthless, aggressive approach displayed by the West Indies. England had drawn the first two Test matches at Trent Bridge and Lord's. At Old Trafford, the West Indies went up a level after suffering a poor first day and England could not respond. The West Indies had more in their artillery that had not been shown until a moment of crisis and England were no answer and were not prepared. It all came like a dramatic shock.

Close and Edrich epitomised what the British admire in their sportsmen. England fell to a large defeat, but with honour as the players stood tall in the face of adversity.

One can argue that the West Indies were the more professional team. They were the more motivated team, accurate, prepared and ruthless in their work. Much was made of a comment by the South African born England captain, saying that he would make the West Indies players "grovel" and, as much as it was an insensitive, crass comment, it in truth made no difference. The West Indies possessed a strong work ethic, worked harder and were more skilled in their craft. They possessed the best bowlers and the best batsmen. Viv Richards, Gordon Greenridge, Clive Lloyd, Michael Holding and Andy Roberts were five world-class players that could walk into any team. It was almost inevitable that they would soon become the best team in the world by developing a team.

The British admire bravery on the field; blood given for the cause and the result is almost secondary.

It is not an uncommon story. In the 2015 Rugby World Cup, the game that most angered observers was the Scotland versus Australia match as victory was denied the brave Scots through a refereeing error. All top sportsmen will state that one just has to accept poor decisions by referees and that it goes hand in hand with the game. However, Scotland had won the hearts of the onlookers as they had been a team that had been one of the poorest performers in the Six Nations over the last five years and with five minutes to go, the Scots took the lead in the match and it was very feasible that they could go further than any other of the home nations in the tournament and defeat the team that had beaten both England and Wales. In that moment, Twickenham, the home of English rugby, had become Scottish. However a poor decision by the referee in the final minute of the game and yet again victory had been denied. There are many Englishmen that will state that they felt more upset by Scotland's defeat than England's elimination for it was unjust and that sport's greatest moments are when the under dog rises to defeat the better team.

The Australians prevailed and reached the Final. Over the course of the tournament they deserved to be in the Final but the view prevailed that Rugby does at times favour the stronger teams and the British love the underdog and the maverick player.

There is little question that over the decades that America and Australia have been viewed as two of the leading sporting nations. There will be many that will argue that they both possess climates that encourage the development of the sporting athlete but this is too simplistic a view. Britain possesses more football, cricket and rugby clubs and players than any other nation and still we struggle to prevail. New Zealand are a small country in population terms and yet their rugby culture is world leading.

No, the answer lies deeper and within culture. America and Australia are relatively new countries and sport is part of their national identity and culture. These countries invested in their sports whilst the British, within reason, relied in their natural talents and flair.

The British adore the flair player; the player that would be a maverick, a rebel and bring genius to the game – George Best, David Gower, Dennis Compton, Ian Botham, Jeremy Guscott, Barry John, Gareth Edwards, Phil Bennett, and Jimmy Greaves. All hold affectionate places in the hearts of fans. Some had a good work ethic; others relied on their natural ability. All though were trusted more than the player that worked hard to achieve the same level.

The Guardian published a relevant story about Barry John, the legendary Welsh fly- half:

> *John kicked with his instep from around the corner. He only kicked one goal in his first season with Cardiff, a long-range effort at Newbridge. "There were better kickers than me," he said. "I guess I took over when the instep style became fashionable, but I was never one to spend hours on the training field kicking. I remember finishing a Wales session when Clive Rowlands [the coach] told me I would be taking the kicks on Saturday, against England, I think."*
>
> *"I walked off the field towards the changing rooms when Clive called after me: 'Barry, don't you want to practise your kicking?' Not really, but I grabbed a ball, placed it 20 yards in front of the posts, kicked it over and told Clive 'I'm in form,' and left with him looking at me open-mouthed. I*

kicked three out of three against England, I recall, including one from the
touchline, and that's how I was: I always backed myself." [26]

(Paul Rees, The Guardian, April 2012)

It is another of the contradictions. It is a strong argument to put forward that other countries were more advanced in terms of investment and structure in sport, but the British did not help themselves – not just through government support – but because there was a love for the maverick player over the hard professional. Maybe the British just love a rebel, the likeable rogue. Maybe and maybe the belief that there was more to sport than just winning still stood at the core of values until the late 90s.

In 1990, Graham Gooch was made Captain of England in succession to David Gower. Gooch rightly brought a stronger, more demanding professional attitude that the England team needed. However, Gower was always the more popular player. It was not long before the two would fall out. They had been close friends. Gooch had even written to Gower after the 1985 Ashes campaign to say how much he had enjoyed his leadership. It was very unlikely that Gower returned the compliment although it can be said that Gooch was loyal to Gower as much as his hard work ethic would allow.

In 1966, there was a great debate over whether it was right that Jimmy Greaves was not selected for the England team to play in the 1966 World Cup Final over Geoff Hurst. Hurst was the less naturally gifted player but more the team player with a hard work ethic. Hurst was selected and settled the argument with a hat-trick in the Final but it almost required such a special feat to settle the argument. Greaves though was always a loved figure.

In fairness, Greaves record as a goalscorer was superb – 44 goals for England in 57 England appearances. Greaves delighted crowds as he was a highly skilled craftsman and also his own man.

George Best was another and from the late 60s to the early 70s was regarded as the best player in Britain. However he was a flawed genius. If he played for one of the major international countries, even England rather than Northern Ireland, he would have been seen as comparable to the games greats of the era. Best was a genius that the Manchester United fans worshipped but he also loved the good life.

Best often would tell a story about a time in the mid 1970s when he was in a hotel room. The bed was covered in money from gambling winnings and Miss World was standing naked in the bathroom. The room service waiter that brought refreshments to their room turned to Best and said; "George, where did it all go so wrong?"

Best would laugh, as he told the story, as he pondered how the waiter could feel that it had all gone wrong for him as he was both rich and had Miss World in the room?

However, Best missed the point. He was loved by the Manchester fans. He was a hero, his name weekly chanted by 30,000 fans and yet he walked out on the club. He suffered from drink problems and arguably lacked discipline. Best may laugh but, to many, money and Miss World came a distant second to the love of the tribe, the supporters, the team and the game.

George Best was a hero until the day he died. It did not matter that he was flawed, had walked out on the club and abused his talent. He was forgiven, as his talent was magical. In other countries, he would have been declared a fool for wasting something so special but not in Britain.

As strange as it may sound, a beautiful woman and all the money in the world was not as important as the support of the tribe. The magic of the talent is something to be loved. It is strange that Britain, that has so often been described as being arrogant and aloof can possess such a deep affection for mavericks.

Maybe the story of the 1981 Ashes illustrates of the contradiction that lies within the British. One would think the British would be supportive of a captain in difficult times but often a change of captain is seen to be a solution to the fortunes of a team. No change was more effective than in 1981 Ashes Series.

England lost the First Test to Australia and as England entered the Second Test, many wanted Ian Botham to be replaced as captain. He had been the star player when Mike Brearley was captain from 1977 to 1980, when Botham was selected to be his successor. However, Botham struggled to maintain his performance levels as captain. He lost two tough series against the great West Indies team when in truth it was unlikely England would win either series. In fact a 1–0 home series defeat and a 2–0 away defeat was not so bad, but the England team did not look like it would play great cricket under his leadership. The cricket was often negative and relatively dull. The Lord's Test marked another uninspiring performance and when he was out for nought in the second innings he walked off to a silent crowd that offered little support and some members of the MCC even turned their backs to the player at a dark moment for the player.

They made their point, for Botham resigned a few hours later and Mike Brearley was brought back as captain. Over the next three games, Botham's performance was extraordinary as he almost single-handed inspired England to beat the Australia in the next three Test matches. England won the Ashes series 3–1 and it will be regarded as one of the great series for its sporting and personal drama. Botham was suddenly a national hero, literally weeks after his lowest moment. It was a truly extraordinary series of events as he scored a match turning 149 in the Third Test at Headingley.

After the match, Botham joked; "*a captain's innings – one match too late.*"[27]

In the next match at Edgbaston, it seemed as England were heading for defeat before Botham took the ball and produced a spell of five wickets for one run. England won a second unlikely victory. In the Fifth Test at Old Trafford, Botham scored a brutal match-winning century that broke the Australians spirit.

It was true that he was never a natural captain and leader of men. He was though a genius who could change the course of a game through his own talents. As he entered the sporting arena, the crowd would light up in anticipation of what may happen. He was one of the few players that could transcend the game. He was never regarded as possessing a high work ethic and over the years he had many controversies that followed him that included allegations of affairs, drugs and drinking. However, he was accepted for who he was and loved for the player he was.

This does sit at the heart of the debate. Many American sportsmen have a greater sporting work ethic and understand that the sport comes first. Simon Barnes, the great columnist for *The Times*, once wrote an article in the late 80s that told how many of the American players understand their need to engage the broader community and be accessible as this, naturally, would lead to greater popularity and merchandising sales. They seemed to understand their commercial responsibilities. In contrast the English footballers of the same era, would always make access related to a fee payable. The culture was less understanding, more selfish and it was no surprise there was friction between the tabloids and the players.

Before World War Two, sport was mainly low paid or amateur and in those days the British more than held their own on the international stage. Arguably, they had the best football team in the 30s as well as the best cricket team. The British offer many contradictions and one of them was the fact that the England Bodyline team of the 30s were arguably as ruthless and professional as the West Indies team in the late 70s. The team was led by Douglas Jardine and he designed a strategy to combat the great Donald Bradman and Australian team. Bodyline was controversial – it caused debate even in both the House of Commons and the Australian Parliament – but highly effective. There is an irony that the England team was almost clinically more professional under Jardine in the 30s than they were forty years later. There is good reason for this as will become apparent.

The war may have changed much, but sport stood at the heart of the culture pre war and it equally did post war as the record attendances that filled the stadiums across the land will testify. Some will argue the introduction of television and easier travel changed the pipeline but this too is a shallow argument. Just consider the names that played during the poor eras when we were not close to being world leading – Kevin Keegan, Billy Wright, Peter Shilton, David Gower, Ian Botham, Graham Gooch, Trevor Brooking, Kenny Dalglish, Ian Rush, Ryan Giggs, David Beckham, Michael Owen, Alan Shearer, Graeme Souness, Michael Atherton, David Duckham, Fran Cotton and the list go on. These were players that would have succeeded in most countries. No, the talent certainly existed and the pipeline is as strong today as it was in the 1950s.

The British may love their sport but they are at their best when it is not the most important thing in life, or when the pressure has not been on. It can be argued that the British know their sport and know its place in life. But why is it that the British have struggled to be as professional as they have needed to be?

This does lie at the heart of the following story as professionalism is about striving to be a winner and be mentally able to handle the crucial moments. Professionals train and prepare for the pressure moments. This appears to be where British teams have been lacking.

So the question, especially in the major team sports, has to be asked – why have British teams so rarely peaked as World Champions? Was it really as simple to explain as a lack of funding and government support?

Of course, there were a whole sequence of factors that created the barriers to success, which included lack of government support, a poor mind-set towards professional sport and there was a far broader social context.

The leading international players possess a natural sporting arrogance and confidence that the British rarely possess as adults. Too often those that play with such flair in their youth are not able to translate their talent to the greatest of stages. One has to wonder why?

Is it any coincidence that England's greatest era in football was probably in the 30s and 40s when football was a real working class man's game and everyone had greater perspective on life after the world wars. The England team during that time was arguably better than the World Champions, Italy.

The England Cricket team of the 40s played with equal flair with Dennis Compton and Bill Edrich amongst others including the Bedser twins. After the war, sport was regarded as what it was – a game for enjoyment and England's players played some of their greatest matches. Arguably England has struggled with the fall of the amateur game and the rise of professional sport. Of course, the balance to this argument is that the decline coincided with the increased focus of other countries on their own sporting structures. During the 60s, 70s and 80s the Eastern bloc governments supported their sports stars to a higher level than any western government. It was this factor that led to the IOC open up the Olympics in the mid 90s as the playing field was no longer level.

Again, one has to ask why the British Government did not do more help to support when the eastern bloc clearly had seen the importance as had the Americans and the Australians and British sport was showing clear signs of decline in competiveness?

British sport was left to its own devices and it had to find the solutions without help. However, the basics were not in place for this to be achieved. There were still many lessons to be learnt in just how to prepare for the biggest games.

It is one of the great ironies that the British are often seen to be aloof and arrogant, but the truth could not be further from the truth. There is a genuine lack of inner belief, which is always one of the reasons that British teams struggle once they do become World Champions. Consider England rugby in 2003; England cricket in 2011 or England football in 1966. England has so often reached the pinnacle but been unable to kick on to become real champions on a consistent basis.

There has been a lack of belief or even arrogance that is their rightful place. The achievement lies in attaining the accolade, reaching the summit but there is no plan for after becoming champions as seemingly there is little belief that as champions the team will kick on. The New Zealand rugby team believe they are the best in the world even when they have lost in the Rugby World Cup. They believe in their players and their culture and it shows. Arguably British rugby only had this belief for a few short years in the 70s after the Lions won in New Zealand (1971) and South Africa (1974) but by 1977 it had gone. The real test of great sporting champion cultures is when it lasts for decades, not just a few years.

It does appear to be a team issue rather than with individuals as teams rely on group motivation whilst individual sport is all about the individual and their desire. Steve Redgrave and Matthew Pinsent did not seem to suffer. Nor Lewis Hamilton. Nor Nick Faldo at his best. Nor James Hunt, Jackie Stewart, Seb Coe, Steve Ovett, Linford Christie, Allan Wells, Kelly Holmes, David Hemmery, Barry McGuigan, and the list can go on.

The real problem lies with the team culture in sport. It goes far broader as British sport is not just about the field of play but the comradeship and the supporters. There is a belief in qualities that are almost more important within the British culture – the tribe, friendship, teamwork, and the pure love of the game. There is almost a fear of professionalism, that it may harm the very qualities that held so closely to our hearts but to be able to fulfil the potential that the sportsmen and sportswomen across the country possess there has needed to be a real change in culture and values.

As the following chapter will explain, the Victorian era set the belief that the importance of sport lay in the game not the rewards. Many players simply felt uncomfortable with the base ethos of professionalism and the nature of celebrity that came with it. Sports players have always been heroes and role models but in the 1960s the notion of celebrity did seem to escalate to another level. As this happened, some naturally talented players would have been lost. One was the great Barry John who had lit up the rugby world with his performances of the British Lions tour of New Zealand in 1971, which made him a household name. Paul Rees, in an article in *The Guardian*, wrote:

> *John was 27 when he retired and there was no way back then because he professionalised himself by writing his autobiography and becoming a newspaper columnist. He was in his prime, but his decision to go out at the top was not taken to preserve his reputation. He was the first rugby celebrity and felt uncomfortable with fame.*
>
> *When he opened a bank in north Wales for his employer – he was a sales rep for Forward Trust, a branch of Midland Bank, a woman curtsied as he approached her. "Everything had got out of control," he reflected this week. "My job was going on the road selling finance, but I would make an appointment and the whole town would turn up. I ended up staying in the office with effectively nothing to do and getting paid for that seemed wrong."*
>
> *If John had an arrogance on the pitch, supremely confident in his own ability and very rarely ruffled, he did not like to be the centre of attention.[28]*

(The Guardian April 2012)

It is often cited that Britain possesses more players and more clubs than almost any other nation in rugby, cricket and football. The issue has laid in the structure itself and how players have been coached and educated. Success, in all walks of life, comes from substance over a sustained period of time and the team trusting that you will deliver consistently and when it matters. When all is stripped way, the reality is that the road to success is not just about skill but about all about what and how each player is as a persona and how a player defines themselves to the outside world and how they influence others through their behaviour. Think Martin Johnson as England rugby captain. Ian McGeehan once stated that he choose Johnson as captain of the 1997 Lions as he wanted the Springboks to face a physically daunting presence from the moment the captains tossed the coin before kick off. "I wanted someone," he reportedly said, "that they had to look up to from the moment they went to toss the coin".

Lawrence Dallagio had a similar presence. He could see his very presence inspired players around him and it is no coincidence that Wasps Rugby enjoyed their greatest era under his leadership of the side.

There is no short cut to success and the best building block is the person you are. This is particularly true in sport when the player is exposed and in front of a large, often worldwide audience. It is about mentally handling the moment and influencing action around you through actions.

This can be seen to be old fashioned, as the argument is that with sophisticated coaching, players are taught to handle each and every situation. This may be true but little prepares anyone for the intensity of a moment and success will be determined by the mind and belief.

Success does not just happen by accident. Some are lucky but luck rarely beats the test of time and those without substance or skill are soon found out. Have you ever wondered why someone with obvious ability and talent never quite makes it whilst others with less talent do? When Jonny Wilkinson announced his retirement in 2014, Nick Kennedy (*The Guardian* May 2014) commented:

"One of the reasons the team is so successful is because it's driven by him. He's the leader and he puts in more work than anyone but he's incredibly humble. It's a team full of superstars but they can't let their egos get the better of them because Jonny's in charge. He's the most famous and the most talented but also the most grounded. In his team talks he speaks first in perfect French and then repeats it in English.

The French absolutely adore him. We'd park under the stadium and he had to have his own security guard – three hours before kick-off. The crowd loves him so much. Once a month we'd go and train at a different rugby club in the area and afterwards we'd do autographs. It would have been a lot quicker if we didn't have Jonny. We'd be there for two hours – in a long line of tables. They had to go past the rest of us to reach Jonny. And with Jonny they'd want a photo and a hug. He never brushes people off and he always makes it special. No other guy could then brush off a supporter and say, 'Oh, I'm busy,' because they'd see what Jonny had done.

It's the same with rugby. There were games last season [Kennedy now plays for Harlequins] where he might've missed a kick. The next day you're bruised and battered and you go for a recovery swim in the sea or spend a day on the sofa. Not Jonny. He would be at training kicking and doing a fitness session. Phenomenal. He does beat himself up because he's a perfectionist but that's why he's been at the top of the game so long. No wonder Toulon want to erect a statue of Jonny".[29]

Wilkinson has maybe been the finest exponent of the sporting professional ethic that has been. He was dedicated and understood what the sport meant to himself, his team and those that follow the game.

It certainly has little to do with skill being the only component for success. *"Most talented players don't always succeed. Some don't even make the team. It's more what's inside."* – Brett Favre[30]

There are a whole number of factors including the obvious – some work harder, listen and learn but more importantly they make the most of the talent that they possess whilst others take it for granted or possess barriers within themselves that they cannot overcome for it takes a courage that they do not have. It is easier to comment on others than put oneself out in the spotlight.

There is a fabulous old quote that states:

"Don't ask yourself what the world needs, ask yourself what makes you come alive, and then go do that. Because what the world needs is [people] who have come alive." – (Rev DrThurman)[31]

And that is what great sport is about – players coming alive in those moments that define a match. Think of Ian Botham's great 149 versus Australia in 1981 or his five for one spell in the subsequent match at Edgbaston; or Jonny Wilkinson's dropped goal in the 2003 Rugby World Cup Final.

Confidence within a team can be remarkably fickle. In 1985, David Gower's leadership as captain was praised for how he gave his players the freedom to express themselves and let them play as they saw fit. England beat Australia 3–1 and Graham Gooch famously wrote a letter to Gower to say how good it had been to play under his captaincy. Within 12 months, Gower was sacked after England were soundly thrashed in the West Indies and the freedom he had allowed the players was ridiculed. The relationship between Gower and Gooch fell to a public low when roles were reversed and Gooch was captain over Gower. Gooch wanted greater concentration and dedication from Gower whilst maybe Gower was more understanding of Gooch and that each player responded to different influences. Both were naturally gifted cricketers. Gooch first played for England in 1975 and was, at the time, viewed to be the middle order stroke maker that Gower became for England. Gooch worked hard to reinvent himself as an opener, which he did very effectively. Both were exceptional players but with different philosophies.

It is no coincidence that the old school English gentleman was universally respected, admired and hailed as a role model for good behaviour. They were seen to be polite, well dressed, gentle in their behaviour, but also calm and considered under pressure. It is again no coincidence that many of the great leaders within sport possess these traits. It is no coincidence that English sport flourished often under the old-fashioned gentleman captain. But it isn't about class, but the person.

Success over a long period of time requires respect from others. Respect comes from many sources but one can gain instant respect through being a step above others in how one behaves. Too many can reduce themselves to mediocrity through a crass comment, a moment of frustration or poor presentation.

This is where modern life does make it more difficult than in past times for there are no simple rules anymore. In today's world, society is more accepting and cosmopolitan. What is right is different for each person. However little is more powerful than great dress in order to make a great first impression.

The challenge – and the reason why people do require coaching – is that the art is to combine character with the ability to let skills and talent feel free and be productive in a socially competent fashion.

So many people do not let themselves be free enough to let their talents be productivity. There are so many obstacles to overcome – shyness, fear, and even just a need to try and do what is right and not stand out. The British love the eccentric character and yet the educational system rarely encourages talent to be brave and different. The system asks for people to conform and yet at the same time we ask for the same people to be brave and not conform when it matters. Coaches can be quick to criticise those that do stand out and then wonder why they get hurt?

To be successful, it is important to learn a couple of basic truths and as obvious as they are, they are very difficult to learn:

If one does not conform and does things differently, it does challenge others and it will create tensions.

Criticism comes naturally with success. It is just part of the journey and one has to accept it. However, it is rarely about you as a person, for the simple reason that few that criticise you will know you as a person beyond the superficial so the answer lies in just accepting it and raising the bar. It is better to win through actions than let the negatives of others influence you not to be as good as you are able to be.

To be successful, it does require bravery as it is not an easy journey and it is easier to opt out.

Not true? One of the recent theories to emerge, as to why our sports teams do not thrive on the world stage is that they are not brave enough. The view is that we have the talent within the system; we have more players, more infrastructure, more financial support and investment but the players are coached to play within systems and structures – so much so that they lack the inner confidence to do what made them successful in the first place – let their inhabitations go and play freely as they would have done in their youth. It is logical. It is no coincidence that the UK possesses so many sports teams, such passion for sport and yet is so rarely successful.

There is an inherent fear of being different and standing out. Get free of this fear and suddenly all kinds of possibilities open up.

Often people defeat themselves at work for the simple reason that mentally they think too much about themselves. They become the barrier to success. They are not brave and they want to stay within boundary lines. But by the very nature of this mind-set, it creates nothing that is new or innovative and success requires bravery to be different.

Of course the whole process becomes a negative cycle as a person's internal reserved nature stops the person doing either what is right or letting their talents shine. They are not true to themselves nor able to be fully productive.

It would be far better if they could just stop thinking about themselves – take themselves out of their thinking and just trust themselves. Let's go back to the sporting comparison and the cricket debate of the last year between Cook v Pietersen. Alastair Cook was probably as free scoring as Kevin Pietersen as a schoolboy and became more restrained with coaching. He has still broken all the records but one wonders how much better a player he could be if he just felt less contained and responsible?

Of course, this is not to encourage irresponsible behaviour but simply to trust one's own natural instincts. A well-behaved person will always be well-behaved because it is in their DNA. The challenge is let their talent not be contained. A free spirit is a different challenge and they need to find self-discipline so that can still be free but within boundaries.

Everyone is different. That is why players are so fascinating but some never give themselves the chance to be successful and the challenge is to free their talents and this does require coaching and learning. The challenge is for the Brits to free their talent.

It was clear that being brave was no longer enough. So what was required to be a winner? The answer lay in greater professionalism and vision amongst administrators, coaches and managers.

CAPTAINS

2 – David Gower

England Cricket Captain 1983–86 and 1989

Gower is rightly regarded as one of England's best ever batsman but his record as captain was less impressive. Gower's captaincy saw victories in India (1984–85) and winning The Ashes in 1985 but also the lows of the 1984 and 1985 Blackwashes against the West Indies and a 4–0 Ashes defeat in 1989.

Gower was such a natural, instinctive player that maybe captaincy did not come naturally to him or was he just a victim of circumstance? Or maybe more likely, was his approach more of the amateur ethos than the modern professional ethos? Gower was a committed cricket player but he was never obsessed by the sport. He understood that there was more to life and that he was privileged to be to play the game.

There are many stories about Gower the man that range from his Tiger moth episode on the 1990–91 tour to Australia, to his love for wine, to episodes in the Swiss Alps to his belief that players are more than able to judge how much they need to train and prepare for matches.

Frances Edmonds, wife of the England spinner Phil Edmonds wrote: "It's difficult to be more laid back than David Gower without being actually comatose."[32]

Gower played 117 Test matches and 114 One Day Internationals (ODI) scoring 8,231 and 3,170 runs, respectively. He was one of the most capped and high scoring players for England during his period.

Gower made his England debut in 1978 and hit the first ball he faced in Test cricket for four. It was quite an announcement of his entry into the Test match arena. From that moment on, the expectations of Gower were of the highest level and in fairness he did not always live up to them.

Gower's generation of England cricketers could have been a golden era with the likes of Ian Botham, Graham Gooch and Bob Willis but the team, never really fulfilled its potential.

Gower took over the captaincy for the West Indies tour of England in 1984. The West Indies won easily 5–0 but in fairness to Gower, England were outclassed. It was often like men against boys. In the final Test at the Oval, the West Indies attack was led by the great Michael Holding. England's attack by Jonathan Agnew. Agnew was a talented cricketer but he was not in the same league as Holding and it did make it appear as though England were firing shots with a pea shooter against Holding thunderbolts. Was this Gower's fault? A captain can only do so much.

It was only in the Lord's Test did England compete and have hopes of victory; only for it to be blown away on the last day as the West Indies batsmen thrashed England's bowlers.

In the winter, Gower led England on a tour to India with fresh faces and built a good team spirit and morale and the team responded some great play to win the series 2–1. The following summer, England's cricket seemed to be on the up as they played positive, winning cricket against Allan Border's Australia and won the Ashes 3–1.

It maybe was not the time to tour the West Indies. England needed another couple of years of building as a team but life is not perfect. Gower endured a torrid time; losing his mother before the tour and then facing a new West Indies onslaught as England were once again outgunned and outclassed 5–0. Gower's captaincy came under scrutiny and criticism as he allowed players time to relax rather than train as England fell to defeat. His argument was logical. He believed that players needed to escape away from cricket in order to recharge rather than just train and practice. However, of course, it seemed as though he was just being laid back and not as professional in work ethic as the West Indies.

Gower tried to face all the criticism as well as he could, but he did build to a crescendo. The harsh reality was that the England team was just not good enough to play the best team in the world and whoever led England, little would have been different. Gower was replaced in 1986. He was briefly reinstated for the 1989 Ashes series, but England again fell to defeat 4–0 at home. Once again the Australians possessed a better work ethic than the England players and Gower was seen to be too laid back. However the issue was deeper. Many of the players had become disillusioned and had signed for a rebel tour to South Africa. It has been throughout this book about the small margins that exist between success and failure and England are unlikely to have been competitive when discussions about the rebel tour were taking place in the background. The tour was to be led by Mike Gatting who had been captain until being sacked in 1988 and some of the players had felt that the sacking had been unfair. In fairness they had a point as he had been sacked for having a hotel barmaid in his room, even though the selectors accepted that nothing inappropriate had taken place.

The 1989 series saw all the criticism of Gower's laid back style return and he did not always help himself. In a press conference in the second Test at Lord's when England were losing, he stormed out saying that he had tickets for the theatre. Life often has a quirky sense of humour as the show Gower was to see that evening was "Anything Goes" which some would argue was aptly titled. He may have handled the situation better, but he may also have been hurting knowing that the mind-set in the dressing room was simply not in the right place and not knowing the answer.

If one looks at Gower through a clearer perspective, without the emotions of sport, one will see a man that is, in truth, very professional and intelligent. He has worked hard to become one of Sky TVs best commentators and offers good insight. He was simply a naturally gifted player that did not see sport or cricket as the be all and end all. Was he not committed enough? Unlikely as his record is one of the best in history and one would not achieve this without dedication and commitment. No, in truth, he was maybe too gifted and expectations were simply too great. The Test series that England lost under Gower were series that would have been lost by any captain. The West Indies were the best team in the world and the 1989 series was arguably lost before a ball was bowled due to issues from the previous summer which had been chaotic and had seen four England captains lead the team against the West Indies. After such a poor period, it would take time to recover but much was expected of Gower and England.

Chapter Three

WHY DO THE BRITISH VIEW
SPORT DIFFERENTLY?

It is an old adage that to understand the present, one must first understand the past. Sport has changed so much that this can be difficult but history tells a fascinating story on the journey that taken sport from the school field to major arenas and explains just why sport is so important in our cultures.

It is always assumed that the three core team sports emerged as real sports in the Victorian age and there is truth in this, but football and cricket have been played for a long time before. There are some that date cricket back to the 16th century although it became a national game in the 18th century and a global game in the Victorian era for reasons that will become clear. The difference was that the games prior to the Victorian era were not governed and organised and that the Victorians did bring order and structure to the games. This allowed the sports to develop and evolve to where they are today.

The Victorian age plays a crucial role in the how the British view sport for they changed the perception of games from being purely recreational to playing an important role in the educational development of young men. Some will argue this was part of the strong, Christian led value set that dominated the age; others that the education system structured sport to have a meaning beyond the game itself as a method of teaching young men how to behave and act. Whichever is true, the era changed the way that games were perceived and played for the next one hundred years.

In the early 1800s, football was on the decline in popularity across the country. Its fortunes were changed as the game was adopted by the country's top private schools, as a method for controlling the boys and building their character. It was a logical step as educational leaders sought to develop future leaders that the schools could be proud of in future years and, of course, reflect well on them in return. The idea was that football, cricket – and later rugby – would be a medium to cultivate athleticism, an understanding of the team ethic and more importantly, how to support the weak. Sport can be about the strong, but teams need to be as good as their weakest links. The Victorian school of thought believed that men should be chivalrous and champions of the weak but also physically strong and robust.

The Victorian age is full of many contradictions. It saw Britain rise as an Empire that at times displayed a bloody and ruthless approach but lived to a strict moral code. Sport was part of the learning of this code.

During the 1800s, Britain did become arrogant in its belief that they should have an Empire. As it became a global power, it built real wealth and authority across the world but working to a deep Christian belief.

Sport came to symbolise both – the best of British talent and how the stronger player is only as good as his weaker member in the team. The belief grew that the sports would cultivate the right behaviours in young men with teaching that the sport was important but there was a greater ethos at heart which said that winning was not everything.

Of course, it was not long before the universities followed the example of the schools and so the game had a new lease of life. At university, it also had a broader social role to play as it allowed boys from different public schools to play together. As the game spread its base, so the rules developed and governing bodies were gradually founded.

As the Empire grew, so did the opportunities and, as the new generation left university they naturally spread the word as they themselves spread across the world. British sports were taken to new countries, new audiences and of course, as the Empire grew so sport was encouraged with a strong common belief in the importance of what sport can teach. It had taught the new leaders the importance of values within the games so it was logical that it could have the same affects on new international audiences governed by the British. Over the years, Britain exported "sport" throughout its empire and alongside trade and organization. The Empire was arguably one of the most respected of empires, as it also gave as well as took. It developed infrastructures and organization with under-developed nations and brought organised recreation and games into their societies. One has to wryly smile to consider that Britain exported football to Brazil, rugby and cricket to Australia, cricket to India and West Indies and we have struggled in matches with them for decades.

In Britain the game of football soon spread too, as it was inexpensive and required limited space and again taught important social values in a method that stood outside of either school or the church. It was natural that the working classes in nineteenth century Britain would soon take the game to their hearts – and of course, its popularity was encouraged by social leaders as being important in the development of a strong value set with the lower social strata.

It can be argued that so effective was the process that this has been one of the key barriers to change as sport moved into the professional era, as our social learning has taught that sport was more about the playing and competing than about the winning. One of the main issues that undermined professionalism in the 70s and 80s especially was almost a reluctance by professionals to do more than train and play the games. It returns to the point made previously about the lack of knowledge and education over rest, diets, preparation and drinking.

An example to illustrate this point was in the mid 1980s when the England football team was struggling to re-establish itself at the top table of the game; Ray Wilkins left Manchester United for AC Milan. Wilkins found that the Italians were ten years ahead of the English game in how the clubs managed and prepared the players off the field. How could England be surprised that they were not competing at the top table when other countries were doing that much more to prepare and ready players for combat?

The answer lies in the fact that the truth was hidden by the fact that the British game valued different values and their club teams competed effectively against the leading European teams. English clubs won the European Cup seven times from 1977 to 1985 through not just one club, but with Liverpool, Nottingham Forest, and Aston Villa. How? The team ethic and commitment of the players managed to hide the weaknesses. If the English game could have had equal preparation to those in Italy and Germany, one wonders what England could have achieved during the 1970s and 80s.

Cricket was the first of the major sports to embrace professionalism. It can be dated back to the eighteenth century, but as an obsession with amateur ethic to sport grew from the success and strength of the public schools and the public school ethos of fair play and playing for the sake of the game. Above all, amateurism was about projecting social position and affluence in a period of social change as the industrial revolution found root. To be an amateur in late Victorian and Edwardian Britain was to play the game with no desire or need to be paid to play. One played for the love of the game. Money would come from prosperity at work.

One can be critical of the public school system, and many have been over the last fifty years, but it did found a strong belief system; the ethos for how and why sport is played in the UK – which is the game is more than just about winning. One can be critical that this core belief hindered a move towards a hard professional ethic but it also makes Britain stand apart for reasons that it can be proud of. As this story unfolds, it will become clear that the countries that most embrace the professional sport are those countries that need sport to give their countries a strong national identity. They was a social and cultural need to be successful and on a personal level the players could play a role in their countries histories. In Britain it was different. Britain possessed a strong national identity and an Empire – and later Commonwealth. Sport was not part of this identity. It had a history and legacy so sport was part of culture and an escape/entertainment from the pressures of daily life. It has simply taken time for Britain to adapt.

The issue does always lie in the concept of professionalism but something slightly deeper. Golf was one of the first sports to embrace professionals. At the turn of the twentieth century, three British men dominated golf so much that they became known as the Great Triumvirate – named after the Triumvirate of Pompey, Caesar and Crassus who governed the Roman Empire in 60 BC. The three players were Harry Vardon (Channel Islands), James Braid (Scotland) and John Henry Taylor (Devon). Between 1894 and 1914, they won 16 of the 21 British Opens. In the five years that they did not win, one finished runner-up. Vardon also open the US Open, beating Taylor.

Vardon will always be known as one of the greats of the game. He is often regarded as the "father of modern golf". His tour of the United States in 1900 was seen to be the first time a golfer united players and fans on both sides of the Atlantic.

As the game of Cricket, in early 1900s, developed and professionals played alongside amateurs, social distinction was preserved through the use of different changing rooms, different ways of writing names and initially requiring professionals to labour with bowling and even menial tasks such as cleaning the kit. Yet, despite the snobbery that underpinned amateurism there was a general reluctance in most sports to impose explicit class-based restrictions on participation.

One has to remember that the Olympics did not allow professionals to compete until the 1988 games, as it was proud to remain a champion of the amateur. However it was forced to change when the IOC was forced to accept and bow to pressure from other countries against the Soviet Union and Eastern Bloc whose athletes were being supported by their government to train full-time. This created a grey area for the IOC to deal with, because the Soviets were not really professional athletes, but since they didn't hold down day jobs and were able to train all day, they weren't amateurs either. The playing field was simply unfairly balanced. So the IOC changed by dropping the distinction between professional and amateur athletes and opened the door to all athletes. In truth, the IOC would have preferred to remain amateur as it encouraged the belief that it was the taking part and competing that was more important than the winning, but there was no option but to change.

From 1870 on, sport in the UK became more organized and players began to emerge who excited audiences throughout the land. Maybe the most famous was one of the great legends of English cricket in W.G. Grace (1848-1915). He was undoubtedly the most famous sportsman of the Victorian era. Grace was a doctor and a gentleman but he was also supremely competitive. He was arguably the sports first superstar and he was certainly a dominant figure of his time. He played first-class cricket for a record-equalling 44 seasons, from 1865 to 1908, during which he captained England, Gloucestershire, the Gentlemen, Marylebone Cricket Club (MCC), the United South of England Eleven (USEE) and several other teams.

During this period, it was in rugby and soccer that the issue of professionalism became most controversial. The growth of socially mixed northern teams led to broken-time payments, where working men were compensated for missing work in order to play. Such payments however not only offended the amateur's principles of some of the elite, but they also threatened to take power away from the middle classes, both on and off the playing field. It may be no surprise then to learn that the first four winners of the English Football Championship were from the North – Preston North End (twice), Everton and Sunderland between 1888 and 1892. A Southern team did not win the league until Arsenal in 1930 and Aston Villa was the southern-most based team to win between 1888 and 1930. It does tell its own story.

The north/south tensions plagued rugby too and this led rugby to split into two codes (which later became known as league and union) in1895. Rugby league became a sport whose whole existence and identity was closely interwoven with ideas of working-class identity in northern England.

One can easily understand how the concept of professionalism was almost a dirty word. It expected different behaviours from that had been taught as the basis for good and strong character. Rugby Union stayed as an Amateur game, taking great pride in its status as being a sport played for the love of the game for the next one hundred years and only became an "open" game and professional in 1995. It is almost as though the Union game took a century to accept the advance of professionalism, Whether the IOC and the Olympics or Rugby Union, there was a fear that professionalism would change the founding principles set by the public schools back in the Victorian era and held so dear as a means for education and developing social comradeship. However, sport needed to change as the audiences – both on TV and in stadiums – were growing and attracting increasing numbers of sponsors so that the governing bodies were being prosperous but the players were still playing for the love of the game and low rewards. Change was inevitable. In fact it is surprising just how long the amateur code survived and players were as loyal to it as they were considering that television had made the players household names and role models.

Of course, in the early days it was still not easy. The problem about professionalism is that it does mean that the players need to be paid and audiences, in the late 1800s, were limited. Clubs could only afford to pay players because soccer and rugby had become something that people watched as well as played. This owed much to the establishment of cup competitions, which gave some purpose and excitement to matches.

In the industrial north of England, the growing crowds began to be charged for the privilege of watching and hosted in purpose-built grounds. This does explain why the FA Cup carried such importance for over a century from 1972 to the late 1990s when the Cup did begin to lose value as the clubs focused more on the Premier League and Champions League. In the 1960s, 70s and 80s, Cup Final day was one of the most important days in the sporting calendar. In those days the only event comparable to the Cup Final was the Super Bowl. In 1923, the FA Cup Final attracted 126,000 to Wembley Stadium. 1938 was the first Final to be televised with an estimated audience of 10,000. In 2005 it was estimated to be 484 million globally. Over the last decade, the Cup Final has decreased in importance, which does sadden many from previous generations as Cup Final day was such a special occasion that was a celebration of football.

After noting that 126,000 attended the 1923 Final, it may seem strange to observe that at first supporters watching matches was a concern to many. Why? It was seen to encourage poor behaviours such as drinking, gambling and partisan behaviours amongst fans. Was it healthy, it was asked, for people to be watching sport rather than playing? Could this trend to undermine the underlying ethos that had been encouraged as the games were developed? In fairness the same questions were asked with the advent of television

When soccer played on after the outbreak of war in 1914 the reputation of professional sport plummeted amongst the middle classes who felt that it was not respectful to the soldiers on the front line. Nonetheless, sport was to play an important role in maintaining troop morale at the front and of course, football stands at the heart of one of the greatest stories of friendship and comradeship from the Great War – the 1914 Christmas Truce match between the trenches.

In the aftermath of the Great War spectator sport reached new heights of popularity. The largest league games in soccer could attract as many as 60,000; yet, disorder was rare. This led the sport to be celebrated as a symbol of the general orderliness and good nature of the British working class at a time of political and social unrest at home and abroad. For spectators, professional sport offered an exciting communal experience, where the pressures of daily life could be forgotten in the company of one's friend's and community.

As such, crowds at professional soccer and rugby league became overwhelmingly escapes for men who sought for something beyond their home and work community.

It gave many a feeling of belonging and identity that they could not find in their daily lives. In the 1970s when hooliganism escalated, many blamed the football clubs but the truth is that the stadiums and teams were the mechanism through which the hooligans acted, but not the reason. The supporters became the tribe and the many could unleash their frustrations in a place where it would not affect either their work or home life. It was almost violent escapism. Those that feared that watching sport would support the development of bad behaviours were right, but for the wrong reasons. It was a broader social issue and little to do with sport bar the fact that it was the venue where men collated together.

Football today is dominant as the national sport, but it was cricket which was the number one national sport of the late nineteenth and early twentieth-century. The contest between the skill and speed of the bowler and the technique and bravery of the batsmen was one familiar to both working-class boys and upper-class gentlemen. Cricket's popularity has always owed something to the rural image of England that it encapsulated. Cricket on the village green was an evocative and emotive image. Over time, cricket spread not only to the masses of the cities, but also the four corners of the vast British Empire, where it enabled the colonies to both celebrate links with the motherland and also take considerable pride in putting the English in their place. As England players and supporters will tell, one of the realities of sport is how so many countries raise their game against England and compete that much harder when playing their old foes. They may not be able to rid themselves of England politically or economically, but a win of the sports field was a great tonic for their people. When England won the World Cup in 1966, one could almost forecast that the first team to beat them at Wembley would be Scotland (3–2 in 1967). In 1977, before a game against England, Phil Bennett – the Captain of Wales – famously said to his players:

> Look what these bastards have done to Wales. They've taken our coal, our water, our steel. They buy our homes and live in them for a fortnight every year. What have they given us? Absolutely nothing. We've been exploited, raped, controlled and punished by the English – and that's who you are playing this afternoon. (33)

Sport may have started as being about teaching young men how to behave and act but by the 1930s, sport has taken on greater importance. International matches were about national pride. Maybe one of the most bitterly contested matches was the 1932–33 Ashes series in Australia which illustrated how the game was no longer just about good and fair play.

In the early 1930s there was no television and it was hard to follow the game bar through newspapers and the wireless. Therefore for a cricket tour to be raised in both the Australian and British Parliaments, the strength of feeling must have deep and strong. There is no doubt that it was one of the most controversial, highly charged tours in the history of the game.

However its importance lay in two other features. Firstly, the tour marked maybe the first example of a strategy being developed – in a coldly professional approach – to combat the strengths of the opposition. The core objective was winning and secondly this objective made many in England uncomfortable, as it was not "cricket's way".

The arrival of the English touring side in Australia for the Ashes series during the summer of 1932–33 was much anticipated by all Australian cricket fans. The Ashes was already one of the great sporting contests and in Donald Bradman, the Australians already possessed one of the greatest players. Bradman had led Australia's victory in a series in England in 1930 and had been such a dominant player that England knew they needed to neutralise his strengths. The only problem was Bradman was regarded as the greatest batsman to have played the game and the only way the objective could be achieved was through a tough, robust approach that would alienate many. The man to lead this challenge was Douglas Jardine whose name even to this day is viewed with disdain by some. Jardine adopted a tactic later to become known as Bodyline.

Bodyline involved the placing of a least five players close in to the batsman and the bowler continually bowling a barrage of short pitched balls aimed on leg stump, these balls would quickly rear up from the pitch placing the batsman in danger of serious injury. To counter these rising deliveries, the batsman would be forced to adopt defensive batting strokes, which would regularly result in catches to the close in fieldsmen.

Jardine had studied Bradman's play for long periods as he prepared for the tour and there is no doubt that Bradman was affected by these close in fielders who interfered with his concentration. A number of the Australian players were subsequently injured as a result of the tactic of Bodyline. It was not only the Australian players who were aghast at the tactics of the English, but also the Australian cricket authorities and many traditionalists in England who felt that it was not in the spirit of the game.

The Australian Cricket Board sent an urgent telegram to the English board demanding that they instruct Jardine to change his approach. For the sake of cricket and sportsmanship the Australians pleaded with the English to refrain. Discussions were even held in the Australian Parliament to find a way to stop the Englishmen from devastating and tarnishing the game of cricket.

High-level diplomatic meetings were held between the English and the Australians. The English went on to win back the Ashes from Australia, and the tactics of Bodyline had served their purpose. They had contained and restrained the great Donald Bradman. However had Jardine's approach been against the spirit of the game? Had he played ethically?

The tactic of Bodyline bowling, a name coined by the Australian press, was referred to as the Leg Theory by the English. Of course, the irony is that the great Australian team under Ian and Greg Chappell was just as ruthless as the team under Jardine. Lillee and Thomson were, in the 70s, the most lethal fast bowling combination to play the game. Keith Miller, the great Australian all-rounder, once quipped about Thompson, "He frightened me, and I was sitting 200 yards away".[34]

"I enjoy hitting a batsman more than getting him out. I like to see blood on the pitch," [35] Thomson once said in a television interview. Whether it was said tongue in cheek or not, it caused a furore but not to the level that was caused by Bodyline.

Bodyline changed the game as it changed the spirit of the contest. The contest was now about winning as well as sport. The laws may have been changed but what could not be changed was the fact that the competition was rising.

Jardine did not help himself. Whether out of design or not, he behaved with arrogance and coldness during that tour. He possessed a single mindedness and cool demeanour to be able to handle all that came in his direction. His objective to stop Bradman scoring and by doing this, undermining Australian confidence.

Jardine was a naturally arrogant man. He was born in Bombay, into a dynasty of well-heeled Scottish lawyers. At the age of nine he was sent to live near St Andrews, and schooled at Winchester College. He once celebrated winning the school's inter-house competition by pinning up an unconventional team sheet. "Cook House: D.R. Jardine, W.M. Leggatt. The following might have been included had they not been unable to bat or bowl, or even to field..."[36]

Maybe it was not the best wording to employ to win friends and hardly in the spirit of supporting the weak and less able.

The teenage Jardine clearly left a strong impression on his cricket master, Rockley Wilson. When he was appointed England captain, a journalist asked Wilson to rate his prospects. The reply was almost supernaturally prescient: "He might well win us the Ashes, but he might lose us a Dominion."[37]

In Jardine's obituary, *Wisden* described this tour as, "probably the most controversial tour in history. England won four of the five tests, but it was the methods they employed rather than the results which caused so much discussion and acrimony."[38]

After Jardine and Bodyline, there was a need for a romantic hero to take cricket back to its heartland and with this need emerged the most talented all-round sportsmen of his generation In Dennis Compton. Compton was the Beckhamesque figure of the 1930s and 40s – well presented, athletic, skilled in both cricket and football, dashing and a bold player that excited the hungry crowds. Compton was one of a series of British sporting heroes that lit up the 1930s and included Fred Perry and Henry Cotton.

"From time to time, in most walks of life, a man appears who rises above his particular job and attracts the attention of people who are not intensely interested in his vocation...Nature came to him with her cornucopia pretty full and she let him help himself to it...Dennis Compton contributes to English life and holiday at the crown of the year; he is part of the English summer."[39] (Neville Cardus)

In Golf, Henry Cotton became the first British Golfer since the days of Vardon to be seen as truly "world class". His win at The British Open in 1934 ended a ten year monopoly by players from the US and he went on to win further opens in 1937 and 1948. Cotton with Fred Perry (Tennis) were great icons for the public to follow.

Fred Perry's success would later become a real burden for all British Tennis players to follow for only Andy Murray has really come close to being at the same level. Perry was a working class man who had a dedicated work ethic that allowed him to rise and become a world champion.

He won 10 Majors including eight Grand Slams and two Pro Slams single titles, as well as six Major doubles titles. Perry won three consecutive Wimbledon Championships from 1934 to 1936 and was World Amateur number one tennis player during those three years. Prior to Andy Murray in 2013, Perry was the last British player to win the men's Wimbledon championship, in 1936, and the last British player to win a men's singles Grand Slam title until Andy Murray won the 2012 US Open.

Perry was the first player to win a 'Career Grand Slam' winning all four singles titles at the age of 26 which he completed at the 1935 French Championships and remains the only British player ever to achieve this feat. Although Perry began his tennis career aged 18, he was also a Table Tennis World Champion in 1929.

In 1933, Perry helped lead the Great Britain team to victory over France in the Davis Cup; the team's first success since 1912, followed by wins over the United States in 1934, 1935, and a fourth consecutive title with victory over Australia in 1936.

However, his background was an issue that followed him around and he became very disillusioned with the class-conscious nature of the game in Britain. Perry turned professional at the end of the 1936 season and moved to the United States where he became a naturalised US citizen in 1938. In 1942, he was drafted into the US Air Force during World War Two. Britain had lost one of its greatest sporting talents for the wrong reasons.

Dennis Compton was the leading sporting role model for boys throughout the country in the 1940s. He was attractive, athletic and skilled. He played cricket for England and football for Arsenal. He made his debut for Arsenal in 1936 and his debut for the England Cricket team in 1937. He played both games with grace and ease. He believed that sport should be played in a positive attitude and hated the negative tactics that would be used in later years. Once he was asked how he made the skill of batting look so easy he simply smiled and replied; "It is amazing that the more I practice, the easier the game becomes".[40]

He was at his height after World War Two, when in four summers and two overseas tours – to Australia in 1946–47 and to South Africa in 1948–49 – he scored 14,641 runs and made 60 centuries. But statistics only tell a part of the story, as his real genius was that he did play the game in the right spirit with daring and improvisation.

His trademark shot as a batsman was the sweep, of which he deployed several different varieties and which he did not hesitate to play off balls that would have hit the middle stump. He played cricket with aggressive intent. He looked to score runs and intimidate the opposition not with his physical presence but with his skill.

Compton's impact on post war England can be best described by Sir Neville Cardus who wrote:

> Never have I been so deeply touched on a cricket ground, as I was in this heavenly summer of 1947 when I went to Lord's to see a pale-faced crowd, existing on rations, the rocket-bomb still in the ears of most folks – and see this worn, dowdy crowd raptly watching Compton."
>
> The strain of long years of anxiety and affliction passed from all heads and shoulders at the sight of Compton in full sail, sending the ball here, there, and everywhere, each stroke a flick of delight, a propulsion of happy, sane, healthy life. There were no rations in an innings by Compton.
>
> Compton was almost a man from the Corinthian image age when playing for Middlesex and England in the summer was fortified in the winter when he turned his attention to football. He was good enough to hold his place in the great Arsenal sides before and after the war, collecting both a League and a Cup medal. He also won 14 wartime international caps for England.

The question is whether Compton's attitude and approach was created by understanding sport's place after the sadness of war. He was certainly a breath of fresh air and he inspired the country.

It is important though not to underestimate the man as a professional and simply to portray as almost an old school amateur in approach. Compton was, in fact, the opposite – a modern professional for a new era. He played the game to win but knew he had the skill to play the game for fun too.

Compton understood that to win at the highest level one had to play with freedom and be brave. In 1993, he commented, "I would dearly love the boys to go out there like playboys, play off the back foot, and enjoy it."[41]

Too often for all those that have followed England over the years has been a stomach churning feeling that the players did not enjoy the game and did not believe they were good enough. Some will argue that it is the pressure of playing for England and the highest of expectations, but the truth is that the greatest players are able to play the game in the moment.

E.W. Swanton, the great writer, once wrote: "What marked Denis Compton's batting from the first was a sense of enjoyment in it all, of risks taken and bowlers teased, that at once communicated itself to the crowd."[42]

When one considers that he lost six wartime summers from the age of 21 onwards, Compton's achievements, numerically speaking were of the highest order

His 38,942 runs, including 123 hundreds, were made at an average of 51.85; his 5,807 Test runs, including 17 hundreds, at 50. He just played the game with a freedom and bravery that made him stand apart.

As time passed and the sports grew as an entertainment so there importance grew too. It is one of life's little ironies that the English are described as being an emotionally reserved race for the truth is that the English are far more emotional than most nationalities. The English may be restrained with any open show of emotion in our day to day lives but that changes the moment they enter a sporting stadium. It is not just reserved for football; the English love their sport – all sports. It is no coincidence that after World War Two, both football and cricket enjoyed periods when attendance levels recorded new highs as people sought to escape their dismal day hardships through sport. On August Bank Holiday Monday 1946, 100,000 attended nine first class cricket matches. In a friendly match between Chelsea and Dynamo Moscow in 1945 at Stamford Bridge it is estimated that over 90,000 filled Stamford Bridge to watch a 3–3 draw. In theory, the gates were closed when an officially full capacity of 74,000 had entered, but still thousands continued to enter the ground. The iconic Tommy Lawton was making his debut for Chelsea. It is estimated that nearly one million attended the opening matches of the season in 1946. Charlton, in 1946, attracted over 40,000 for each home match. At the time The Valley (Charlton's home stadium) was one of league's largest stadiums, for a match in 1938 versus Aston Villa had attracted a record 75,000. Football – and sport – had a new central importance within society.

There is an argument that England could really have been genuine world champions for long periods between 1870 and 1950. Without consistent international tournaments it is impossible to answer this question, but England won the football gold medal in the 1908 and 1912 Olympics and it seems clear no other nation had overtaken England by this point. How they would have coped with the 1920s Uruguayans or travelling to and playing in South America in 1930 raises some doubts, but it could be argued that they were the best team in Europe, if not the world, in the 1940s and before this may have even have won one or both of the 1934 or 1938 World Cups had they competed. Is it too much to suggest that if there had been a European-based World Cup in the 1940s then England would surely have won it?

This claim to greatness is chiefly substantiated by England's results against Italy, still reigning World Champions until 1950, and still under the guidance of the great coach, Pozzo, in 1948. Italy never beat England when they were world champions and on 16 May 1948 England beat the Italians 4–0 in Turin. The Italy team contained seven players from the great Torino side of the era. This was seen as a major victory at the time and justified England's high opinion of her own footballers. Also in 1948 England beat Portugal an incredible 10–0 away in Lisbon. This was a Portuguese side that had recently ended the record unbeaten run of the great emerging Hungarian side. And, of course, England remained unbeaten at Wembley until 1953 when the Hungarian team of Puskas came to Wembley and won over the nation with their natural flair and skill. The Hungarians, on that day in 1953, showed England that the game was changing and evolving with new ideas, tactics and approach.

This was a golden period for the English game with matches that will always be recognised in history and include the day when England played the World Champions, Italy, in 1934; the day England beat the Germans in 1938 which is a symbol of England's stubborn refusal to be intimidated. The next forty years witnessed real ups and down but football prospered.

The Great Matches

November 1934
The Battle of Highbury
England v Italy

England played the newly crowned World Champions at Arsenal's stadium in north London in a tense and often bad tempered match. England had not taken part in the 1934 World Cup so the match has special meaning. England to measure how they fared against the best team in the world and for the Italians to prove conclusively that deserved the title World Champions. England went 3–0 in the first 12 minutes through goals from Eric Brook (3 and 10 mins) and Ted Drake (12). The Italians though were not World Champions for nothing and came back in the second half with goals through Guiseppe Meazza (58 and 62). Stanley Matthews later recounted it was one of the most violent matches he had ever played in and Italy did play most of the game with only 10 fit men after their centre-half, Monti, had his foot broken after only two minutes.

Sir Winston Churchill once said, "Italians lose wars as if they were football matches, and football matches as if they were wars."[43]

September 1938
Germany v England

The England soccer team were even told by the appeasing Foreign Office to give the Nazi salute when playing an international in Berlin in 1938. With war looming, England played Germany in Berlin in front of a crowd of 110,000. Despite the players' reluctance, the Foreign office ordered the players to show respect to their hosts with the Nazi salute prior to the match. Stanley Matthews later recalled:

> The dressing room erupted. There was bedlam. All the England players were livid and totally opposed to this, myself included. Everyone was shouting at once. Eddie Hapgood, normally a respectful and devoted captain, wagged his finger at the official and told him what he could do with the Nazi salute, which involved putting it where the sun doesn't shine.[44]

None the less, it clearly motivated the players to show less respect during the match as an England team inspired by the great Stanley Matthews outplayed Germany to win 6–3 through goals from Cliff Bastin, Jackie Robinson, Stanley Matthews, Frank Broome and Len Goulden.

The game was watched by 110,000 people as well as senior Nazis, Hermann Göring and Joseph Goebbels. England won the game 6–3. The game included a goal scored by Len Goulden that Stanley Matthews described as, "the greatest goal I ever saw in football". According to Matthews:

> Len met the ball on the run; without surrendering any pace, his left leg cocked back like the trigger of a gun, snapped forward and he met the ball full face on the volley. To use modern parlance, his shot was like an Exocet missile. The German goalkeeper may well have seen it coming, but he could do absolutely nothing about it. From 25 yards the ball screamed into the roof of the net with such power that the netting was ripped from two of the pegs by which it was tied to the crossbar.[45]

16 May 1948
Italy v England

In Turin, England produced display that has gone down as one of England's finest. Italy were still World Champions as no world cup had been played during the war years. England dominated the match from the start and won easily at 4–0 with goals from Stan Mortensen (4 mins), Tommy Lawton (23 mins) Tom Finney (70 and 72 mins). It was a lift to post war England wanting heroes to cheer and in the likes of Frank Swift (captain), Billy Wright, Wilf Mannion, Stanley Matthews along with Finney, Mortensen and Lawton, England has a team that made a nation feel proud.

It was also marked England's first win on Italian soil.

29 June 1950
The Day that Shook England to the core
The 1950 World Cup group Stages
USA v England

England first played in the 1950 World Cup and in a match they were expected to easily win they fielded a side that included Bert Williams, Alf Ramsay, the Captain Billy Wright, Jimmy Dickenson, Stan Mortenson and Tom Finney some great names and players, but yet England managed to lose 1–0 through a goal from Joseph Gaetjens on 38 mins. When England had beaten Italy 4–0 in 1948, it was felt we were world champion contenders and two years later we had lost to an amateur footballing nation. Our inner confidence was suddenly punctured and the 1950s were a period of some difficulty. Bert Williams, the England and Wolverhampton goalkeeper was later to say:

> "But you've got to give the Americans some credit for what they did. As soon as an English player picked up the ball, everyone in the American side retreated into their goalmouth. You couldn't see the goals for legs."[46]

25 November 1953
The Day Modern Football began
England v Hungary

In front of 100,000 people at the old Wembley Stadium an England team was outplayed by a Hungary team that played a new more modern brand of football than had been seen before. It was a match that confirmed England's decline as a world power, but also excited many observers with the skill and approach of a very skilful Hungarian team led by the great Ferenc Puskas. The story grew worse as England lost the return match in May 1954 7–1 in front of 92,000 in Nepstadion.

30 July 1966
World Champions
England v Germany

Every England knows the story of Geoff Hurst's hat-trick and how England won the World Cup at Wembley Stadium. Led by the young, charismatic Bobby Moore and with a team that included the great Gordon Banks, Martin Peters, Alan Ball, and Bobby Charlton, England at last fulfilled the dreams of English fans as they resisted the stubborn resistance of a very capable West German team. Germany scored first through Helmut Haller but by half-time, England had wrestled control through goals from Hurst and Peters. Webber then equalised in the last seconds of the match, which led to the dramatic twists of Hurst's third goal which bounced off the underside of the bar onto the line. Was it a goal or not? The debate has raged on for years but Hurst's third goal was worthy of winning a match. Bobby Moore's calmness under pressure, his long pass to Hurst. Hurst's run toward goal and how he hit his shot beyond the German 'keeper with raw power.

England may have had better players but the England team of 66 will always be the benchmark as it combined truly world class players with good players such as Jack Charlton, Nobby Stiles, George Cohen, Roger Hunt and Ray Wilson to create a real team that faced moments of adversity pressure, great play, aggression and still came through.

7 June 1970
A Game for the Memory
England V Brazil

In the group stages of the 1970 World Cup in Mexico, England faced the favourites Brazil in the second match. It is a game that is generally regarded as one of the greatest of England's games as it included some inspiring moments such as Banks "wonder" save off a Pele header and Moore's calm tackle of Jairzinho in full flight. Brazil went on to win the World Cup playing some of the most exciting and free flowing football ever seen. No team came close to beating them bar England who should have drawn the match save for Jeff Astle missing an open goal. But that is sport.

The game though is remembered for two great moments. The first when Brazil broke to the by-line and crossed for the rising Pele to head the ball with all his power towards the goal from 10 yards from the goal. The great player cried "Goal" as the ball left his head. Probably every supporter in the stadium, in Brazil and in England thought it was to be a goal, but Banks, who had been on the near post, flew his body through the air to tip the ball over the bar. Bobby Charlton described it as "the greatest save I have seen". It was one of those sporting moments that makes you stop in your tracks and respect the moment whichever side you may support.

In the second moment, the great Jairzinho – one of the players of the 1970 tournament – picked the ball up and ran with guile and speed at the England Penalty area. Only Moore stood in his way. Bobby waited with calm authority as the Brazilian attacked. Moore waited and then slid his foot in and stopped Jairzinho in his tracks. It was like a young boxer attacking an older, fading champion but the experience and skill of the latter won the moment.

It has often been argued that the England team of 1970 was a better team than the 1966 team. Did this hold validity? Charlton was still a powerful player, even though in his last days. Banks and Moore had reached their peaks as had Peters and Ball. They had been joined by Alan Mullery, Terry Cooper, Brian Labone, Keith Newton and Francis Lee who were seen as more skilful players than the ones they had replaced. This was one of England's greatest teams.

Post War Britain

There is a school of thought that argues that as economic prosperity returned in the 1950s, so spectator sport suffered a downturn in popularity, as it competed against the lure of shopping, cars and increased domestic comforts, of which television was one of the most alluring. One consequence was the rise of a youthful football fan culture that changed the character of the supporting crowds from one of community respect and banter to a more aggressive even violent undertone.

In truth sport flourished during the 1950s. It can be argued that it had not been for the Munich Air Crash which sadly killed so many of Manchester United's first team including the great Duncan Edwards, then England would have possessed a strong team for both the 1958 and 1962 World Cups. It can also be argued that it was the game in the 50s that lay the foundations for the 1966 triumph.

This is true but there were also great failures. In 1953, England discovered they were no longer world leading. In front of 100,000 people at the old Wembley Stadium an England team was outplayed by a Hungary team that played a new more modern brand of football than had been seen before. It was a match that confirmed England's decline as a world power, but also excited many observers with the skill and approach of a very skilful Hungarian team led by the great Ferenc Puskas. The story grew worse as England lost the return match in May 1954 7–1 in front of 92,000 in Nepstadion. However defeat inspired a new generation.

If fate had not dealt its cruel hand with the great loss of life in the Munich Air Crash of 58, it is very feasible that England would have had a competitive team in the 1962 World Cup with Duncan Edwards and some of the "Busby Babes" such as Tommy Taylor, Mark Jones and David Pegg. These were seen to be some of England's finest young talent to come through and it appeared that success was their destiny. 1958 would still have been early in their development but by 1962, these players could have joined the likes of Johnny Haynes, Jimmy Greaves, Bobby Moore, Ray Wilson, Bobby Charlton, Jimmy Armfield and Bobby Robson to form a formidable England team. The whole of the 1960s could have been a golden age for the England side, led by Duncan Edwards. Edwards was an awe-inspiring player who possessed both strength and skill. He had become the heartbeat and leader of the Busby babes that were winning admirers across Europe. The 1962 World Cup in Chile would have been his stage.

But fate did change destiny's course and England were a solid side in 62 but not more. Every great side needs five world-class players and three great talents. The 1966 had five world-class players in Moore, Banks, Bobby Charlton, Martin Peters and Ray Wilson. The three great talents were Ball, Hurst and Wilson. In 62, England could have had 5 world-class players in Haynes, Charlton, Moore, Edwards, and Greaves. These five would match in talent the five from 66. Then add in the possible strengths of Mark Jones, David Pegg, Tommy Taylor, and Bobby Robson and it could have been a very special team.

The road to the 1966 triumph had begun back in the mid 50s with the rise of a new generation of class players led by the likes of Duncan Edwards, and Johnny Haynes. The Hungarian win in 1953 at Wembley may have shocked many, but is also inspired a new generation to develop and hone their skills. The Hungarians showed a new dimension to the game and, although there was no joy in losing to the Hungarians, the English did take note and learn lessons. The Busby babes excited many across England as they developed and would have provided England with a strong talent base, able to compete in 62 bar the Munich air Crash, but the seeds had been sown and success was achieved in 66.

It is hard to argue that sport declined in the 1950s, it did change, but then again the world was changing at speed. The 1960s saw great political and social change so, of course, sport would change too.

The advent of television brought sport into people's homes and televised sport was to become hugely popular and influential. In the 1960s, coverage of the Olympics and the 1966 World Cup won mass audiences and turned the events into shared celebrations of a global sporting culture. Wimbledon a television event rather than a live tennis championship while rugby league began to be seen by southern audiences.

Television also opened up the opportunities to commercially utilise sport, not least through sponsorship. Athletics was one sport where television and sponsorship increased its profile and popularity, but this also created tensions between the amateurist traditions of the administrators and the commercial demands of the stars.

Interestingly, cricket proved the most willing to embrace change and even innovate, as was shown by the decision to introduce a one-day Sunday League as early as 1967. One can argue that cricket has, over the decades, been more innovative than any sport as it has worked hard to develop its audience. The development of twenty-twenty has opened the game up to new audiences and again shown a commercial expertise by those that run the game.

The real commercial boost from television came in the 1990s, with the development of satellite television. Soccer was seen as the key to securing an audience for the new medium. Rupert's Murdoch's Sky thus spent enormous sums on securing and then keeping the rights to televise the game's senior division. After the 1980s – when hooliganism and the fatal horrors of disasters at Bradford, Heysel and Hillsborough had seen English football sink to its lowest ebb of popularity and standing – Sky's millions enabled the game's upper echelons to reinvent itself in the1990s. New all-seater stadiums (enforced by the government to avoid a repeat of Hillsborough in 1989) made watching soccer both safer and more sanitised, an influx of talented foreign players raised standards of play. Players were the main beneficiaries as their profile, wages and sponsorship opportunities rapidly escalated in the now hugely fashionable and celebrity-conscious game. David Beckham epitomised this transition, with his wife being from The Spice Girls, countless sponsorship deals, merchandising and a high profile lifestyle. Beckham represents the modern professional and is a far cry, not just from the sportsmen of the 30s and 40s, but from those that he started his career with. He became a brand in his own right.

One of the fun questions to debate with friends is, "Who has been the best player in the football history?" The debate will include players such as Pele, Bobby Charlton, Bobby Moore, Maradonna, Ronaldo and Messi.

However, ask the question, "who is the most commercially successful player of all time?" and Beckham's name will be near to the top. Only a handful of players have ever reached the very highest level in this field. In some ways, Beckham is almost forgotten for his footballing exploits and is seen as a fashion icon. However few have made as much money out of sport and been more professional. Beckham's big-name status was confirmed when he left Manchester United for Real Madrid in 2003. The £23 million transfer fee was repaid within days from shirt sales in Asia alone.

At the time it was written; "Purely from a football perspective, Beckham is a terrific player, but Real Madrid is so good that Beckham may not make the starting line-up. His real value to the team is in the branding of the club worldwide. He is yet another star that Real Madrid can sell as they try to enhance their world image." (says Scott Rosner)[47]

Beckham's brand has broken new barriers. He has had a major film have his name included in the title – Bend it like Beckham. In historical terms, Beckham arguably marks the age when Britain finally embraced professionalism and the rewards. It is sad that Beckham's achievements as a player are beginning to be forgotten for he was an exceptional player, but he has transcended the sport and become part of modern culture just as the Beatles achieved such heights in the 1960s.

British Sport had finally come of age.

Captains

3 – David Beckham

Most people today only see David Beckham, fashion icon, modern man and multi millionaire who married a pop star and made a fortune from playing for some of the best footballing sides in the world including Manchester United, Real Madrid, AC Milan, Paris St. Germain and England.

However, Beckham's story from 1998 through to 2002 was one that the writers of *Roy of the Rovers* would have been justly proud. Beckham made his debut for England in 1996 and by the 1998 World Cup in France, it was clear that Beckham would become a regular England player and star player. However in the second round match against Argentina, Beckham soon became a national villain. The match was tied in an exciting tense 2–2 scoreline as early in the second half, the Argentine player Simone slid into Beckham from behind. It took the legs from Beckham. In a moment of anger and petulance Beckham flicked his leg against Simone who collapsed on the field. The referee had seen the whole incident and sent Beckham from the field of play. It was simply naïve play. The flick could not have hurt Simone but the Argentine had made the most of the incident. In truth his tackle had been far worse but he had been streetwise whilst Beckham showed his immaturity. It left England to play the second half and extra-time with just 10 men and England bravely left the tournament to the dreaded penalty shoot out.

Of course, it was disappointing and many turned their anger onto Beckham. He became a villain figure during the summer period. However, come the new season the hate seemed to just inspire Beckham to a greater level of play. In 2000, after Kevin Keegan's resignation as manager, the caretaker manager, Peter Taylor, appointed Beckham as captain of England. Many were shocked but it proved to be an inspirational choice as over the next couple of years, Beckham almost carried the England team through to World Cup qualification on his own shoulders. In the early days under Sven Goran Erickson as manager, Beckham played a series of heroic games that inspired England to play a more positive brand of football that reached its peak with the 5–1 victory in Munich in late 2001. In the final qualification match for the 2002 World Cup, England looked as though they would blow their automatic opportunity for qualification by losing to Greece at home until Beckham came forward in the last minute of the match to score from a free-kick to send the nation into celebration.

The 2002 World Cup team was probably the last truly competitive team to represent England in top competition until after the 2014 World Cup. The team played a good brand of football under Beckham. Sol Campbell and Rio Ferdinand were arguably two of the best central defenders in the competition and Michael Owen was at his best. England lost in the quarter-final to Brazil after an individual error by David Seaman, but Beckham's England had its followers dreaming of success once again.

Beckham became a marketing dream for his clubs and he became arguably the most successful footballing export as he moved from Manchester United to Real Madrid to LA Galaxy, AC Milan and Paris St. Germain. He became a star in the USA as well as England and has adapted his character and approach with each environment that he has been in. During this period, he had a very successful British movie carry his name in the title *Bend it like Beckham* and was a fashion icon across the world. He was also named in a speech by Hugh Grant's Prime Minister in the film *Love Actually* as Grant named David Beckham's left and right feet as something that makes Great Britain a great nation.

Beckham's story is one of great success and an example of the power of the modern international sportsman. One could argue that no Englishman was more influential than Beckham at his peak and he played a central role in both the unsuccessful World Cup Bid but also the successful Olympic bid for the 2012 Games.

Was a Beckham a great captain? He was certainly proud to play for England and led from the front when confidence was low. Keegan resigned after a 1–0 home defeat to Germany. If England did not improve they could well have failed to qualify for the 2002 World Cup and it was Beckham that did lead the team from the front. One could make a comparison to the 1973 team, which fell away when it mattered and failed to qualify for 1974 after world success in 1966. In 1996, England excited the nation in Euro 96 and also had a good team at the World Cup in France 98. However Euro 2000 had seen England eliminated in the group stages and supporters feared a new decline until Beckham – with Owen, Gerrard, Ferdinand, Scholes and Campbell – stepped forward. Beckham was one of the true world-class players of his generation and was one of the best examples of the modern sportsman. He was a figure that made the most of his time.

One can argue that England underachieved in the 2006 World Cup and the blame was laid at with the "WAGS" and the culture within the squad but it was illustrated how far England had come under Beckham from 2001. However the team should have gone further than it did.

Chapter Four

THE ROAD TO PROFESSIONALISM

T here is an old saying that the test of a player's mental ability to play at the top level can be witnessed by the moment a player walks into a high profile match and a cauldron of supporter expectation. Can the player handle the moment they walk out at Wembley Stadium in front of 100,000? Many players freeze and many players rise to the occasion. In the 1988 F.A Cup Final, the Liverpool team of Kenny Dalglish just did not rise to the occasion and were beaten by the underdogs of Wimbledon 1–0. The same story happened with the famous Sunderland win over the great Leeds United team in the 1973 F.A Cup Final. At the time both Liverpool and Leeds United were the most formidable teams in the country. Both games were seen as straightforward wins for the teams but for whatever reason, neither team played to their highest levels. It is more likely that both teams were complacent and believed all the accolades that had been said about them. They both underrated the opposition.

For football fans of the 1970s, most can still name the majority of the Leeds United team without needing any form of reference – Billy Bremner, Allan Clarke, Peter Lorimer, Eddie Gray, Norman Hunter, Johnny Giles, Paul Madeley, Gary Sparke, Paul Reaney and the names go on but they arguably did not win as much as they should have. They won the Championship in 1974, the FA Cup in 1972, reached the European Cup Final in 1974 and the 1971 Inter-Cities Fairs Cup Final. Liverpool's record from 1976 to 1990 was far greater but the Leeds United team of the early to mid 70s will always be known as one of the greatest of teams whether they underachieved or not.

That is the nature of sport. A player may be talented but it does not mean that he or she is mentally able to handle a moment in time and build consistent success. It does certainly separate the great from the good. One of the arguments against British players is that their sporting psychology has just never been strong enough. It relies too much on the moment and great competitors do train their minds to handle every sporting eventuality so that they are prepared for the moment when it comes. The professional ethic is not just about fitness, but about training the mind. Many leading sports coaches will talk about the importance of visualisation to create both a positive mind-set but an ability to handle the unexpected when it happens. Sally Gunnell, the Olympic Gold Medalist, used to visualise every eventuality before a race so if something did go wrong, she would not panic and would instinctively know how to respond.

It will be no surprise to discover that the US led others in the use of sports psychology with the discipline really taking hold in the 1960s with many of the major baseball and American football teams and in 1988, the US Olympic team was the first of their national teams to have a specialist appointed to the team. The British did not really take it seriously even into the early 2000s. This is part of a common trend and part of the reasoning for how Britain took longer to evolve from seeing sport as recreation and entertainment to being a real profession. Glenn Hoddle, as England football manager, tried to bring into Eillen Drewery to work his players but it was seen to be a sideshow and a distraction. Clive Woodward had more success and arguably he is the one that made it accepted, but through the success of the team.

In America, sport psychology's roots date back to the late 19th and early 20th centuries when several psychologists started conducting sports-related studies. The person viewed to be the founder of sports psychology is Coleman R. Griffith (1893–1966)

He started studying sport psychology as a graduate student in 1918. His research then focused on how vision and attention predicted basketball and football performance. A few years later, he was teaching a course specifically on "Psychology and Athletics." He also was appointed assistant professor at the University of Illinois. In 1925, he opened the first-ever research lab on athletic performance at the university

In the 1950s, sports psychology really grew. In the 1960s, the Philadelphia Phillies teamed up with some University of Delaware professors to found a "Research Program for Baseball". In the 1970s, the Kansas City Royals created a science-based "academy" of baseball development. By the 1980s, tests such as the Athletic Motivation Inventory were becoming a standard tool of professional baseball scouts and managers. Also in the 1980s, the then Chicago White Sox and Oakland A's manager Tony La Russa brought the laptop computer and the digital database into the dugout to stay.

Maybe the often unspoken question to consider is – have players in Britain handled the demands of professionalism as well as could be? And more controversially, handle the wealth?

Wealth is an interesting subject as increased rewards, even for failure, has often been cited as a problem area. How can one expect an England football player earning £50–70,000 per week to be as motivated to succeed as those in the Moore and Charlton era?

In an interview in 2009, Jack Nicklaus the great American golfer ponder the subject talking about the 2009 generation of player:

> If they don't win, they still walk home with a big check. They don't have to do some of the things the Watsons had to do, the Normans, the Lehmans and that to gut it out...when we played golf, it wasn't to make a living. It was to make a name for yourself so that you could make a living. When I started on tour, maybe one or two guys might have made enough money to make a living. Then it got to five or ten. Now there's a couple of hundred guys who make a living playing golf. We had to play really well and scratch it out to be in a position to get endorsements. But we worked to try to build the tour so they didn't have to do that... you try to create a system that allows a lot of people to be able to make a living doing something. And they're successful doing it and then your system destroys the desire for the guys to work hard.
>
> I always took the attitude that the harder I worked at my golf game and the better I played, the money would take care of itself. If I had that trophy on the shelf, the money would come with it. [48] (Associated Press)

Nicklaus's comments maybe highlight just how a small shift in perspective changes much. He played the game for the love of it and worked hard to make a living. His primary focus was on the game and not the money, believing that money follows success. There are many observers today that believe that the primary focus of many is the money with the sport second.

In a BBC radio Interview on 28 April 2016, there was an argument put forward that Leicester would do better to finish second in the Premiership as they could well make more money that way. Why? Because of the extra bonuses that would need to be paid to the management team and players. If this view held, then it does make sport become cynical, as it takes away from the very essence of what sport should be about which is striving to the best one can be.

In fairness to the interview, it did go on to stress that this would be an accountant's viewpoint, but ignores the extra prestige that winning the premiership would bring to the City as well as the feel-good factor that would be generated amongst the fans.

Great sport will always be about more than money. Money is just the reward but yes it can ruin many along the way.

A number of thoughts for consideration:

If one lists out the great British sporting heroes, it is staggering how many of them stand before the age of high financial reward and how few have come since?

In the era when sports players were not rewarded with high wages, players not only played with greater freedom but there were genuine moments that made you rise from your seat. Consider Gareth Edwards, Barry John, Fred Trueman, Derek Underwood, Alan Knott, Geoff Boycott, Johnny Haynes, Bobby Charlton, Gordon Banks, Alan Ball, Len Hutton and Bobby Moore. These players may have had comfortable lifestyles, but not one possessed the high wages of today.

It can be fairly argued that rugby is the one sport where the top players have managed to be able to be both professional and handle wealth. The best two examples would be Jonny Wilkinson and Lawrence Dallagio; both of whom will always be regarded as genuine greats of the English game. Wilkinson is not only revered in England, but Toulon who adopted him as one of their favourite sons.

In contrast, the so-called golden generation of England's footballers (2002–08) underperformed against their potential. England possessed a range of great players including David Beckham. Frank Lampard, Steve Gerrard, Michael Owen, Paul Scholes, Rio Ferdinand, Ashley Cole and yet the team were never a genuine threat at the top level bar for the historic 5–1 win in Germany whilst qualifying for the 2002 World Cup and for half a game v Brazil in the 2002 quarter-final of the World Cup. England promised much but delivered in truth very little.

It can be argued that the only English footballer to be able to prosper with foreign clubs was David Beckham with a career that included Real Madrid, AC Milan, and LA Galaxy.

The British sporting structure does possess more players and more clubs than any other nation, but has under performed in all the major team sports since the era of professionalism really took off. The England Cricket team briefly were the number one side in the world for just a year. The England rugby team became World Champions in 2003 but in the following four years, England played some appalling rugby and reached the 2007 Rugby World Cup Final only through the strength of character in their great players led by Phil Vickery, Jonny Wilkinson, and Lawrence Dallagio. The England team has underperformed from 2003, but the hope again has risen with the 2016 Grand Slam. As was written in Chapter three, the percentage between success and failure as so fine but for long periods in the thirteen years between 2003 and 2016, England were losing the one percent margins.

The English football team has not threatened the top teams in major competition since 1996 and arguably not since 1970. The 1990 and 96 campaigns were moments of sunlight in between the storms of failure of 1973–74, 1977–78, 1983, 1993–94, and 2007–08 – all campaigns where England failed to qualify. No other World Championship nation has struggled as badly.

For some reason it appears that the professional ethos in sport has been a struggle for the British. Professional sport at the highest level seems to bring fear with it and many players have struggled with meeting expectation. Some have argued that the problem is the expectation placed on the player's shoulders by a public desperate for success. Maybe? But is it really more than other nations? The New Zealanders often struggle with elimination from the Rugby Wotld Cup. The Italian fans are renowned for having high expectations of the football teams. Same with the Australian Cricket team. No, it must be something that lies a bit deeper within the psyche.

For the British, sport is about a moment; about flair; about putting ourselves on the line for our friends and teammates but sport is not about money. Sportsmanship is about the character.

Does the answer lie in a fear of failure? And does that fear undermine the sheer joy of playing top-level sport and more importantly stop players performing in the games of the highest level?

Consider for a moment:

The England football team is renown of losing key matches in major tournaments on a contest of penalties – Germany in 1990 and 1996; Argentina in 1998 and Portugal in 2006. Is it just bad luck? Bad technique? Or do the players just struggle to cope with the pressure of the moment?

How many times have the England batting collapsed in key moments under pressure? Think Lord's 2015

Why are there so few English players playing in the premiership? England has for a long period produced players of the highest calibre throughout a long history – Stanley Matthews. Tom Finney, Duncan Edwards, Bobby Moore, Martin Peters. Bobby Charlton, David Beckham, Gordon Banks, Paul Gascoigne, Gary Lineker, Peter Shilton, and the roll call can go on. Does great English talent not exist as in previous eras or is there a reason why English and Scottish players are struggling in the top end of professional sport?

There are just many signs and coincidences that British player struggle to maintain their love of playing with freedom in the highest levels of the game. There are a number of key questions to explore:

Are British Sportsmen neither professional enough in preparation nor mentally strong enough in moments of high tension?

Is the British mentality towards sport still one of the amateur sportsman?

Does wealth corrupt the British more than with other nations?

Do the fans and nation's expectations intimidate the players?

Is there an inherent fear of failure?

The answer, of course, lies in a mix of all. This leads to the age-old question of whether money has changed sport for the worse?

The argument between professionalism and amateurism has been raging ever since professional sport really took hold in the 60s. Some will argue for a hundred years. The British can argue that they invented football, rugby and cricket but sport was seen by its Victorian founders as a moral instrument, a tool for inculcating discipline and forging character. This was the founding platform from which the games in this country evolved.

The public schools fiercely resisted professionalism, arguing that the sporting ethos was incompatible with financial gain. What mattered was the taking part – sport for its own sake – not the vulgar win-at-all-costs mentality of professionalism. When the FA legalised professionalism in 1885, the aristocratic players largely abandoned the sport.

Did football become poorer for becoming a professional sport? If the game had remained amateur it would have been an elitist sport. Amateurism, by its nature, is a privilege only afforded to either the wealthy or those willing to make major sacrifices.

Yes, money and professionalism changed sport but only for the better. It allowed for players from poor backgrounds to change their lives, raise the bar and let talent from all backgrounds express themselves. The British exported the game and as the game took hold in other countries it did so without the same founding social platform. Without these changes, the world would arguably not have seen the likes of Pele, Maradonna, Cruyff and Messi.

The argument is some of the financial rewards today have gone too far and the balance has been lost but the players that receive the high rewards have excelled in their disciplines and they need to be exceptionally skilled in their craft to achieve such reward. Maybe the rewards are too high but the counter is that it forces the craft to continuously evolve, test the boundaries and improve. It will not be many years before an African nation is close to winning the world cup and other nations too are emerging. Professionalism has freed a global game to inspire millions.

The real issue is that as the British began their journey to professionalism from a different base then it has been a harder journey. It is not the game in Britain has not embraced professionalism. It has without a shadow of a doubt. The battle is that it has done so whilst trying to maintain the balance of some of the founding principles and that balance has been difficult to achieve.

In the 1980s and 90s, as England's football teams went from the great highs of Italia 90 and Euro 96 to the lows of Euro 92 and World Cup elimination in 1994,

Euro elimination in 1984, as well as brave exits from the 1986 and 1998 World Cups. England possessed the talent. The coaching and management arguably controversially strayed from the wisdom of Bobby Robson to the international inexperience of Graham Taylor to the clear skills of Terry Venables and Glenn Hoddle. There was a desire to play at the top table with the likes of Alan Shearer, Pail Gascoigne, Paul Scholes, Gary Lineker, John Barnes, Chris Waddle, Terry Butcher, Davis Seaman, Peter Shilton, Bryan Robson, Ray Wilkins and the list can go on. The England team flattered to deceive. Maybe the coaching was, at times, at fault. There is little doubt that Graham Taylor was out of his depth but maybe England never truly deserved to play at the highest levels, as the players themselves were not professional enough in attitude?

Graham Taylor was an honourable man but the pressure of the role told. Maybe one of the most memorable and public illustrations of the pressures of the role came in a Channel 4 documentary on how the England football team struggled in the 1993 World Cup qualifying campaign, culminating in the away match against Holland.

England needed to win, but a poor refereeing decision saw Koeman not sent from the field for a professional foul on David Platt when he had a clear goalscoring opportunity. Not long later, Koeman then stepped forward to score the first decisive goal which lead to England losing the match and failing to qualify for the 1994 World Cup Finals in the USA. Far worse followed as Graham Taylor lost his composure on the touchline.

There were reasons and excuses that could be made for England's failure. England's two leading "world-class" talents in John Barnes and Paul Gascoigne were injured, but regardless the squad struggled with the emotion of the moment. The loss against Holland was bad enough but the TV documentary televised how Graham Taylor literally and sadly came apart in front of everyone's eyes. The documentary illustrated just how poor England were in their preparation at international level.

It was a truly tragic tale of how a good man was just not equipped for the highest levels. Or was it that England was not mentally ready?

> Six months later the documentary came out and Taylor's reign as England manager ended up looking like a Monty Python film rather than the sort of David Attenborough documentary he'd hoped it would be. [49]

(Rob Shepherd in the *Daily Mail*)

Throughout this period there was a culture of heavy drinking and gambling. It is naturally going to be difficult for a top international athlete to compete when players either drink too much, have poorer diets than their opponents and have gambling habits. This is all well recorded and there have been many tragic stories. At Euro 96, England was led by Tony Adams, who had spent four months in prison for drink driving in the early nineties and had a serious alcohol problem at the time of 1996. His wife also suffered from a drug habit and after their divorce, her life fell further. Paul Gascoigne, England's leading player of 96, has had a torrid and sad fall from grace.

This is not about morality or judging other's lives. This is about the fact that the players did not possess the self-discipline to be successful at the highest level. The coaches can be partially blamed, but maybe the clubs needed to be better at coaching and educating their players in what was required. The players cannot be blamed as they lived life hard and played hard and were adored by their supporters. They were young men living life. The issue was that the clubs and structures needed to do more to educate and support players so they understood what was important in a professional lifestyle.

There is no blame. It was simply that the professional code was not embraced and as a result, England – and others – did not achieve what they could have. So often, the team was so close. What could have been at Italia 90, Mexico 86, Euro 96 if only the players had an extra five percent either mentally or physically? Those players had the opportunity to have succeeded Bobby Moore and Bobby Charlton but it did not happen. Maybe it was just not destined to be but there is a strong argument that players from other countries would have prepared better.

The counter will naturally be that the players from other countries are hardly saints – Tiger Woods, Pele, Maradonna – but the real question for debate is whether they were mentally and physically better prepared? Tiger Woods clearly was not the most faithful of men but he was faithful to the game of Golf and worked with a strong work ethic to be the best player in the world. Of course, Woods should have – and may still do – surpassed Jack Nicklaus's record for major wins but he has never been the same player since the stories erupted. Yes he has carried a series of back injuries but one also suspects that mentally he will never be as he once was.

Ray Wilkins stormed onto the football scene at the age of 17 in the mid 70s and was soon made captain of Chelsea. Wilkins was soon promoted as a future England captain and went on to be captain plus win 83 International caps. Wilkins was a charismatic young leader with talent to match. There is no doubt that his career has been a success but it has taken its toll and one has to ask whether he was both managed and supported as well as he could have been through his career. When he was appointed Chelsea captain in his late teens, the doctor at the club would give him valium to help him sleep and prepare for the games. As his career evolved he fell into the trap of drinking and he suffered from depression and this has plagued him ever since until he has started talking openly in the issue.

Wilkins was a superb player. A modest, intelligent man who played for a number of major clubs across Europe – Rangers, AC Milan, Paris St. Germain, Manchester United and Chelsea. He has often stated that when he first went to AC Milan they were 10 years ahead of the English league in terms of diet and physically preparing players. He will also note that the Premier League has caught up and overtaken, but one has to wonder that if the game in England was 10 years behind in its preparation of players in the 1980s, what could have been under Bobby Robson in 86, and 90?

One also has to ponder how much better could Wilkins – and others – have been with extra support?

Was it different in rugby and cricket?

Arguably yes dramatic and open but both have had their problems. In1986, David Gower led his Ashes winning team to the Caribbean to face the might of the West Indies. It was a one sided affair and England were soundly thrashed. During the tour, Gower would often argue that he would let the players determine how much they trained and practiced. There was a sound logic. Firstly, he argued the players knew their craft and bodies and how best they should prepare. They were professionals and adults, he argued. Secondly, when a team is being beaten it is not always helpful to push the players into tough training regimes. Sport is about psychology and the need to relax to compete.

In fairness whatever Gower had done the result would have been the same as the West Indies team were so strong under Viv Richards. The problem was that the England team did not compete even though it possessed such players as Gower, Botham, Gooch, and Allan Lamb. Gower was soon striped of his leadership on the basis that the professional work ethic was not strong enough and replaced by Mike Gatting who arguably was the lesser player but the tougher taskmaster. Gatting went on to win the Ashes again in 1987 but would the result have been different under Gower? Gower has led a great victory over Australia and India (away) in 1984–85. Was it not simply that the West Indies were the better team?

The problem was that Gatting was heralded for his more direct style of leadership and approach and maybe this was helpful at first, but Gatting ended up having an open argument on the field of play in Pakistan with an umpire. Maybe fairly so as the umpire was not the most competent, but it was unseemly and could have been handled with more grace. Later in the year Gatting was himself stripped of the captaincy after a naive incident with a lady in a hotel room. England then went through a summer against the West Indies under four captains. It would be hard to argue that the thinking or behaviours of the England team was professionally strong.

Changing the captain was an easy solution and the administrators needed to look deeper at the structure of the game. Both Gower and Gatting were good men and their fortunes declined even lower as first Gower was reappointed as captain for the 1989 Ashes series but the Australians arrived with a stronger, more combative mind-set that set them above the England team, although on talent alone it should have been an evenly matched series. To make matters worse, a number of England players including Gatting signed for an unsanctioned "rebel" tour to South Africa and the English mind-set was clearly not close to being correct. Again Gower took the blame and Gatting was seen by some as betraying the cause. The reality was deeper.

England in the early 90s struggled to compete. Emma John in her engaging book *Following on* wrote of the England Cricket team in the early 90s:

"At the time, England's cricketers were losers. Literally losers. They got beaten by almost every team they played against and often in the most depressing and humiliating way possible. Ennobling them, idolising them, and preserving memories of their less than triumphant progress under sticky-back plastic – that was weird."[50]

Emma John went on: "For the first decade, the England team I knew and loved led me a not-so-merry dance of false hope and false starts. Their results were woeful and their performances sometimes staggeringly awful... if there was one thing that was consistent about England in the 1990s, it was their ability to snatch defeat from the jaws of victory".[51]

The real sea change came with the appointment of Duncan Fletcher as coach and Michael Vaughan as captain. Vaughan just fitted the English leadership mould – intelligent, charismatic, a great player but also believed in setting a structure so that the players could express themselves freely. The 2005 Ashes series was one of the greatest of any era and for the first time since 1985, England's players expressed themselves as elite sportsmen.

Under Andrew Strauss this went to another level and in 2011, England did become the Number one ranking Test team. English found the professional balance to their cultural – social – sport equation arguably in the early 2000s.

Has the British game now adapted to the professional era? Yes. The premier league is one of the best in the world. However it is a league of mercenaries with a relatively low percentage of British players. There are many that disapprove and feel it is a problem for the English national team and there is a strong argument as the England team has not been truly competitive at the top level since the 2002 World Cup. However, the clubs and league is very professional. One has to ask why England's players have taken time to compete in their own league and stadia?

The answer is that the home born players have not been good enough but there are signs that change is in the air and that there is a new generation of British players breaking through that could herald a new era. Tottenham and Leicester in 2015–16 have excited and amazed supporters and observers and the likes of Harry Kane, Dele Ali, Eric Dier and James Vardy have been the best in the premiership. All are English.

Cricket and Rugby too are professional although after the 2015 Rugby World Cup, there is no doubt that there is a gap between the Northern Hemisphere and Southern Hemisphere teams. There is still work to be done.

CAPTAINS

4 – Michael Vaughan

England Cricket captain 2003–08

Michael Vaughan's approach as captain of England was almost a throwback to the eras of Compton, Hammond and Edrich, as he believed in players being relaxed and allowing the players the freedom and courage to express themselves. Under his leadership, the England team blossomed to be one of the most exciting in thirty years with a mix of exciting stroke makers and dangerous bowlers. He was the captain of the England team when they regained the Ashes in 2005, eighteen years after having last won the trophy. For England fans, it had been a long disappointing period of time when the England team did not seem able to compete with the Australians. The 2005 team not only competed, but took the Australians on in an aggressive, positive manner that delighted the nation.

In truth the 2005 series could easily have been lost, but Vaughan's team had the belief and courage not to be fearful of another defeat and instead backed their own abilities. The first Test was lost and other England teams would have lacked the belief to continue to play in a positive mind-set but Vaughan – and Duncan Fletcher (Coach) – had seen enough in the game to suggest that England could compete by meeting fire with fire. On the first morning of the first Test, Steve Harmison, England's fast bowler, has unsettled the Australians with his aggression and Vaughan had seen areas where England could attack even as the side slipped to defeat at Lord's.

Vaughan's great ability was to create a framework that allowed players to express themselves and have positive intent. Freddie Flintoff played his best cricket under Vaughan. Kevin Pietersen certainly enjoyed his time with Vaughan as Captain and arguably Vaughan would have got the best out of the mercurial player.

Vaughan was ranked as one of the best batsmen in the world following the 2002–03 Ashes, in which he scored 633 runs, including three centuries. He could play almost at any position in the batting line-up. He had been an opening batsman as well as a middle order player. One of his greatest attributes was a calm temperament. Even in his first Test match against South Africa, he entered the lion's den with England 2–4 (two runs for four wickets down) and helped steer the ship to some respectability.

Vaughan captained England in 51 Tests between 2003 and 2008, winning 26 and losing 11; England won all seven home Tests of the 2004 summer under Vaughan.

It was unfortunate that Vaughan did not have more time at the helm as he was hampered by injury. The team had just beaten Australia when injuries began to hinder Vaughan and England struggled to replace him. Flintoff led the team to Australia for the following Ashes but the panache of 2005 was not there and England were crushed 5–0.

Was Vaughan the difference? One man never can be but he was a natural leader with an astute tactical mind. Flintoff was more of a Bothamesque character – full of good intent and bravery, but without the tactical insight. It was a shame as it took England back to the dark days as Flintoff struggled and his relationship with Vaughan became strained. Vaughan did come back as captain, but it was never the same. He struggled with Peter Moores, who became coach in succession of Duncan Fletcher and it was clear that England would never recapture the belief of 2005.

Vaughan was never just an establishment captain. Vaughan was respectful of the history and legacy of the game but played to win. He just understood that to win, players had to be bold and play to the best of their capabilities, which meant that he needed a framework that took the pressure off the players. This worked in 2004 and 2005 to great effect. His relationship with Moores was always strained as he felt that Moores over analysed the game and placed too much detail into the minds of the players. At heart, Vaughan – like many of the very best – understood that the game was simple in essence but to play well one needed both intelligence and confidence to play the game.

In 2015, the England hierarchy appointed Andrew Strauss to lead England's management. Strauss has been an excellent appointment but one wonders whether the establishment should try to involve Vaughan more as he is an innovator and understands players. Too often in England's history, players have been expected to fall in line rather than be given the freedom to play. That was Vaughan's strength and his legacy – his teams played positive cricket to win.

Chapter Five

AMERICA, UK AND SPORT

"I've missed more than 9,000 shots in my career. I've lost almost 300 games. Twenty-six times, I've been trusted to take the game winning shot and missed. I've failed over and over and over again in my life. And that is why I succeed." – **Michael Jordan**[52]

American sporting heroes are a major part of their history and have been a major part of the global identity of the US. Over the years, the leading sportsmen have been the greatest ambassadors for the American culture and dream. In the 1970s, Muhammad Ali was probably a more well known personality – and certainly more popular – across the world than Presidents Gerald Ford, or Jimmy Carter. One can certainly argue that Ali and Foreman did more good in Zaire with their 1974 fight than much of US foreign policy in the region. The local Zaire community took Ali, especially, to their hearts and it served to break down barriers.

In 1936, Jesse Owens was a symbol of a nation that stood up to Hitler's Nazism. It was a sportsman who did this far better than any politician and moreover, it was a black sportsman, which in 1936 was still an issue:

> *"The Berlin Olympics of 1936, which Hitler used to promote the idea of Ayran superiority, though the black American athlete Jesse Owens upset those plans badly by winning four gold medals."*[53]

Sport often was the lead in social change and nowhere more so than in the US;

> "Jackie Robinson the first black man to play major league baseball, helping set in motion the necessary change of consciousness that would lead to big social changes in America"[54]

To a level, it is very natural that US sports players have played such an active role on the international stage, as the country is still relatively young. However, over the last one hundred years, America has been a major world force – a super power – with a list of influential leaders, so it is a statement that many of the best known Americans are sports players.

America is close to being 250 years old and over the last one hundred years, their sporting heroes have played leading roles on the international stage – Bobby Jones, Ben Hogan, Jack Nicklaus, Carl Lewis, Jesse Owens, Muhammad Ali, George

Foreman, O.J. Simpson, Joe Namath, Jesse Owens, Mike Tyson, Arnold Palmer, Joe Frazier, Tiger Woods, Michael Johnson, Michael Jordan and the list can be endless. As sports have become global businesses, the best players naturally become global icons. Maybe one day sports players will be more influential in a foreign country than their political leaders?

The most famous Americans globally are the presidents, film stars and sport players. A few business leaders compete, but only business superstars such as Bill Gates and innovators such as Mark Zucherberg. One could make the argument that more people globally know Muhammad Ali, or Tiger Woods than all the American Presidents bar J.F.K., Reagan, Clinton, Bush (maybe for the wrong reasons) and Obama.

There are so many great American sports films based on true stories – stories that depict different periods of American history and often the fight of the athlete against adversity. The list of films is endless – the *Cinderella Man*, *Sea Biscuit*, *Secretariat*, *The Legend of Bagger Vance*, *Coach Carter*, *Blind Side*, *Raging Bull*, *Ali*, *The Wrestler*, *Race*, *Concussion*, and *Remember the Titans*.

How many great British sporting films have there been? Maybe *Chariots of Fire* alone can stand the test of sitting with the above. It does illustrate how sport in America has played a more important social role than in the UK. Sport is a symbol of how anyone can achieve success and embody the concept of the American dream.

One of the great attractions of American culture is how they love to see the unheralded rise to the top, overcome every challenge and barrier placed before them through talent, courage and determination. Sport is a crucial part of the national identity and daily culture. Sport reminds everyone of the core US principle that all are equal and anyone can excel and rise to the top through hard work and talent. The U.S culture celebrates success and this naturally encourages people to strive to be the best they can be. In the traditional old societies often class structures and prejudice makes the journey far more difficult and there are so many artificial barriers to success. The US culture works hard to make the system as open as is possible.

Sports naturally enjoy high popularity in America, but it is a vehicle for transmitting such values as justice, fair play, and teamwork. American college matches are a community event in themselves. Britain can boast the Varsity marches between Oxford and Cambridge, which attract a strong following, but it does not equate to the following the American High Schools attract for their American football, basketball and baseball matches. These play a central role to the community at large. In Britain a school match is just a school match – important for the schools but no real meaning beyond. It does illustrate how sport is just higher the social scale in the US.

Sports have contributed to racial and social integration and over history have been a "social glue" bonding the country together. One can argue that the base ethos of sport in the US is not far different to those determined in the Victorian Age. The difference is that they were more comfortable with the concept of winning because their culture was determined by a need to build a life from scratch. American society came with no historical legacy. It needed to be built and hence striving to be the best that one can be sits at the very heart of their beliefs.

In Britain, few politicians over the years have really connected with sport. Sport and politics, until Major and Blair, have sat at very separate tables. In America, politics and sports are closely connected and many of the Presidents have encouraged and promoted the importance of sport. President Dwight D. Eisenhower founded the President's Council on Youth Fitness in 1956 to encourage America's youth to make fitness a priority. The Council later became the President's Council on Physical Fitness and Sports, including people of all ages and abilities and promoting fitness through sports and games. Today, the Council continues to play an important role in promoting fitness and healthy living in America;

It is said that sport in North America pre-dated the settlers. Native American peoples played a variety of ball games including some that may be viewed as earlier forms of lacrosse. The typical American sports of baseball, basketball and football, however, arose from games that were brought to America by the first settlers that arrived from Europe in the 17th century. These games were re-fashioned and elaborated as time progressed.

From the late nineteenth century to our present day, professional and college sports have served as two of the nation's most powerful community-building institutions, helping to define American identity on the grassroots level, as powerfully as our political system, our broadcast media, or Hollywood film. In a huge and diverse nation experiencing waves of immigration, struggling with racial divisions, and undergoing a pace of economic change unmatched by any society in the world, the importance of sports cannot be ignored. Sport has provided many Americans with more than a much-needed escape from the hardships of their daily lives; it has given them a visceral connection to our nation's lived traditions and cultural values.

The role of sports in Americanizing immigrants has been written about extensively by historians and journalists. Professional boxing and baseball, both of which achieved heightened popularity at the dawn of the twentieth century, became important vehicles by which waves of immigrants marked their progress in American society. The hero-making machinery of these two sports, enhanced first by mass-circulating newspapers then by radio, allowed for individuals from immigrant backgrounds to achieve the status of popular cultural icons while the majority of their ethnic cohorts struggled with poverty and marginality.

For European immigrants, even those from eastern and southern Europe, sports—guided by an ethos of fair play and open competition—proved far more accessible to talented immigrant youth than the nation's banks, corporations, and universities where discrimination was often masked behind "gentlemen's agreements," and where progress in breaking barriers was often painfully slow. Boxers John O'Sullivan, Jim Corbett, Benny Leonard, and Rocky Marciano and baseball players Joe DiMaggio and Hank Greenberg became symbolic representatives of the potential of Irish, Italian, and Jewish Americans to win success and acceptance in a nation that had often looked on their presence with suspicion. And this filtered down to the neighbourhood level where the American-born children of immigrants seized upon sports as the best way of affirming their American identities and opening up opportunities for economic and educational success.

One of the central features of American sport – and culture – is that it is focused on individual achievement. The team concept, although important, is secondary. All the lead athletes whether in American football, baseball, golf or athletics will have personal statistical date that runs alongside their records. So an American running back may be a team player, but he will be judged by the amount of yards he has gained/made with the ball. American culture and sport is about what the individual achieves.

The following chapter analyses the Australian perspective towards sport and interestingly they do possess a far more advanced concept of team and the importance of the team before the individual. It is just differing perspectives but ones that sit at the heart of their national psychology towards sport. It is this very belief structure that gave immigrants the confidence that they could change their lives and create a new life in the US and encouraged athletes from all backgrounds to embrace sporting endeavour.

Sport also played a crucial role in the breakdown of racial barriers. It has been well reported about America's long battle on the race issues from slavery to the acceptance of racial equality. During the first half of the twentieth century, African Americans were barred from participating in most professional sports leagues no matter what their talent level, and unable to play on most college and recreational teams. In 1900, baseball was the single most popular sport in black communities throughout the nation, and the pool of black talent was deep and strong. It was not until Jackie Robinson joined the Brooklyn Dodgers in 1947 that the system began to change.

Jackie Robinson is arguably one of the most important figures in the history of all sport. It is hard to explain the barriers and adversity that Robinson had to overcome but his lasting legacy is that he helped change the way Black players were viewed. Jackie Robinson made history in 1947 when he broke baseball's colour barrier to play for the Brooklyn Dodgers. He won the National League Rookie of the Year award his first season, and helped the Dodgers to the National League championship – the first of his six trips to the World Series. In 1949 Robinson won the league Most Valuable Player award, and he was inducted into the Baseball Hall of Fame in 1962. Despite his skill, Robinson faced a barrage of insults and threats because of his race. He was often made to stay in separate hotels to his team mates but he jsut took it in his stride and he did inspire a generation of black athletes to compete and break down the system. It was the courage and grace with which Robinson handled the abuses that won over his detractors and awakened a greater understanding that change was needed.

Over time, sports would become an important arena in the battles against segregation and racial discrimination. In the 1930s, boxing and track and field—two sports in which segregation was never as complete as it was in baseball—produced two black athletes who became genuine American sports heroes: Jesse Owens and Joe Louis. In both instances, these athletes won their victories against athletes from an ascendant Nazi Germany, a nation whose racial theories stigmatized much of America's immigrant population as racial inferiors.

Jesse Owens' victories at the 1936 Berlin Olympics and Joe Louis' 1938 victory over Max Schmeling at Yankee Stadium marked the first time in American history that large numbers of white Americans perceived a black athlete as fighting for them, and joyously celebrated their triumphs. These moments helped set the stage for the gradual steps taken by coaches at schools like NYU, UCLA, and the City College of New York to recruit black players for their football and basketball teams as well as for the much bigger step taken by Major League Baseball executive Branch Rickey to integrate the national pastime.

It was not a major rise in the number of talented black athletes but changes in the political climate in the nation and the world that led to the integration of sports, but sport played a central role.

> *"For historians, there is no better way to teach students about the creation and destruction of the colour and gender lines in twentieth-*

century America than to draw examples from the history of race and gender in sports, a history which is now richly documented in biographies, historical works, novels, and documentary film. Educators can see how useful an examination of sports can be in raising important themes in American history. Sports history provides a point of entry into American culture."[55]

It is easy to see why one immediately thinks of America as a country that seems to possess an advanced belief in the importance of sports. This is maybe where the contrast with Britain becomes most acute. The Americans believe in sports from an early age; not as a teaching methodology, but for building physical strength and robustness and it is celebrated to a higher level as the major High School events and teams bring together the communities in support.

In Britain a 2011 report on sport stated:

> We know that there is a tendency for pupils to drop out of sport during secondary school. Sport Wales' surveys consistently show that participation in sport decreases as people get older.[56]

The 2011 School Sport Survey in the UK said that:

> The School Sport Survey shows that the majority of primary school pupils have a positive experience of sport in school and this is reflected in participation rates. This message was reinforced in the focus group discussions, where participants in the groups recalled a strong onus on the fun and play aspects of sport. The primary school experience was perceived as being inclusive, regardless of ability.
>
> Participants reported that their experience of PE and school sports clubs in secondary school had a strong influence on whether they continued taking part, with the early years at secondary school being a key point for some in terms of disengagement.
>
> In many cases, the experiences that put young people off doing sport were the same regardless of gender. There were some specific issues reported by girls however. Non-sporty girls reported that sport was no longer fun due to the following reasons:
>
> - having fewer sports available to them, so they became repetitive and boring;
> - less of an emphasis on enjoyment and more on technical skills; and
> - competitiveness went against their preferences for enjoyment and sociability.
>
> At secondary school, girls may not be able to continue with the

football and rugby that they had played as mixed classes at primary school if there was no one to run a girls' club or class. Some reported they wanted to play less traditional sports because they were more fun, but there wasn't always somewhere to do them. The non-sporty girls from the focus groups did note the opportunities provided through 5x60 for trying new things, and these were welcomed, although it was noted that there were sometimes limited opportunities to follow through the things they did enjoy due to lack of availability/accessibility.

The influence of PE teachers and PE lessons on young people.

Participants in the focus groups who had dropped out of sport or never really engaged said that the most influential factor on their decision had been their experience of PE. The issues that they described were:

- *favouritism – they felt the teacher was only interested in those who were good at sport and did not encourage everyone to participate and enjoy. This was reflected in choosing teams for PE activities – either being in the "good" team or the "also-rans";*
- *feeling useless – if they weren't competent they felt "better" classmates (and sometimes their teachers too) could make them feel useless and were not encouraged to do their best and find something they enjoyed;*
- *limited choice – few sports were available in the PE class so if the young person didn't enjoy the activity or excel then there wasn't an alternative (often driven by a lack of facilities or equipment);*
- *no fun – the PE class and teacher didn't focus on enjoying the sport or the physical exertion;*
- *tolerating excuses – PE teachers readily accepting "excuse" notes so it was easy to get out of doing sport;*
- *inconsistency – some PE teachers were reported as bowing to pressure from young people to do classroom sessions in bad weather, so not instilling a positive attitude about sport and activity.[57]*

Clearly there is work to be done in terms of improving the PE structure and coaching but arguably the underlying point is that sport and PE is not as important in schools as maybe it should be. It has been known that there is a gap between sport in the leading private schools – which is still strong – and the state school system.

The difference is that sport is more centrally important in the US system and in the community. Athletics begin at a young age. They continue at more competitive levels throughout primary school to university, with extracurricular programmes playing a development role, and training students to perhaps even eventually become professionals. Sports remain a leisurely recreational activity even afterwards, as friends catch up at golf and tennis clubs. The large number of sports is not limited to baseball, ice hockey, basketball, American football and soccer, but rather includes a wide scope of athletic activities. At the professional level, spectator sports have become a staple of American traditions and culture. Families gather around the television or endure hours of traffic to support their favourite teams. The difference is that in the UK, it is less likely to be a family affair. When sport is on, the family splinters into different activities. It can be argued that the American wife and mother will be far more educated on sports than their UK counterpart as it is so much more part of family life.

In America, many children are exposed to sports at a young age to instil a habit of remaining active and fit, while also enjoying themselves. The system promotes sport as a key part of developing one's body, just as education is for the mind. The two are of equal importance. In the UK, sport is a recreation, an add on. In the UK, the average time spent playing sports in secondary school is 98 minutes per week (2011 school report). In the US, The Bureau of Labour Statistics issued figures that suggest that an American child will spend an average 28 mins a day playing sport during weekdays and 33 mins on weekends. This equates to 3.4 hours per week.

A report in the *Daily Mail* (April 2016) reported on a survey by Mothercare that in the UK:

> *Modern children play outdoors just half as much as their parents did when they were young, a study has revealed.*
>
> *Today's youth are more inclined to stay indoors and watch television, play computer games and, in some cases, even do their homework, than go outside to play, according to researchers.*
>
> *Figures show that those growing up in the during the 1970s and 1980s enjoyed more than two hours of outside play each weekday, and a further nine hours at weekends – whatever the weather.*
>
> *"But today's youngsters venture outside for just over an hour each weekday, and fewer than five hours on Saturdays and Sundays.*
>
> *The study of 2,000 parents revealed the average parent spent ten hours and 26 minutes playing outside during the working week when they were children – double the five hours and 32 minutes children head outdoors today.*
>
> *Weekends identified similar results, with youngsters spending just four hours and 32 minutes outside over the two days, compared to the nine hours their parents played outdoors during the same period.*

It also emerged that 44 per cent of parents wish their children played outdoors more often, with 58 per cent saying their children don't play outside as much as other youngsters they know.

And 54 per cent seriously worry their child doesn't spend enough time playing outdoors

Instead, 43 per cent say their children would rather watch television than go outside to play with friends, while another 42 per cent prefer to play computer games.

Parents also said their children would rather surf the Internet and listen to music, with almost one in ten claiming their offspring would even choose to do their homework over venturing out of the house.

A third of parents polled said their children will only play outside when it is sunny, with just 17 percent going outdoors whatever the weather.

In comparison, almost one in three parents said they enjoyed the fresh air come wind, rain or shine.

An astounding 43 per cent of parents even admitted they rely on school to ensure their children are getting plenty of time outdoors through PE and play times, and spend very little outdoor time with their children themselves.

The statistics emerged in a study by JCB Kids to mark the launch of its "Fresh Air Campaign".

Sam Johnson, spokesperson for JCB Kids, said: "It is alarming the extent to which today's children are missing out on the outdoor play time which we enjoyed as children.

"Playing outdoors is so important for children – not only to help them stay active and healthy, but also to socialise with friends – and create those treasured childhood memories which we look back on so fondly.

"There are many distractions which divert kids' attention from going outside, but as parents we need to encourage adventurous spirit and create imaginative, and of course safe, opportunities for them to get out there.

"Today's children are spending a lot of time in front of the TV, playing on consoles and staring at computer screens.'

Cath Prisk, Director of Play England, a UK wide charitable organisation who promote outdoor play for children and are supporting the JCB Kids Fresh Air Campaign added: "It's a sad reality that many kids don't get outside to play every day anymore.

"And because they don't go out, they don't know their own communities as well as their parents did, they don't have as many friends in the area and they don't have the same opportunities for fun that many of their parents did." [58]

Top ten things children would rather do than play outside

1. Watch TV
2. Play computer games
3. Play games
4. Play with toys
5. Read books
6. Go on the Internet
7. Listen to music
8. Read magazines
9. Do their homework
10. Do chores [58]

In America, the debate has been over whether sport is invested in too much at High School. The Atlantic offered a fascinating insight with a feature that asked why The United States routinely spends more tax dollars per high-school athlete than per high-school math student—unlike most countries worldwide?

EVERY YEAR, thousands of teenagers move to the United States from all over the world, for all kinds of reasons. They observe everything in their new country with fresh eyes, including basic features of American life that most of us never stop to consider.

One element of our education system consistently surprises them: "Sports are a big deal here," says Jenny, who moved to America from South Korea with her family in 2011. Shawnee High, her public school in southern New Jersey, fields teams in 18 sports over the course of the school year, including golf and bowling. Its campus has lush grass fields, six tennis courts, and an athletic Hall of Fame. "They have days when teams dress up in Hawaiian clothes or pyjamas just because – We're the soccer team!" Jenny says. (To protect the privacy of Jenny and other students in this story, only their first names are used.)

By contrast, in South Korea, whose 15-year-olds rank fourth in the world (behind Shanghai, Singapore, and Hong Kong) on a test of critical thinking in math, Jenny's classmates played pickup soccer on a dirt field at lunchtime. They brought badminton rackets from home and pretended there was a net. If they made it into the newspaper, it was usually for their academic accomplishments.

Sports are embedded in American schools in a way they are not almost anywhere else. Yet this difference hardly ever comes up in domestic debates about America's international mediocrity in education. (The US ranks 31st on the same international math test.) The challenges we do talk about are real ones, from undertrained teachers to entrenched poverty. But what to make of this other glaring reality, and the signal it sends to children, parents, and teachers about the very purpose of school?

When I surveyed about 200 former exchange students last year, in cooperation with an international exchange organization called AFS, nine out of 10 foreign students who had lived in the US said that kids here cared more about sports than their peers back home did. A majority of Americans who'd studied abroad agreed.

Even in eighth grade, American kids spend more than twice the time Korean kids spend playing sports, according to a 2010 study published in the Journal of Advanced Academics. In countries with more-holistic, less hard-driving education systems than Korea's, like Finland and Germany, many kids play club sports in their local towns – outside of school. Most schools do not staff, manage, transport, insure, or glorify sports teams, because, well, why would they?

When I was growing up in New Jersey, not far from where Jenny now lives, I played soccer from age seven to 17. I was relieved to find a place where girls were not expected to sit quietly or look pretty, and I still love the game. Like most other Americans, I can rattle off the many benefits of high-school sports: exercise, lessons in sportsmanship and perseverance, school spirit, and just plain fun. All of those things matter, and Jenny finds it refreshing to attend a school that is about so much more than academics. But as I've traveled around the world visiting places that do things differently – and get better results – I've started to wonder about the trade-offs we make.

Nearly all of Jenny's classmates at Shawnee are white, and 95 percent come from middle- or upper-income homes. But in 2012, only 17 percent of the school's juniors and seniors took at least one Advanced Placement test – compared with the 50 percent of students who played school sports.

As states and districts continue to slash education budgets, as more kids play on traveling teams outside of school, and as the globalized economy demands that children learn higher-order skills so they can compete down the line, it's worth re-evaluating the American sporting tradition. If sports were not central to the mission of American high schools, then what would be?

On October 12, 1900, the Wall School of Honey Grove played St. Matthew's Grammar School of Dallas in football, winning 5–0. The event was a milestone in Texas history: the first recorded football game between two high-school teams. Until then, most American boys had played sports in the haphazard way of boys the world over: ambling onto fields and into alleys for pickup games or challenging other loosely affiliated groups of students to a match. Cheating was rampant, and games looked more like brawls than organized contests.

Schools got involved to contain the madness. The trend started in elite private schools and then spread to the masses. New York City inaugurated its Public Schools Athletic League in 1903, holding a track-and-field spectacular for 1,000 boys at Madison Square Garden the day after Christmas.

At the time, the United States was starting to educate its children for more years than most other countries, even while admitting a surge of immigrants. The ruling elite feared that all this schooling would make Anglo-Saxon boys soft and weak, in contrast to their brawny, newly immigrated peers. Oliver Wendell Holmes Sr. warned that cities were being overrun with 'stiff-jointed, soft-muscled, paste-complexioned youth.'

Sports, the thinking went, would both protect boys' masculinity and distract them from vices like gambling and prostitution. "Muscular Christianity," fashionable during the Victorian era, prescribed sports as a sort of moral vaccine against the tumult of rapid economic growth. "In life, as in a football game," Theodore Roosevelt wrote in an essay on "The American Boy" in 1900, "the principle to follow is: Hit the line hard; don't foul and don't shirk," but hit the line Athletics succeeded in distracting not just students but entire communities. As athletic fields became the cultural centers of towns across America, educators became coaches and parents became boosters.

From the beginning, though, some detractors questioned whether tax money should be spent on activities that could damage the brain, and occasionally leave students dead on the field. In 1909, New York City superintendents decided to abolish football, and The New York Times predicted that soccer would become the sport of choice. But officials reversed course the next year, re-allowing football, with revised rules.

The National Collegiate Athletic Association had emerged by this time, as a means of reforming the increasingly brutal sport of college football. But the enforcers were unable to keep pace with the industry. Once television exponentially expanded the fan base in the mid-20th century, collegiate sports gained a spiritual and economic choke hold on America. College scholarships rewarded high-school athletes, and the search for the next star player trickled down even to grade school. As more and more Americans attended college, growing ranks of alumni demanded winning teams – and university presidents found their reputations shaped by the success of their football and basketball programs.

LAST YEAR IN TEXAS, whose small towns are the spiritual home of high-school football and the inspiration for Friday Night Lights, the superintendent brought in to rescue one tiny rural school district did something insanely rational. In the spring of 2012, after the state threatened to shut down Premont Independent School District for financial mismanagement and academic failure, Ernest Singleton suspended all sports – including football.

To cut costs, the district had already laid off eight employees and closed the middle-school campus, moving its classes to the high-school building; the elementary school hadn't employed an art or a music teacher in years; and the high school had sealed off the science labs, which were infested with mold. Yet the high school still turned out football, basketball, volleyball, track, tennis, cheerleading, and baseball teams each year.

Football at Premont cost about $1,300 a player. Math, by contrast, cost just $618 a student. For the price of one football season, the district could have hired a full-time elementary-school music teacher for an entire year. But, despite the fact that Premont's football team had won just one game the previous season and hadn't been to the playoffs in roughly a decade, this option never occurred to anyone.

"I've been in hundreds of classrooms," says Singleton, who has spent 15 years as a principal and helped turn around other struggling schools. "This was the worst I've seen in my career. The kids were in control. The language was filthy. The teachers were not prepared." By suspending sports, Singleton realized, he could save $150,000 in one year. A third of this amount was being paid to teachers as coaching stipends, on top

of the smaller costs: $27,000 for athletic supplies, $15,000 for insurance, $13,000 for referees, $12,000 for bus drivers. 'There are so many things people don't think about when they think of sports,' Singleton told me. Still, he steeled himself for the town's reaction. 'I knew the minute I announced it, it was going to be like the world had caved in on us.'

First he explained his decision to Enrique Ruiz Jr., the principal of Premont's only high school: eliminating sports would save money and refocus everyone's attention on academics. Ruiz agreed. The school was making other changes, too, such as giving teachers more time for training and planning, making students wear uniforms, and aligning the curriculum with more-rigorous state standards. Suspending sports might get the attention of anyone not taking those changes seriously.[59]

A week later, the Huffington Post responded with:

Last week, a provocative article appeared in The Atlantic titled "The Case Against High-School Sports." In a publication known for great journalism, the piece has received thousands of "Likes" on Facebook and evoked hundreds of comments, as it argues that high school sports hinder America's academic performance compared to other nations.

While it's imperative that we constantly strive to improve the educational experience for America's youth, the article's representation of high school sports in our country is short-sided. It suggests that high schools should not subsidize sports teams, stating, '(in other countries) most schools do not staff, manage, transport, insure, or glorify sports teams, because, well, why would they?'

Here are few reasons, well, why they would.

The goal of high school is to educate our young people so that they may become productive citizens, not to simply score well on the 'international math test' to which the article makes several references.

The benefits of sports as part of the education process are abundant and sometimes beyond quantification, but the article merely brushes them off with only a slight acknowledgment. Today's employers, however, recognize those benefits in evaluating potential employees.

According to Forbes, incorporating sports into a woman's education is perhaps even more critical in preparing her for the future, stating

In 2002, a study by mutual fund company Oppenheimer revealed that a shocking 82% of women in executive-level jobs had played organized *sports in middle, high or post-secondary school. Moreover, nearly half of women earning over $75,000 identified themselves as "athletic."*

There is a long list of proven leaders that can attribute part of their development to sports like Jeffrey Immelt (General Electric), Meg Whitman (Hewlett Packard), and even President George H.W. Bush.

The article states that sports are overly emphasized in American high schools, commanding significant budgetary dollars. Yes, sports are a big deal in America, and it affords Americans the freedom of choice. In other countries, sports and academics are often mutually exclusive. In China, for example, a girl who wants to pursue competitive gymnastics must be identified at a young age, may then be removed from her family, and thrust into rigorous habitual training. Academics become secondary. The same happens around the world in soccer, as Lionel Messi, now one the world's best players, was plucked at a young age and placed into a soccer academy.

Thanks to high school sports, American children can be both students and athletes.

But if we fail to support high school sports, this American freedom is threatened. If you're not exceptional at an extremely young age and in possession of the financial resources to play, you would have a bleak future in that sport. Michael Jordan, who didn't excel in basketball until later in high school, wouldn't have had the opportunity to become 'Michael Jordan.' And Ronald Reagan, who developed a love of football at Dixon High School before captaining the team at Eureka College, may not have acquired the skills to become president.

The article suggests that in place of high school sports, kids could play on club teams outside of school. But that misses the critical role that high school sports play in America's unparalleled sports infrastructure.

High school sports supply talent to college sports, and college sports supply talent to professional sports.

This infrastructure is significant because sports can lift a country in need. In the aftermath of the 9/11 terrorist attacks, perhaps the country's darkest hour, sports became therapeutic. 'The games people love became an integral part of the healing process...the athletes, some with absolutely no ties to the city but a uniform, became a source of inspiration,' according to CNN.

A single sports team can lift a city, as the New Orleans Saints did for theirs in the wake of Hurricane Katrina. "The Saints gave the city hope.

It's something very emotional. We just love the team," one woman told The New York Times as she sobbed softly.

Even a high school volleyball team can lift an ailing community, as HBO's Real Sports showed with the story of Caroline Found, who was tragically killed in a moped accident. Her teammates, united with the community, rallied to win the state volleyball championship in her honor.

Sports make our country better, and high school sports play a vital role.[60]

In the United States, sport and the community are bedfellows. It is one of the contradictions of the US, sport is a community feature and yet, as previously outlined, the system is geared towards the importance and skills of the individual. Logic would suggest that the team ethos would be as potent as it is in Australia or the UK. One can argue that the system is fairer and the analysis is of individual performance and contribution rather than team dynamics. One could argue that it is more brutal as there is nowhere to hide, no team ethos to protect poor performance and it leads to every individual contributing and consistent delivery.

One could also argue that in the US, the family and the community is the team. There is a greater affiliation with the broader community than just a team. The team represents the town or city whilst in the UK it is far more about the smaller group of the team. This is supported by the fact that it is the towns and communities that organise and own sports in the locality itself. Towns often create youth leagues that allow children to compete against other towns. These programmes, which are run by volunteers, stress not only skill development, but also values of sportsmanship and enjoyment no matter what the outcome. This commitment to athletic engagement at the local level is evident throughout all ages, as one sees families jogging around town and supporting their kids' baseball games on a regular basis. The government echoes this sentiment through the "President's Council on Physical Fitness and Sports," which is tasked with recommending physical fitness and health through athletics.

The governing body of university sports is the National Collegiate Athletic Association (NCAA). With 1,281 member schools, the NCAA oversees the majority of sports at the university level. These college sports, especially basketball and football, draw numerous crowds and sometimes are more popular than the respective professional sports. Several university head coaches command multi-million dollar salaries. In March, for instance, Americans anticipate the NCAA Division I Basketball Tournament "March Madness," a knockout championship featuring the top 68 teams in basketball. Either supporting their alma maters or their states' school, Americans watch the games passionately.

Professional sports in the US are largely dominated by the Big Four Leagues: American football in the National Football League (NFL), baseball in Major League Baseball (MLB), basketball the National Basketball Association (NBA), and ice hockey in the National Hockey League (NHL). The teams operate in a franchise system, in which a set number of clubs field one team representing a region. These clubs are different than other systems such as the English Premier League, as American franchises are able to move their team to different regions, often renaming them to demonstrate this change. However, this relocation does not happen often. Furthermore, within any of the major leagues, there is no promotion or relegation process. Instead, the NBA has a developmental league system, and hockey and baseball have minor league systems; these allow rising athletes to hone skills to eventually pursue their dream at the professional level. Sports in America also do not follow a league system as the Premier League. Instead, the teams play over a season and the select best teams are given berths in playoff tournaments, which operate in a knockout method, with the winner being deemed the champion.

America possesses a strong infrastructure that suggests that sport will continue to grow and prosper for decades to come.

The Special Relationship... The close bond between the US and UK in Golf

In team sports there is very little that links the UK and the US. The UK has no real strength in American Football, Ice Hockey, or Basketball. The UK has teams, but of no real significance. Similarly the US is not as strong in soccer or rugby – although they are arguably closer to being competitive than the UK is in US based sports.

However, there is no doubt that there is a very close relationship between the two nations when it comes to golf. Many of the American greats will view the British Open Championship with genuine affection and there have some superb performances over the years by American players seeking to win this crown.

The Ryder Cup

The Ryder Cup is one of the great sporting contests that takes place between the US and Europe every two years. Great Britain's professionals first played their American counterparts at Gleneagles in 1921. The second match too place in 1926 at Wentworth and it was this match that inspired Samuel Ryder, of St Albans, to create the bi-annual contest. The first Cup match was played in 1927 in Massachusetts. In this first match, Walter Hagen captained the US team and Ted Ray the British team. However over the years, the US team were the dominant team. By 1957, the score stood at nine matches won by the US and two by GB. Great Britain won the 1957 match but then did not win again until the 1985 match when GB had been enlarged to be a European team.

However, since 1985 the contests have been more equally contested – in fact they have become fiercely contested. Since 1985, Europe has won 10 matches to the US's four. In that time there have been some dramatic matches such as The Battle of Brookline in 1999, and the Meltdown in Meldinah in 2012. The matches are intense and players on both sides are desperate to play, which is odd as the players are so generally conditioned to being individuals and singular.

As is so often the case, there are so many contradictions. The European golfers seem to come together far better than the Americans. It is strange as the Europeans can be often fragmented in approach that one would expect the US to have a stronger team ethic but the facts show the opposite to be true. The Ryder Cup has seem some explosive personal battles but also great sportsmanship between the teams.

The British Open

The British Open is generally regarded as the premier of the majors although The Masters has grown in importance and prestige in recent times. The first Open was played in 1860 at Musselburgh. The first American to win was Jock Hutchinson in 1920 and between 1920 and 1939, American players won 12 British Open Championships. The two most famous would be Bobby Jones and Walter Hagen. Jones won in 1926, 1927 and 1930. His 1930 success was part of the Grand slam when he won the US Open plus the amateur titles of both countries. After the war, not so many Americans competed until Arnold Palmer reinvigorated interest in the great old tournament. The 1960s saw the arrival of maybe some of the greatest ever players in Palmer, Jack Nicklaus, and Gary Player. They were followed in the 1970s by Tom Watson, Johnny Miller, Lee Trevino and Tom Weiskopf. If one looks at these players records, it is impressive:

Walter Hagen won the Championship in 1922, 1924, 1928, 1929

Bobby Jones in 1926, 1927 and 1930

Jack Nicklaus in 1966, 1970 and 1978

Arnold Palmer in 1961, 1962

Lee Trevino in 1971, 1972

Tom Watson – 1975, 1977, 1980, 1982, 1983.

Bobby Jones

It has been well recorded that Bobby Jones possessed a very strong affection for St Andrews. Jones was an unique sportsman and maybe one of the most intelligent – he was a Graduate of Atlanta School of Technology and of Harvard. He had degrees in Law, Engineering and Literature.

He was US Open Champion on four occasions in 1923, 1926, 1929 and 1930. He was British Open Champion three times. He won the U.S Amateur Championship five times in 1924, 1925, 1927, 1928, and 1930. He won the British Amateur Championship just once in 1930. He won the Walker Cup five times and was captain of the wining US team in 1928 and 1930.

However, there is a touching story of the love for St Andrews that Jones possessed and it became mutual. St Andrews University boasts The Robert T. Jones Memorial Trust Scholarships, which support students for one year of study at Emory University in Atlanta. They cover all mandatory costs at Emory as well as the transatlantic airfare and a substantial stipend for personal spending. The year at Emory is taken as an extra year of study after graduation. St Andrews boasts a Bobby Jones Place – named after the golfer.

So why the great bond between the two?

The 19-year-old Jones had first played at St Andrews, regarded as the home of golf, at the British Open in 1921. He famously tore up his scorecard in disgust during his third round after failing to get his ball out of a bunker on the 11th hole. He publicly expressed his dislike of the Old Course and in return the local press labelled him as an "ordinary boy".

Six years later, however, he returned to St. Andrews to successfully defend his British Open championship, which marked the beginning of a long and special relationship with the course and Scottish golfing fans. In 1930 he won his Grand Slam, winning the British championship at St Andrews. He effectively retired from the game after 1930, but continued to be active in the world of golf. Later in his life, he was quoted saying; "If I had to select one course upon which to play the match of my life, I should have selected the Old Course."

In 1948 Jones was diagnosed with a rare, incurable spinal cord disorder, which gradually crippled him. In 1958 he was appointed as team captain of the USA for the World Amateur Team Championship at St. Andrews. At the packed and emotional dinner at the Younger Graduation Hall to mark Jones becoming an Honorary Burgess (he was the first American since Benjamin Franklin to receive the honour), the golfer, who by now could only stand with the aid of leg braces, spoke movingly of his career and the special role St. Andrews had played in it. After he received the key, he was quoted saying; "*I could take out of my life everything but my experiences here in St Andrews and I would still have had a rich and full life,*"[61] which is a testament to the Old Course and the town's support.

Why the bond? Maybe they first witnessed a boy and recognised his genius. Maybe it was the venue that saw him fail, and he felt that failure; only for him to return and conquer. Maybe St Andrews was his greatest challenge?

As for the town's support, it again showed the hallmark of the British ability to forgive sporting genius.

CAPTAINS

"When considering the stature of an athlete or for that matter any person, I set great store in certain qualities which I believe to be essential in addition to skill. They are that the person conducts his or her life with dignity, with integrity, courage, and perhaps most of all, with modesty. These virtues are totally compatible with pride, ambition, **and** *competitiveness –* **Don Bradman**[62]

5 – *Bobby Moore*

England's World Cup Winning Captain

Maybe Bradman's words could have been written for Bobby Moore, England's Captain for the 1966 triumph.

The name of Bobby Moore has had iconic status down the decades since that moment in 1966 when England won the World Cup. Moore just stood apart as a captain and as a player.

When he died, his authority was maybe summed up by Jeff Powell who wrote after his early death from Prostate cancer in 1993; "Heaven's XI can now play. The captain has arrived."[63]

Moore was the Golden boy of English football who grew into one of the world's greatest players by 1970 – a man of genuine global stature. In the match against Brazil in the World Cup of 1970, Moore's brilliance at reading a game was shown as Jairzinho raced at him with aggression and speed. Moore just stayed calm and timed his tackle to perfection. The man was "cool" under pressure and a man's man. At the end of the game, the world's great player, Pele, walked over to Moore and they swapped shirts and showed their mutual respect to the world. Here stood the world's greatest attacker and defender and they had just done battle.

The strange debate over Moore was the bemusing reason for why he was shunned by the game after his retirement. Maybe the best description appeared in the book Harry by Harry Rednapp (2013). Harry Rednapp played with Bobby Moore at West Ham and they remained friends. In his book, Rednapp writes with a care and admiration for his friend and Captain:

> What a man. I mean it. The straightest, most honest bloke you could meet in your life. Not an ounce of aggression in him, not a hint of nastiness. Won the World Cup, and even the opposition loved him.

Brazilians idolised him. Not just Pele but all of them: Jairzinho, Rivelino. People say the 1970 Brazil team was the greatest of all time and Bob would have walked into it; in fact, he would have made the team of the tournament at any World Cup throughout history. I remember the game England played against Brazil that summer in Mexico. He was the best player on the field...Everyone wanted to meet Bobby, everyone wanted a night out with him. And Bobby loved the social side of the game. He captained the England football team, but he would have captained the England drinking team too if we had one...You'd have thought that someone, somewhere, would have snapped Bobby up (after his retirement from playing) and given him a second chance. They only had to see him play to know the way he read and understood the game. And he was Sir Alf Ramsey's captain. That should have meant something. Surely? I won't have it that Bob couldn't have become a good manager. His footballing brain was on a different level when he played, so surely that would have converted to management, over time. To this day I will never know why he could not get a break. I still believe that with the right support, he could have been the greatest manager in West Ham's history. But we'll never know...He could have been fantastic for England and for English football. Germany put Franz Beckenbauer centre stage. France did the same with Michel Platini, so much so that he ended up President of UEFA. Meanwhile, Bobby Moore holds the same rank of honour in this country as Des Lynam. How didn't he get a knighthood? Why didn't he get a knighthood? How did we end up with Sir Dave Richards and Sir Bert Millichip but not Sir Bobby Moore?

We think of scandals in football as a player diving, or high transfer fees, but this, for me, is what scandal really means. The way that football treated Bobby, changed my attitude, professionally, because seeing him struggle confirmed to me that nobody in this game really gives a monkey's about you once you've served your purpose.[64]

It will always be hard to explain why the game in England did not nurture or even look after Bobby Moore better than they did. Many, including Rednapp, believe it was because of Moore's reputation for drinking. Maybe but there were many that liked to drink in all walks of life including no few of England's leading politicians at the time – George Brown, Harold Wilson and Roy Jenkins to name a few. If this was really the reason, the level of hypocrisy in England would have been remarkable.

Maybe the problem was more simple? Moore simply stood taller than most. He was a natural leader and maybe most people would have been intimidated by his presence. Bobby Moore was a hero and sometimes it is hard for anyone to work with such characters as it presents a no win situation – if he does well, it is because he is a natural. If not, and many great players are not good managers, would you want to be the person to shoot the great legend? It was easier to look at other options.

This still does not excuse the fact that he was not recognised better and he could have been a superb coach and mentor. Moore's greatest talent lay in the fact that he could be one of the boys and let lead them into battle with full respect the next day. Bobby Moore was a special leader because respect came from the man himself. It was not just that he was an exceptional player but he would lead through example; he would rarely talk about his own problems but he would be there for his teammates and friends to support them; and he would not be fazed or intimidated in even the most pressurised of situations.

Jeff Powell, in the *Daily Mail* (Nov 2012), noted how even the Scots respected Moore like few other Englishmen:

> The Scots never took to Alf but Bobby was a different matter. No matter how feisty the sporting enmity, admiration of greatness at the "fitba" resides deep in their soul.
>
> The score that day was 5–0. Take good note of the nil.
>
> When, after games like this in which their finest foundered on his haughty defending and they called him "that bastard Moore", it was said with enormous respect. When the bloody English failed to knight him, the Scots were first to take to calling him 'Sir Robert." [65]

Moore had the aura about him that commanded respect. When he led a team, he looked confident, assured and as though he could face any opposition and still not be fazed.

Moore was, in most people's minds during the late 60s and early 70s, England undisputed leader. Given the tribal aggressive nature of England's football landscape, this was a special compliment but he just stood a step apart, He inspired others but asked little for himself.

Chapter Six

AUSTRALIA, THE ASHES AND SPORT

Australia has long been one of Britain's great rivals over the decades and most especially in cricket where The Ashes is such an important battle for national pride. The Ashes have been the centre of many exceptional sporting stories over the years from the infamous Bodyline series which pitted Douglas Jardine against the great Donald Bradman to the exploits of Ian Botham, Freddie Flintoff and Alaistair Cook for England to those of Lillee, Thomson, Marsh, Warne and McGrath for Australia.

Australia has such a strong sporting heritage with many icons and heroes that also include the likes of the Chappell brothers, Michael Lynagh, David Campese, Shane Gould, Greg Norman, Rod Leaver, John Eales, Ian Thorpe, Cathy Freeman and Pat Cash. The names represent some of the greatest of sporting moments over the last seventy years.

Australia is a land that is a natural environment to nurture sport. The immediate image is one of sand, sea, sun. In fact, the surfing championships in Australia are one of the major highlights in the sporting calendar. The Australian Surf Life Saving Championships sees members from Australia's 313 Surf Clubs come together annually to compete in more than 400 beach and ocean events over just nine days. In 2016, this will equate to over 7,000 competitors.

There is little doubt that it provides an idyllic backdrop to playing sports all the year round. There also are no restrictions on space, and no shortages of suitable land for playing fields. Of course, one cannot say that the climate alone is responsible for the sporting passion that exists within Australia, but combined with a desire to win it is a significant contributor.

It is, though, the desire to win that has often sets Australia slightly apart from anyone including the US. There is a greater ruggedness within Australian culture. It can be argued that this is derived from the fact that Australia is still a relatively young country and success in sport has helped in developing a strong national identity and pride. Australia was almost created at the will of the European powers who exported their "undesirables" to this distant land. Unlike America where its founding fathers travelled to the continent in hope and in search of a new life, many arrived in Australia with far less expectation. It was in their interests to build a strong society and culture and the early population embraced that challenge. The result is there is a real desire within Australian culture so that they can stand equal to anyone as they came from a lesser start.

However, it is always dangerous to underestimate Australia or Australians. Whatever the origins of their country, they are – maybe as a result – open-minded with a thirst for culture and to learn. Whilst America can be criticised for sometimes being blinkered to life beyond the US, the same cannot be said of Australians. They are quick to travel, to experience the world and to learn.

For this reason, one of the driving strengths in their culture is the base Australian ethos is that everyone is equal, only divided by the talent they possess. In Australian society any game is open to anyone at any time – if a person is capable, they can play. Sport is not restricted to social classes, race or gender. This allows the maximum involvement of youth. The Australian ethos is tough and no nonsense and part of the no nonsense approach is a belief in equality and that all can play.

Europeans began to arrive in Australia in the late 1700s and soon focused on expansion and change. Though the first European settlement was in 1788, there were no "free settlers" until several years later. Early arrivals consisted mainly of convicts. With later arrivals of upper class Europeans, new leisurely activities were created. New sports such as cricket, rowing and boxing were brought to Australia from the UK.

However, it was very different to the story of America, which grew from immigrants moving to a country to come together to build a new country. Many arrived in Australia against their free will. The criminal background meant that the Victorian sports were not immediately the leading sports of interest sports but those that encouraged gambling – sports which included boxing, cock fighting and kangaroo hunting.

The beginnings of a sports consciousness can be traced to England. When the land was first settled, the scarcity of recreational opportunities may have created a hunger for sport and leisure. One academic traced a *"surging passion for sport back to the colonial era and argues that sport flourished because of the weakness of high culture in a culturally-deprived society"*.[66]

Sport played a major role in the lives of colonial leaders and they played a significant role. Through the interaction of the British Army, the development of cricket was enhanced where matches between officers and civilians were organised and recorded. The military was responsible for the development of a permanent cricket club and playing ground in Sydney. Officers also helped establish other sports such as rowing and rugby. The later arrival of larger numbers of free settlers created an environment in which organised sport on a greater scale emerged.

In 1876 there occurred the first of Australia's significant successes, and this was in a sporting event. Edward Trickett won the sculling (rowing) championship of the World. This was suddenly evidence of Australia being the best in the world at something. The same year a combined New South Wales and Victorian cricket team beat an all-England team in Melbourne. These stimulated a nationalism and a growing desire for sports which dramatically increased in following years and coincided with increased sporting success.

The establishment of some of Australia's first recreational clubs includes boxing in 1814, horse racing in 1825, cricket in 1826, rowing in 1835, billiards and sailing in 1836, shooting in 1842, lawn bowls in 1846 and golf in 1847. During this period in Australian history, from pre 1788 to 1850, sport changed from that originally created to serve as survival means to that designed for leisure and cultural means. Society began to find its feet in Australia and began directing itself toward more social diversions such as cricket and horse racing rather than the more violent games.

The real change in Australian sport came with the increase and ease of travel. Suddenly, teams from across the country could play each other and international teams could travel to Australia and this gave Australia the opportunity to prove itself as a nation. It was natural. Any success in overseas sporting competitions thus boosted the national pride and confidence of the Australian population.

The increase of matches between regions led to a new game, Australian Rules, being created with characteristics of English and Australian football games, soccer and rugby. Although both soccer and rugby shared a commonality in traditional folk football, the Australian football was the first sport to be unique to Australia; there was no single game in Britain upon which this new game was modelled. An increase in competition resulted in a rise in need for the standardization of rules. Some organisations thus formed included the New South Wales Cricket Association in 1858, the Northern (Queensland) Rugby Union in 1874 and the Victorian Football Association (Australian Rules) in 1879.

Australia today is a strong country but it is important to understand that its roots were from weaker foundations and this has acted as a real motivation to build a brave new world. Historically, Australian society has been perceived as a male dominated area as the first Europeans were predominantly male convicts and officers. This contributed to the sporting image in Australian social history. This image encompasses what Keith Dunstan describes as a; *"correct and manly will-to-*

win attitude".[67] In fairness, there was little choice. The country was under developed as the first immigrants arrived and it was not going to be a land for the faint hearted. Society was a ground zero too and all had to be built. It was always going to take courage, determination and steel to build the country from its starting point.

Arguably, Australia's development was helped by the belief in social equality. It arguably was one of the first countries where women were viewed as being able to compete openly in sport. As sport became more organised, so women's sports emerged. In the decades following settlement, while women rarely succeeded in executive or political positions, they could always succeed in sport and gain widespread admiration. In contemporary public surveys for popularity, sporting heroes both men and women, have always been near the top. Jack Kramer once stated, "*You're somebody in Australia if you're a sportsman. People will recognise you, in a way that you like, and they want to talk to you*".[68]

Over the years, sport has developed a nationalism, which has unified Australia and has helped bridge inequalities of race and gender.

Following the end of World War One, people turned to sport and other recreational activities as an escape, to put the horrors of war behind them. It was during this time that sports for women became widely accepted. This period saw the organisation of many large-scale competitions. There was also the creation of two exclusively female sports: vigoro and netball.

In 1929, even while massive economic losses from the Great Depression affected many aspects of Australian life, sport continued to thrive. Again, sport was seen as an escape, this time from harsh economic realities. Extensive Australian success in all levels of sporting competition, from local to Olympic, expanded the importance and significance of sport in Australian life.

Australia's greatest success though came in cricket, which enjoyed one of its golden eras with the great Donald Bradman at the helm. He is widely acknowledged as the greatest Test batsman of all time. Bradman's career Test batting average of 99.94 does set him apart. One can understand why Jardine developed Bodyline to combat Bradman's skills.

During a 20-year playing career, Bradman consistently scored at a level that made him, in the words of former Australia captain Bill Woodfull, "worth three batsmen to Australia" (69). Following an enforced hiatus due to World War Two, he made a dramatic comeback, captaining an Australian team known as "The Invincibles" on a record-breaking unbeaten tour of England

World War Two had, like for other countries, a devastating effect on Australian life. A significant drop off was seen in sporting participation because all eligible men were going off to fight. But, immediately following the war an upsurge was seen in sport popularity. Thousands of immigrants from numerous countries increased cultural diversity in Australia and also introduced new sports into the society. In addition to the rise in popularity of new sports, economic prosperity during this time allowed for greater leisure time available to the average Australian worker.

The post war era needed new heroes and out of the horror and grief of the war years, rose a new mentality in sport. It was natural. It had a fresher perspective and players played games with greater freedom. Just as in the 1940s, England's greatest idol was Dennis Compton, so Australia had Keith Miller – a player that like Compton – brought new audiences to watch the game of cricket. Miller was an exceptional all-rounder. Miller was an "action man" and also a war hero who enthused a generation of cricket lovers both in England and Australia. He was charismatic, outspoken, handsome and troublesome.

Ian Chappell, a great Captain in the 1970s, wrote an article for the *Sydney Morning Herald* that outlined Keith Miller's charisma and charm for audiences:

Every time I went to the Adelaide Oval as a kid to see either NSW or Australia play, my father Martin would urge me: "Watch Miller. Watch what Miller does."

Consequently, I grew up idolising Keith Miller, which is like saying Australians enjoy beer. Years later, I got to know him. I'd enter the lounge room of his house in Newport and two photos either side of a table would catch my attention. One was of a young Peg Miller, a long-legged beauty from Boston with long, dark hair and a shy smile. In the other photo was a debonair young Keith, with a glint in his eye and a face that was ruggedly handsome, a man adored by males and females alike.

Keith Ross Miller was born in November 1919, served in the air force and had a four-boy family, the same in every respect as Arthur Martin Chappell, except my father sired only three boys. My first Adelaide Oval cricket memory is of Miller in the 1950–51 Ashes series. He took four wickets and made 44 and 99. I don't remember any wickets or attacking shots, but I do recall a moment when he was completing a quick single and the toe of his bat dug into the turf and stopped abruptly. Miller had to adroitly hurdle the bat to avoid a nasty inconvenience. I was immediately hooked as a Miller fan.

His athleticism profoundly impressed me. There was the nonchalant flick of his hair as he walked back to his mark or faced up to the bowler, the short but energetic run-up that generated surprising pace, yet could easily be adapted to accommodate the occasional googly. These mannerisms were an integral part of my Miller impersonations in my backyard fantasy games, whether I was bowling at an unprotected set of stumps or tossing a ball in the air and dispatching it to the wooden fence.

The Miller escapade I most admired was one of quick-thinking ingenuity. He was lounging around at mid-on and the pro-South Australian crowd was baiting him over the lack of interest he seemed to be taking in the thrashing NSW were administering. When a lofted shot went over his head, to the right, he loped after it, casually got his hands under the ball, then let it fall to the ground. The crowd erupted, calling Miller a mug. What they didn't realise was there'd been an early no-ball call under the old back-foot law. Once the batsmen saw the ball hit the turf, they called for a second run. Seizing his opportunity, Miller pounced on the ball, whirled and threw to the bowler's end. John Drennan was run out for nought.

It was sheer genius. It also hushed the raucous Adelaide Oval crowd.

It was easy to be fooled by Miller's apparent nonchalance, to judge him as a captain lucky to lead a supremely talented NSW side. Yet years after that, when I talked cricket with Miller, I occasionally felt embarrassed that I'd captained Australia and he hadn't. Miller's knowledge of the game flowed through his conversation and I was impressed by his gambling instincts, which came through in every discussion of tactics.

Miller and Ray Lindwall were comfortable in each other's company. They were a classic case of opposites attract. Miller was gregarious and a larrikin, with a gambler's nature. Lindwall just enjoyed a beer and a chat with his mates: the most humble champion I have ever met. The pair of them attended a late 1980s Ashes function at the MCG and a few of us were invited for a beer afterwards at the Australian Cricket Board offices. Rod Marsh, Neil Harvey and myself walked there while the two hobbling fast bowlers rode in a car. I ambled over to Miller. "Look at you fast bowlers," I said. "You're limping on your left leg and Lindy's right leg is gimpy. You're buggered."

Glaring at me, Miller took a swig from his beer. "That's because batsmen never do anything." He took another swallow, looked me in the eye and spat out: "I f---in' hate batsmen." I was glad he was in his seventies and hampered, otherwise he might have invited me into the nets.

In the late 80s, my wife Barbara-Ann and I moved to Sydney's northern beaches. A young kid asked me to obtain Keith's autograph, and this led to regular visits to Newport. At first, Miller told mostly cricket stories. He also made it clear that we had similar opinions about Don Bradman – the man, not the batsman. He was reluctant to recall World War Two but did tell a tale about bowling to Englishman Bill Edrich on a dangerously damp pitch at the Gabba. It was December 1946. Miller explained how receiving the Distinguished Flying Cross early in the war was the equivalent of winning a Victoria Cross. Edrich had been awarded an early DFC, and when a couple of Miller's quickest deliveries nearly decapitated him, Miller slowed down. This was not well received by Bradman.

"Bowl fast, Keith," Bradman said. "They're harder to play when you bowl fast."

Miller replied: "This guy survived the war, Don. I'm not going to, ahem, kill him with a cricket ball."

And he tossed his skipper the ball.

As my visits became more regular, Miller began to open up.

He told me how pilots had to report any faults with the plane after flying a mission. "I reported a fault with one plane and went off to bed. When I awoke, ahem, I was told the next pilot to fly that plane had been killed in a crash."

Hearing the stories made it easier to understand his casual approach to life in general, and to family life in particular. Almost as a way of explanation, Keith once confessed: "I'm the most selfish bastard on earth." It was a one-off admission but it hardened my opinion on the futility of war. At Peg's funeral, Jan Beames, a daughter of Keith's brother Ray, recalled her father saying Keith was "a different guy after he returned". Perhaps Miller was acknowledging this when, occasionally, he'd confide: "Peg's way too good for me."

Miller was never one to mince words. On one occasion, I arrived at his house only to have a piece of paper thrust in my hand. "Read that, ahem, and if you want to throw up, don't do it in my direction."

It was a copy of a sycophantic letter Ian Johnson sent Bradman after the successful 1948 tour of England. Johnson gushed like a schoolboy about Bradman being the best batsman and captain he'd ever seen. No exaggeration there – but he overstepped the mark when he described a century partnership they'd had on tour, of which Johnson made very few, as the greatest thrill of his career. Many good judges thought Miller should have got the Australian captaincy ahead of Johnson. After reading that letter, it was easy to see why Miller had little chance: at the time, Bradman was chairman of selectors.

Vice-captain Miller and captain Johnson had several run-ins. After English spin twins Jim Laker and Tony Lock bowled Australia out for 143 at Headingley in 1956, Johnson made a typical rah-rah rallying speech suggesting Australia could still win. Miller was reading a form guide in the corner, and he looked up just long enough to say: 'Six to four we can't'. [70]

Government and Sport

For sport really to flourish at the highest levels, it is clear that it does require support from Government and the development of an infrastructure to help in the development of talent, coaches and facilities. As previously stated, the British performance levels improved as sport began to receive Government support.

The sea change for Australia began earlier and dates back to 1941, when the United Australia Party Government, led by Robert Menzies, passed a National Fitness Act which set up the Commonwealth Council for National Fitness and six state councils.

The Budget for the National Fitness Council was set for £20,000 for five years. While the stated intention of the National Fitness Act was to improve the overall fitness of the population. One of the prime motivations for the Act was that the fitness level of many Australian men who had enlisted to serve in World War Two had been defined as low. It is strange as this counters the argument that Australia was an environment that encouraged sporting prowess and physical activity but one also has to note that life in those early days was difficult and conditions were still relatively poor. It would still take time to build a strong sporting culture but this was a start in that process.

In 1972, The Labour party began to formulate a plan for sport and recreation. The ALP plan was underpinned by Labour leader Gough Whitlam's view of sport as a means for improving the overall welfare of the nation. Labour's development plan was later the foundation for what was to become a modern sport system in Australia.

After it came to power, Labour set up a Department of Tourism and Recreation who then commissioned Bloomfield to report on the status of sport and recreation in Australia and to recommend future direction. Bloomfield made a number of recommendations in a report in 1973; the first and most fundamental of these was that the existing elite sports system needed to be professionalised. At the same time, Bloomfield was insistent that grassroots programmes to improve physical fitness levels in schools and the community needed to be developed.

After Australia's poor performances at the Montreal Olympics in 1976, there was general outrage and the Government was forced to rethink its policies with regards to the funding of elite sport. Considerable pressure was applied by sports lobby groups and the press for the Government to take action to redress what was labelled as the decline of Australia as a sporting nation. The Government responded by allocating some funding for sports development and assistance to the Australian Olympic Federation, as well as assistance to the Queensland Government for the staging of the 1982 Brisbane Commonwealth Games.

The Fraser Government of the 1970s and early 80s initiated programmes which have been built upon by its successors. However, the pace really began to change with the Hawke Government, which re-established a department which was responsible for sport – the Department of Sport, Recreation and Tourism. In his speech during the opening of Parliament the Governor-General cited the great cost of ill health as the motivation behind establishing the department.

In 1985, the Government also created an independent statutory authority, the Australian Sports Commission (ASC). The ASC was intended to fulfil the role of a coordinating body for sport – to foster cooperation, to allow for greater involvement of sports bodies in decision-making about sport and to broaden the financial base for sport.

One of the first jobs the ASC undertook in 1986 was to find a way to increase children's sports participation in response to concern that young people's activity levels had declined and that an over emphasis on competition was discouraging participation. The solution to these problems, Aussie Sport, adopted a non-traditional approach, stressing that sport was not just about winning; it was also about having fun.

The Aussie Sport strategy proved successful, and by 1990, not only had half a million children participated in the programme, it had been expanded to include options for students in secondary schools. Funding for the programme was directed to the states and territories, which in turn provided money to participating schools. For the three years from 1986–87 funding of $1.7 million was set aside for Aussie Sport; from 1989–90 the programme was allocated $5.8 million over a four year period. The Government's Next Steps and Maintain the Momentum packages expanded the programme and in 1995 the Government claimed that Aussie Sport was played in 96 percent of Australian primary schools.

In August 1989 the Minister for the Arts, Sport, the Environment, Tourism and Territories, Senator Graham Richardson, launched the Next Step initiative, a $239 million package, which the Government intended would be mostly allocated to the ASC to develop elite sport and grassroots participation programmes.

Funding for elite sport in the Next Step package included commitment of an additional $27 million to the AIS for the development of intensive training centres across the country and $18 million to assist athletes to participate in the 1988 Summer and Winter Olympics, the 1990 Auckland Commonwealth Games and in competitions in the lead up to the 1992 Olympics. From 1983, Direct Athlete Assistance grants had helped athletes to prepare for competition (from 1988, coaches were eligible for these grants), and the package allocated an additional $8.5 million to this programme over a four year period.

To maintain the momentum, a further funding package, which was announced in 1992–93 by Ros Kelly, committed another $293 million to sports and physical activities.

Under Hawke and Keating, sports policies had successfully evolved to develop associations with other policy benefits. Sports and physical activities could deliver health and economic benefits. In addition, sport delivered on traditional expectations – increasing national pride and enhancing Australia's reputation as a sporting nation.

Sport from 1950 onwards

The period from 1949–66 was also known as Australia's "golden era" in sport. Such prolific success in world sporting events emphasized the world image of the average Australian being that of a bronzed, strong, healthy athlete. In 1956 the first Olympic Games held in the southern hemisphere took place in Melbourne. The five Olympic Games between 1950 and 1970 saw Australian athletes earning a total of 37 gold medals.

In the 1970s, the Australian Cricket team became the world leading force led by the likes of Lillee, Thompson, the Chappells and Rod Marsh. In so many ways, this team – as talented as they were – created the image of Australian players as hard nosed, competitive, hard drinking, no nonsense players. They also had astute cricket brains and build a formidable team. In 1974, they destroyed the England team winning The Ashes 4–1. They were the natural successors to Keith Miller's legacy.

In 2014, Martin Williamson published an article titled: "Shell Shocked and Bloodied";

England set off for Australia in October 1974 on the back of a drawn series in the Caribbean the previous winter and a summer in which they had whitewashed India and drawn with a strong Pakistan side. Under Mike Denness, they possessed a good fast-bowling attack, even though they controversially omitted John Snow, the hero of the previous tour. They were also without Geoff Boycott, who had gone into a self-imposed international exile a few months earlier.

Australia seemed to pose few threats. Their one known fast bowler, Dennis Lillee, was on the comeback trail after a career-threatening back injury and few thought he would be anything like the force he had been in the 1972 series. England watched him in action during a state game soon after they landed. "He was not employing the high kick and jump, which he had used just before delivery," Denness said. "Neither did he look as quick as before."

One other bowler's name had cropped up in the local media: Thomson. He was erratic but fast and with a unique action, and looked as if he would be more at home on the beach with a surfboard under his arm. He had played one Test, almost two years earlier, when he had taken 0 for 110; unbeknown to anyone at the time he had played with a broken foot.

The tourists got a chance to see him first hand when they played Queensland. For a couple of overs he was sharp, but then he cut back and the feeling was that he was quick but wayward. "Most of us found it a little difficult to pick up the ball, because when the arm goes back the ball is hidden behind the body, and could not be seen again until just before delivery," Denness said. "At that time we were very open-minded about the threat he posed."

What England did not know was that Thomson was under orders from Greg Chappell, his captain, to rein himself in. "Just **** around," Chappell told him. "Don't show the English batsmen what you can do." Chappell had already been alerted to his potential in a state match. 'He was quick through the air, hitting the bat and the gloves hard…and he hit a couple of players as well.'

"I followed his instructions," Thomson admitted, "and just toyed around and bowled within myself." Even so, he let rip in the second innings after Peter Lever and Bob Willis had peppered the Queensland tail with a barrage of short stuff.

England were surprised when Thomson was included in the Australian side for the opening Test in Brisbane. 'We never thought they'd pick Jeff,' recalled David Lloyd. "We thought it was a different Thomson...Froggy, who played for Victoria."

In the days before the Test, Thomson upped the hype in a TV interview when he said: "I enjoy hitting a batsman more than getting him out. I like to see blood on the pitch."

The night before the match Lillee came across Thomson in the bar drinking scotch. "When I go out to bowl I want a hangover from hell," Thomson explained. "I bowl really well when I've got a headache."

When the game got underway Australia batted first, leaving Thomson in the pavilion to nurse his hangover. Towards the end of their innings Tony Greig, who could bowl briskly and generated significant lift from his 6ft 7in frame to trouble decent batsmen, bounced Lillee. The ball reared at his head and he could do no more than glove it to Alan Knott. "Just you remember who started this," muttered Lillee as he trooped off.

Although England were not outgunned in the first innings, largely thanks to a brilliant counterattacking hundred from Greig, they were blown away by Thomson second time round. He took sox for 46 to give him nine for 105 in the match. "He frightened me, and I was sitting 200 yards away," wrote Keith Miller. There was no looking back.

Denness had an early taste of what was in store when he was hit on the collarbone by Thomson. In those days there were no helmets and no body protection. 'Of course it hurt, but you couldn't show any signs of distress against the Aussies because they will always smell blood. In those days, I used to wear a gold St Christopher pendant, and it was only when I got back to the dressing room that I found the ball had literally embedded the pendant in my chest. For any bouncers aimed at your head, you had to rely on your reflexes, or, for those brave enough to take on the hook shot, you had to be prepared to lose your front teeth.'

In the first four-and-a-half Tests Thomson took 33 wickets at 17.93 and left England battered and beaten. He seemed set to break Arthur Mailey's Australian record of 36 wickets in a series when on the rest day of the penultimate Test in Adelaide he tore muscles in his shoulder playing tennis.

By then, England's morale was in tatters. Lillee's form had increased as the series went on and Thomson's raw pace had left nerves shattered.

"When I batted at Perth I didn't even wear a cap," said Lloyd. "All I had was an apology for a thigh pad." It was in that Test that Thomson struck Lloyd so hard in the groin that his protective box was turned inside out. "You didn't feel fear," he added, "but you did feel a hopelessness at times, a feeling that you couldn't cope."

Denness noted Lloyd's reaction when he returned to the dressing room after one innings. 'Within seconds his body was quivering. His neck and the top half of his body in particular were shaking. He was shell-shocked.'

"There was no respite," added Dennis Amiss, who the previous year had set a record for the most Test runs in a calendar year but ended the tour a shadow of the batsman he was. "They were in your face the whole time."

Only years later did it emerge that Greig almost became the first man to use a helmet in Test cricket. A man came to see Denness in his hotel with some new head protection. "It looked like a motorcycle crash helmet, and it weighed half a ton. Tony was staying in the room next door, so I invited him to come and have a look. Greigy was all front, all bravado, and he was all in favour of wearing one in the next Test. I told him, You can't wear that against Lillee and Thomson. It'll be like a red rag to a bull".

Australia won the series 4–1 – England's sole win came in the final Test when Thomson was absent and Lillee broke down after four overs. It served to underline the impact the pair had on the rubber.

"As the plane left Australia for New Zealand, some of the lads said they were glad to get out alive, even if some of them didn't exactly get out all in one piece," Denness said. "That was difficult for me to take. They had spent three months fearing for their livelihoods and wondering if they were going to get hit on the head, and I was upset I hadn't picked up on it earlier." [71]

It was a crushing defeat for England. As an aside, Mike Denness did later tell an amusing story against himself.

"Scotsman Mike Denness tells an amusing story of how he received a letter addressed, simply, to 'M. Denness, Cricketeer'.

Inside was a short note: "If this gets to you, the postman thinks more of you than I do".[72]

Today, sport is something that most Australians would admit is a part of their recreational lives. In Australian terms, "sport" has come to encompass everything from direct participation to loose associations with sport. In fact, it has been observed that Australians place an unusually high value on sport and leisure. In 1973 one observer noted:

> *Sport has been used as a channel of self-esteem both individually and to the nation as a whole. In some situations fervent dedication to sport has helped overcome societal class divisions. Energy was put into the support of and participation in sport rather than into class bitterness and other prejudices. The idea was that if a person was skilled enough, they could play.* [73]

Over the last thirty years, Australia has also been a dominant force in both Rugby Union – winning the World Cup in 1991, and 1999 and finalists in 2003, and 2015 – and in Rugby League where they are often been the best team in the world and possess a proud history.

It is fascinating how fast rugby spread around the world. The Blackheath Club was founded in 1858 in London. In contrast, Rugby Union formally began in Australia with the formation of the first clubs, the oldest of which is the Sydney University Club, formed in 1864. By 1874 there were enough clubs to form a Sydney Metropolitan competition, and in that year the Southern Rugby Union was established.

The "Wallabies" became a world power in the mid eighties and by the Lions tour of 1989, were already one of the two best teams in the world alongside the All Blacks. In 1991, Nick Farr-Jones's team lifted their first World Cup and rightly so, as they were one of the best ever teams for they combined rugby intelligence, natural flair and physicality. The back line alone is arguably one of the best in history with Farr-Jones, David Campese, Michael Lynagh, Tim Horan, and Jason Little. It was England's misfortune that they came up against one of the best ever teams in the Final. The 1991 Final was seen as a battle between English forward supremacy against the Wallabies strength in the backs. In the end the English tried to meet fire with fire by playing through their backs, which helped the wallabies to a tight 12–6 win.

Other key notable moments for Australian sport were:

-   Australia Two winning the America's Cup in 1983 after a 132-year stranglehold on the cup by America. The win transcended the sport and became a symbol of Australia's prowess in sport. It was one of those victories that sent shock waves around the world. Prime minister Bob Hawke went on national television and said if any boss sacked a worker for having the day off they were a bastard.

- In 1971, Aboriginal teenager Evonne Goolagong beat Margaret Court to win Wimbledon . In 1980, then a mother and supposedly past her best, Evonne Goolagong Cawley became the first and only mother to win Wimbledon when she beat Chris Evert in 1980.
- Mark Taylor reached 334 at stumps on the second day against Pakistan at Pershawar in 1998 and declared overnight out of respect for Sir Donald Bradman, who had long held the Australian Test record on the same score.

The last example is important as it does say much about the Australian approach to sport – play to win but respectful of its history. In truth, it is hard to think of many British players that would have acted in the same manner. The Australians have always played a "hard" game with the view to win but with an acute sense of fair play. It has been an important feature of the Australian approach. They ask for no quarter and will not complain. They will also play an aggressive hard game but after all is done will be respectful and shake the hands of those they have played. They possess an excellent approach to sport.

Brian Mossop characterised the context of Australians sporting passion when he said, "we are obsessed in the broadest sense, but can be grouped as devotees, fanatics, zealots and in some cases, even worshipers..."[74] Sport has been called an Australian super-religion.

The character of Australia's sporting passion has also influenced politics, literature and the media to name a few. It is this character that has added to the uniqueness of Australia in the past and will continue to add in the future.

CAPTAINS

6 – Tony Greig and Mike Brearley

Mike Brearley is known as one of England's best captains, but Brearley may not have achieved as much without Tony Grieg. It was Grieg that called Brearley into the England side and made him vice-captain for the tour to India, which was a big move as Brearley had been dropped during the West Indies series. It was Grieg that built the team that Brearley inherited.

Tony Greig

"The Prince Charming, the Golden Giant who comes from afar to set to rights our tottering state."[75]

In 1974–75, England were humiliated in the Ashes series in Australia as Lillee and Thomson tore the English batsman apart. England had been brutally exposed. In the summer of 1975, England hosted the first World Cup and it was followed by a four Test series against Australia for the Ashes. England had still not healed their wounds from the winter and it showed with the loss of the First Test. The English Selectors sacked Mike Denness as Captain and appointed Tony Greig.

Tony Grieg's was not an universally popular choice as captain as he was South African born and could be controversial. However he was a real competitor. One of Grieg's first acts as Captain was to bring into the team a player – David Steele – who looked like an English bank manager but he had heard from others on the English county scene could play fast bowling better than most others. Over the summer, Steele became a national hero as the "Bank manager" with a cap and glasses stood up to the best of Lille and Thomson. England lost the series 1–0 but had regained respect. Grieg, like Vaughan and Johnson, gave his players confidence, as they led from the front and asked their players to play a bold, aggressive game.

Grieg is often under-rated as a captain. He could have been one of England's best. He did not hide and he was unafraid of change. In 1976, the West Indies battered the England team in a 3–0 Test victory. Historians will often cite how the West Indies were motivated by a silly, banter comment made by Grieg before the series started when he said that he would make the West Indies "grovel". There is no doubt that he could have selected better wording. However this is not to mask the fact that the West Indies were the better team. After the Old Trafford Test when the West

Indies took a 1–0 lead, Grieg had almost accepted that England would be defeated and started a rebuilding process during the remaining matches. He brought in new players during the Test Series and one day series that would go on to form the basis for the successful team that would tour India.

The India Tour saw England triumph 3–1 and play a bold attacking game that gave real hope for a bright future. The Indian crowds loved Grieg for his demeanour and approach and Grieg seemed to relish captaining the team.

After India, England travelled to Australia for a Centenary celebratory match and saw a highly competitive game won by Australia but it was clear that England were on the up.

In the early summer of 1977, the story broke of the Kerry Packer circus which saw the media mogul Packer start a competitive Test series against the establishment. Packer signed many of the world's greatest players on higher paid contracts. Grieg was seen to be one of Packer's key recruiters and supporters. The establishment reacted with anger and Grieg was soon dropped as captain and replaced by Mike Brearley.

Mike Brearley

Brearley has gone down in history as one of England's shrewdest and best captains and he was, without doubt, a superb captain. He was especially skilled in motivating players and getting them to play above themselves – maybe most especially Ian Botham who played his best cricket under Mike Brearley.

However, one has to wonder how successful Brearley would have been without Grieg's work as captain. Brearley inherited a team that won the 1977 Ashes in England 3–0. It was essentially Grieg's team. Over the next few years, England played teams that had been ravaged by the Packer Circus so the results look very impressive but is hard to judge. England won an Ashes campaign in Australia 5–1 in 1978–79 but Australia did not play any of the Packer players. When England did face Australia with the packer players again in 1979–80, England lost.

There is no doubt that Brearley was an astute man-manager and he will always be best known for the 1981 Ashes when England came back from the dead and Ian Botham had three match winning performances that turned Test matches on its head. Brearley was never a Test class batsman, but he was a shrewd tactician and understood players. Grieg and Brearley together were a formidable double act in India (Brearley was Vice captain) and could have built a new great England team for the 1980s but we will never know.

Chapter Seven

THE FOOTBALLING SUPERPOWERS – GERMANY AND BRAZIL

There are four teams in international football that represent the highest benchmark for England to play against. These are Brazil, Germany, Italy and Argentina. However, without doubt, it is Brazil and Germany that strike fear into the hearts of the British.

Brazil

If England founded the game of football then Brazil is the spiritual home. Brazil's teams over the years have captured and inspired generations. There are many arguments over which has been the best team – the team of 1958, 1970, 1994, 2002 or even the team of 1982.

Football is so deeply ingrained in Brazilian culture to the extent that much of world sees the nation through the lens of the football team. The team is the national identity of the nation.

England has enjoyed some memorable matches against Brazil with Brazil generally coming out on top. The 1970 World Cup match will always be regarded as a classic and arguably boasting the two best teams the respective countries have ever produced. It certainly produced moments of brilliance including one of the greatest ever saves from Gordon Banks and one of the best ever timed tackles by Bobby Moore. England have come out on the wrong side of results against Brazil just as they too often have against Germany. The difference is that the English admire Brazilian football for its bravery, skill and innovation. It has a freedom of expression that the British game just does not possess.

Football came to Brazil in 1894 on the shoulders of two British residents, Oscar Cox and Charles Miller. The game began with the social elite playing with the European residents. Over time the game filtered down to all classes and became a game for all the people. Over the years, football in Brazil has become more than a game. It is part of their culture and daily life. In some way or other, Brazil has always found that football is its greatest pride and joy. Despite the country's huge problems, the Brazilians themselves are considered the best football players in the world. Brazilian life isn't anything close to being as beautiful to their view of the game. It has, over the years, been full of corruption, violence, poverty and unstable economy. Football though presented a different perception of the country – one which is world leading and which other countries look towards.

It is one of the great aspects of sport – that wealth has no place on the field of play. Most of the other countries that have been analysed have possessed real strength in their social infrastructure and economy. Not Brazil. Football is the game for all classes. It is a game where the poorest have thrived with the ball at their feet. It is simply an expression of Brazilian life.

The early history of Brazilian football is a strange one, as the game was originally for the elite but popularised by the masses. The game just seemed to find its home and the popularity quickly spread through the poor city areas and into the villages.

The country's poor classes gave football its 'Brazilian' character as the game spread through the Indian and Black populations. What made the game stand apart in Brazil was a belief that football allowed both children and adults to play together with a freedom of expression. It is for this reason that football became so important in the social consciousness as it was a unifier and arguably the one unifying force in the country.

The international success of the Brazilian team was rooted in the initial squads of the 1930s and 1940s. Although Brazil was knocked out in the first round of 1930 World Cup, the team's best player Preguinho caught the imagination of the watching audience with his style of play. Brazil's exciting style of play excited fans and was a breath of fresh air to the methodical, formulaic European style of play. With flair and flamboyance, Brazil was now on the football map. They hosted the World Cup in 1950 – although this tournament is best remembered for England's 1–0 defeat to the USA; a result that shocked the footballing world and marked the open evidence of England's decline from a footballing superpower.

Brazil won their first World Cup in 1958, led by a young 17-year-old Pele. They won the hearts and minds of the Europeans with their speed, flair, and creativity. The Brazilian National Team would go onto have even greater success, winning the World Cup in 1962, 1970, 1994, and 2002.

One cannot underestimate the importance of football to the Brazilian people as both politics and the economy were consistently unstable and football provided hope and release from the concerns of daily life. There is little doubt that the generation of players from 1958 through to 1970, led by Pele, became the symbols of Brazil. They played a game that was brave, exciting, innovative and constantly on the move. During this period, the government had little interest in football as a means of a social or political control; rather, the state merely saw football as a source of revenues. The more popular the game, the more revenue to the government.

The 1958 team was the one that started the excitement of Brazil led by a 17-year-old Pele. David Goldblatt (*Telegraph* 31 May 2014) wrote of the 1958 team:

> *"In the Final, they faced the hosts, Sweden, and though Brazil went 1–0 down early in the game, they gave an untroubled, commanding performance of inventive football that saw them win 5–2. The Times declared: "They showed football as a different conception; they killed the white skidding ball as if it were a lump of cotton wool".*[76]

In 1962, the team continued their success winning the World Cup again in Chile. In 1966, the World was ready and played a more cynical game to counter the threat of Brazil and the team struggled to prevail and fell at the first hurdle. England played a more efficient, structured game and won the Cup.

David Goldblatt continued:

> *It is hard to overestimate the importance of these two footballing triumphs. Of course there were phenomenal celebrations in the streets, gigantic crowds gathered in the cities to see the team and cup parades. Both victories were followed by presidential receptions and speeches, and a torrent of memorabilia.*
>
> *But these moments left a deeper legacy. The Brazilian anthropologist José Leite Lopes recalled of the 1958 final: "It was so intense. I don't think I was ever more moved by a few minutes of football in all my life. It was football's turning point."*
>
> *Football columnist Nelson Rodrigues thought Brazil could kick its "mongrel-dog complex" forever. Brazil had won not once but twice; and they didn't just win, they won in their own style. Brazil was the football nation.*[77]

Brazil in the 1970 World Cup

The Brazilian team of the 1970 World Cup is often hailed as being the best national team in all of football history. The team featured what many have called the "Five Number 10s," with Pelé, Tostão, Rivelino, Jairzinho and Gérson combining for 17 goals en route to the title. The high acclaim it received, however, can also be interpreted by the incredible importance the team had to its countrymen and women at the time. In many ways, the 1970 team gave Brazilians hope that their country would succeed beyond the political turmoil it was experiencing at the time. By winning the 1970 World Cup, Brazilians were shown that their country refused to be defined only by the political instability and unrest it had come to view as norm. In football, they were the world's best and this gave the country great pride. Jeff Powell (Daily Mail 2 July 2012) wrote of the 1970 team:

"A team of superstars? Pretty much. Pele, Tostao, Jairzinho and Rivelino were stellar forwards, Carlos Alberto an inspiring captain as well as an exemplary full-back, Clodoaldo a creative maestro. And at the hub of it all was Gerson, the fearsome template for the modern, all-purpose midfielders of today...In distilling the greatest international football team of all time, the willingness to take risk is one of the most potent ingredients".[78]

One of the consistent themes throughout this book is that it is bravery that makes the best teams move beyond to another level. The 1970 team possessed a deep belief and confidence in each other and also their ability to defeat any opposition. This team is known as "The beautiful team" but they were also ruthless and in the Final of the 1970 World Cup, they destroyed Italy 4–1, making Italy almost appear pedestrian in comparison. Most observers will regard the 1970 team as the greatest of all time

Jonathan Stevenson (12 May 2010 BBC) noted:

Pele, who had wowed the world with his sparkling skills throughout the tournament, set an individual record that may never be broken with his third World Cup triumph, 12 years after arriving on the world stage as a precocious 17-year-old in Sweden.

The last word must go to Burgnich, tasked with marking "The King" on his final appearance on the global stage: "I told myself before the game that he's made of skin and bone like everyone else. But I was wrong."[79]

The 1982 World Cup Team

Some will argue that the 1982 team was the closest team to match the brilliance of the 1970 team. They certainly enthralled the global audience and were exciting. However, they also lost (to Italy 3–2) when they should have won, but maybe they had begun to believe all the good reports and PR. They seemed complacent and Italy scored three counter-attacking goals through Paolo Rossi. The game made Rossi a legend and set the platform for Italy's eventual triumph as World Champions but one also wonders what might have been.

The Brazilian team were led by Socrates, a player trained as a doctor, a smoker but a footballer of great elegance who became a global name in just a few weeks. The story of the 1982 team could have been written in Britain as it was one of glorious failure – defeated just a victory seemed certain.

Adam Powley (*The Mirror* – 10 June 2014) wrote:

"Brazil 1970? Wonderful, but too obvious. France 98? Pah. Spain 2010? Nope.

Ignore the "best team not to have won the World Cup" label – the best team in the history of the World Cup full stop was Brazil 1982.

It's not unheard of for the finest team to be the one that isn't the last man standing. But Brazil in 1982 did something more than record a glorious failure. They played the game the way the Selecao should play it, were stuffed full of incredible individuals, and were architects of their own downfall. Brazil were so good they had to beat themselves to lose.

'Key to their appeal was that, for British viewers at least, very little was known about them. Zico was the superstar most of us had heard of, but aside from one or two others, they were an unknown quantity. This was in an age before wall-to-wall coverage of every game from every league, and English teams populated by Brazilian internationals. It was a time when the golden shirt was something exotic and mysterious, rather than just a marketing tool.

Everyone knew that Brazil had a certain way of playing. The magnificent team of 1970 had defined that template of beautiful flair merged with supreme confidence

So, when the class of 1982 took to the field, we expected the cliché of proper "samba soccer". But boy, did we get it. To a backdrop of pulsating drums, the searing heat of a Spanish summer, and under the bright floodlights of Seville, Brazil dazzled through the first group stage. With flicks, tricks and sublime footwork they beat the Soviet Union 2–1.

Then, after the letting their opponents score a cracker of an opener from David Narey, they saw off Scotland 4–1, leaving Alan Hansen, Gordon Strachan and co. red faced and sweating like Brits on a first-time Mediterranean holiday. New Zealand were dismissed 4–0.

Brazil looked unbeatable. They scored phenomenally great goals. But who were these geniuses in unfeasibly tight blue shorts?

Who were these magicians who probably went direct from the Copacabana beach to the Maracana and then straight back again for a spot of keepy-uppy with bikini-clad beauties from Ipanema?"[80]

Brazil has had its great highs such as 1958, 1962, 1970, 1994 and 2002 but it has also had its disappointments such as 1982 and 1998 when in the final the team that was everyone's favourites failed to turn up to play against the hosts France. Brazil's star player, Ronaldo, was taken ill before the match and although he played, it was as though the magic and belief had deserted them. There were many that watched the final bemused as France cruised to a 3–0 victory. In 1974, Brazil was a pale shadow of its 1970 self and although it reached the semi-finals, they fell to a Dutch side that had won the hearts and minds of the global audience. It was like the handing over of the baton from one great team to another except that Holland themselves lost in the final to West Germany.

Of course in 2014, the country truly mourned as its team was thrashed at home by a powerful Germany team 7–1 in the semi-finals. It was a game that left audiences around the world in profound shock. Would Brazil ever be the same again?

The answer is yes of course, they will recover as football is so important. In football terms, Brazil stands apart. It represents a freedom and enjoyment of the game that so few other countries can match. The name of Brazil conjures up the memories of some of the greatest ever players to have played the game such as Pele, Carlos Alberto, Rivelino, Jairzinho, Zico, Socrates and Ronaldo. In Brazil, football is classless and true.

Germany

Germany have long been one of the England's greatest rivals and often, in football, their nemesis. Ever since the 1970 World Cup in Mexico when West Germany came from 2–0 down to win 3–2, so England have struggled to overcome them.

Gary Lineker, the former England striker, once famously joked: "*Soccer is a game for 22 people that run around, play the ball, and one referee who makes a slew of mistakes, and in the end Germany always wins.*"[81]

West Germany were the opposition on the day that England won the World Cup on a summer's day in 1966. It was England's greatest moment in sport but it also marked a turning as West Germany would soon come to be the dominant force, not just over England, but in Europe. After the 1970 defeat, West Germany travelled to Wembley in 1972 for the quarter-finals of the European Nations Cup and tore England apart winning 3–1. It was arguably the game that indicated England's decline as an international team. From that game, England's fortunes seemed to be in terminal decline as they failed to qualify for the 1974 World Cup in West Germany.

As England suffered, West Germany went on to win the Nations Cup (versus Russia in the Final) in 1972 and the World Cup in 1974. This was the team of Franz Beckenbauer, and Gerd Muller at their best. Both had played well in the 1970 World Cup but 1974 marked their peaks as players. Muller scored in the 74 Final and Beckenbauer lifted the cup as captain.

In 1982, West Germany again reached the Final as England went home proudly unbeaten, but maybe lacking the courage to really attack Germany in their second round group match which ended 0–0. It was a game of limited opportunities but many observers felt that England should have been bolder. Germany was always likely to prevail in a game of tactical cat and mouse and England needed to play a bold, traditional English game to upset the odds. It didn't happen and after another 0–0 draw against the hosts Spain, England departed, proud that they had held their own, but with thoughts of what might have been. West Germany's performance in 1982 is best remembered though for the moment their goalkeeper Harald Schumacher committed an aggressive, almost violent, professional tackle on Patrick Battiston in the semi-final in Seville against France. It was so aggressive that Battiston lost two teeth and cracked his ribs. At the time the game was tied at 1–1 with minutes to go in the game. Michel Platini played Battiston through and if he had scored, France could have progressed to their first Final. As it was Schumacher ensured that did not happen. The outrage after the game was so intense that both the West German Chancellor, Helmut Schmidt, and French President François Mitterrand eventually released a joint press release to ease tensions and the players appeared at a joint press conference. West Germany progressed the Final but had lost the public's goodwill. Many saw it as fair justice as Italy won the Final and reclaimed the World Cup for the first time since the 1930s.

In 1986, West Germany again reached the Final and then won again in 1990, but only after heartbreakingly overcoming England on penalties in the semi-finals. One could argue that England were the better team until it came to penalties but seemed to lack composure at the crucial moment.

In 1996, the reoccurring theme continued as England once again lost on penalties to Germany in the semi-finals of Euro 96 and again could argue that they were the better team. In 2010, England were well beaten 4–1 in the World Cup, but will argue misfortune as a perfectly good Frank Lampard goal was disallowed by the referee when the scores were 2–1. If the goal had been awarded, would the momentum have shifted towards England? Maybe, but in truth the young German team were the far better team and were worthy winners.

The story of England versus Germany has been a forty year story of England coming up short when it mattered most. Maybe there have been small margins between the teams on occasions and the Germans do seem to possess a mental strength that has been better than that of England's.

The German national team is one of international soccer's most consistent powers in the major finals. German teams – including those from the Nazi era, post-war West Germany, and reunified Germany – have qualified for 18 of 20

World Cup tournaments and missed the quarter-finals of those only once. The team has also made it to seven finals – a 35% appearance rate – winning three of them. Only Brazil, Italy and Argentina are able to argue similar records. These are the four strongest teams in football.

Germany has always had a culture that has striven to achieve. Germany's history as a country began in the late 19th century. In 1871, a collection of 39 sovereign states loosely federated to create the singular state of Germany. The German determination to develop its strength and influence has always been a common thread and by 1914, Germany was pressing for war and so started World War One. It is just remarkable that a country that was really only united 45 years earlier could be at the heart of such conflict. One might have assumed that old divisions would have opened and reason prevailed but one of Germany's strengths has been how it unites together. After the 1990 fall if the Berlin Wall, Germany's reunification process was not easy, but it was relatively smooth as East and West came together.

Germany suffered defeat in World War One and was forced to sign the treaty of Treaty of Versailles in 1919. The harshness of the treaty and the humiliation it inflicted upon German pride fuelled a victim identity. During the 1930s depression, National Socialism gripped the population and led to the rise of Adolph Hitler. World War Two was initiated and again Germany was defeated. The Nazi regime left much for the more reasonable German to feel a desire afterwards for rebuilding and the country did so with real purpose.

In the post-war years, both West and East Germany were successful in their own way. West Germany built a strong economy. East Germany built a country in which everyone had a job, an education and a home. In that regard, it basically achieved the communist aims that it set out to achieve. However it was a bleak culture.

Germany and Britain have been the greatest of rivals on almost every level – sporting, intellectual and in military. Germany has produced a great number of Nobel Prize winners and lies just behind the British who have 117, winning most in Chemistry, Physiology and Medicine.

Isn't it interesting that few in Britain will know of the nation's great success in this arena? Is it taken as just natural or do we not regard the awards winners as highly as our sportsmen? The United States has had the most Nobel Prize winners, with 336 winners overall. It has been most successful in the area of Physiology or Medicine, with 94 laureates since 1901. The United States tops the rankings for all prizes except Literature – where France, Germany and the United Kingdom perform better.

Why has Germany seemingly always had the upper hand against England since 1966?

There are two key points that are often overlooked. Firstly, football is the premier sport in Germany by a long way. In Britain there are a number of national sports. In Germany their football team is their core pride. Germany's three major soccer leagues each take in over €100 million, and their combined revenue is €2.8 billion. There's really only one major sport in Germany, with a few second-tier leagues running far behind.

Secondly, one of the common trends is that there appears to be a link between success in sport and how that success relates to their national identity and pride. After World War Two, Germany needed to rebuild. It had been embarrassed and humiliated. There was a real desire, within the country, to build a new future and for there to be a difference. Between 1945 and 1990, the country was divided into East and West. West Germany was the football stronghold. East Germany has success whilst part of the Eastern Bloc. They used sport to gain recognition. During the period of 1960s the communist athletes started winning medals for various sports activities. Those Germany sports include track and field as well as swimming. However the suspicion was always that the East Germans "cheated" through the use of steroids. One should not underestimate the drive and motivation that the Germans possess to build a future that is removed from their chequered past. The BBC published a feature on just how bad the East German's approach was towards building a winning team at sport.

The report was by Mike Costello in 2013:

> They talk of stolen childhoods and long-term health traded in for medals, of dissenters bundled into wooden crates and young women growing up to look and speak like men.
>
> The history of doping in athletics has no more haunting chapter than the one covering the era of global dominance by East Germany. The well-being of the country's youth was sacrificed in the name of glory and propaganda – and still the scars are being healed.
>
> To mark the 30th anniversary of the first World Athletics Championships in Helsinki, where the East Germans finished top of the medals table, BBC Radio 5 live has been to Germany to hear harrowing testimony from those who once were silenced and now want to shout.
>
> In Helsinki, athletes bedecked in the blue and white of the GDR won 22 medals, including 10 golds. From 1976, across a period of just over a decade, East Germany won more medals than any other nation at three Olympic Games and two World Championships.

"We were a large experiment, a big chemical field test," says Ines Geipel (pictured at the top of this article), a former world record holder in the women's sprint relay.

"The old men in the regime used these young girls for their sick ambition. They knew the mini-country absolutely had to be the greatest in the world. That's sick. It's a stolen childhood."

The fall of the Berlin Wall in 1989 exposed the depth and extremities of the systematic doping programme on the eastern side of the bricks and barbed wire.

"It originated for one reason, that was national importance," according to Professor Werner Franke, a fearless campaigner who gained access to many files belonging to the Stasi, the secret police, and uncovered the sins of the past.

"Annually, about 2,000 athletes were added to the programme. We know this very exactly because there have been many court cases with all the details. The youngest athletes were around 12 or 13. And it was not just pills, injections also."

The Stasi kept hidden files on all international athletes. In some cases, athletes and coaches were spying on each other. Geipel's file contained more gruesome details than most.

In 1984, at a training camp in Mexico, she fell in love with a local athlete and made plans to flee East Germany to study and "start a whole new life" in the United States. She returned home to break the news to her boyfriend, only for him to reveal he was in the secret police.

At that stage, the full power and authority of the "machine" came bearing down on Geipel. At her home in Berlin, she told me of a plot that belongs in one of the novels she now writes.

"Firstly, they wanted to find a man in the GDR who looked like the Mexican I'd fallen in love with," she explained. "They thought if I met a man who looked like the Mexican, then everything would be good again. There wasn't such a man."

"Then they tried to force me to commit to the Stasi. But I didn't do it."

"The last stage was that they didn't see any other option than to operate on me and cut through my stomach."

"It's all in the files... they cut the stomach in such a way, through all the muscles and everything, so that I couldn't run any more and didn't have a way of getting to the rest of the world any more."

"The plan started with the sentence: 'She is to be strategically extinguished.' That's Stasi speak. It means she's to be thrown out of the sport."

In another file, Geipel remembers reading about the system in place at the 1972 Olympic Games in Munich.

"There the Stasi had built wooden crates, like rabbit crates, in hotel rooms," she said. "If they believed an athlete was going to flee – because the Games were in West Germany – they would put this athlete in the crate and carry them back to the GDR.

"I find it so symbolic. We were objects, we weren't people."

Geipel is now president of a group called Help for Victims of Doping, explaining that her sadness and pain have been converted into action.

It is believed that as many as 10,000 athletes were part of the programme. The drug of choice was Oral-Turninabol, a steroid targeted particularly at young females because the effects were more dramatic, at a time when women's sport internationally was under-developed and therefore ripe for domination.

In 2000, 32 women filed a lawsuit against the perpetrators and the court in Berlin heard tales of woe regarding hearts, livers, kidneys and reproductive organs, with mothers blaming the disability of their children on the wrecking ball of drugs.

One of the plaintiffs was Andreas Krieger, who represented East Germany as Heidi Krieger in the mid-1970s and underwent a sex-change operation two decades later.

I visited Krieger in Magdeburg, where he now lives and finds it hard to conceal his resentment.

"I still say today that they killed Heidi," he said. "Through administering these pills to me, Heidi was killed and she's not there any more."

At its height, the programme employed up to 1,500 scientists and doctors.

"It's difficult to say whether I would be Heidi today or not, but I could have decided on my own. That decision was taken away from me. And Mrs Geipel put it this way...I was thrown out of my gender."

Like many others, Krieger was enrolled in the programme as a teenager.

"In our country, we had an economy lacking many things, like fruit," he continued. "So we were told we were taking vitamin pills that would compensate for our lack of nutrition. They played God with us back then."

A compensation fund of £2.5m was set up by the unified German government and the Berlin court case ended with suspended sentences for the head of the East German Sports Ministry, Manfred Ewald, and the chief doctor, Manfred Hoeppner.

More than 300 athletes were each awarded around 10,000 Euros (£8,500, $13,000). Thousands more failed to come forward to stake a claim. For some, there was lingering embarrassment, for others a reluctance to relive the agony.

State Plan 14.25 was responsible for many victories at the world's great sporting events. For an impoverished, inward-looking nation, the meticulous and wide-ranging policy left a huge dent in the national budget. The cost in human terms is impossible to measure.

A crime against humanity?

"That's the least it was," concluded Professor Franke.

The history of Germany is unique. They do not accept defeat. Humbled by World War One, and World War Two. Hurt by the split in their nation. Many countries would have been psychologically struggling for decades but not Germany. They do possess a culture that seems to give them a unique strength to move forward and achieve new heights. How many countries divided as Germany was after World War Two win the World Cup within a decade as West Germany did in 1954? Even during reunification, Germany did not break stride.

The Guardian published a feature entitled "Germany, Europe's reluctant Goliath, is hiding its true strength". It was a political feature but carried some messages that were valid in relation to this story as it argues that Germany works hard to hide the fact that it is strong:

The explanation goes deeper. "It's because of our history," says Janecek. Later a leading publisher tells me power makes her fellow Germans "uneasy", that the message drummed into them from childhood is that "a powerful Germany is a dangerous Germany". When I meet Jochen Arntz, features editor of Süddeutsche Zeitung, *he says: "We make ourselves smaller than we are. This is a German habit that we've learned over the last 50 or 60 years – for reasons we all know."*

The war ended closer to 70 years ago, but the shadow it casts is still long and inescapable. Stroll to the Marienplatz in the centre of Munich and you'll find branches of Diesel, Zara and the inevitable Starbucks. But you'll also see a tour guide addressing a group of students from across

Europe, holding up an archive photo of a Marienplatz rally in the 1920s. There, circled, is the face of Adolf Hitler. Nearby, a klezmer quartet play the haunting melodies of a European Jewish culture whose extinction was sought by the movement Hitler launched on these very streets.

That legacy informs every aspect of German political culture" [82]

It is a harrowing tale and one can understand the motivation to build a new society. In football's culture, they strive to be strong. The answer is the same as it is for Australia and America. Sportsmen are the new global warriors that can make their countries feel pride in their nation. Germany has always been a nation with a culture that is disciplined and driven during any age. The Germans are well known for their hard work ethic.

The difference though from America and Australia is that the German focus is predominantly on football. If a nation is going to place that much emphasis on one sport, it will naturally be strong. Look at New Zealand and they their love for Rugby. The All Blacks are crucial to their national pride. They are dominant as they place so much focus on the sport.

So often England has been left feeling disappointed by the Germans. However the truth is that England do well to compete. England and Britain have so many excellent champions of sport in so many disciplines. It is not an equal comparison. Germany has many strong players and athletes in minor sports too, but Britain has three dominant national sports and play endless other sports. It does make a difference. It has never been a fair debate, as Germany commit more to football than the British. Germany possesses the record that they deserve.

However, one of the causes of tensions is less jealousy and competitive jealousy, but an underlying belief that the Germans cross the line between fair and unfair. There have been a number of scandals that had an undercurrent that suggest that the Germans will do anything to win. In 2013, The *Daily Mail* published an article a provocatively titled feature entitled:

"Did Germany cheat the world... including when they beat England in 1970 World Cup?" [83]

The article commented:

Two World Wars and two World Cups, doo-da – as the politically incorrect ditty England fans sing doesn't quite go.

But perhaps it should after devastating evidence emerged of a state-run doping programme that implicates the West Germans in cheating in their win over the finest England football team to leave these shores – in the World Cup quarter-final at Mexico 1970.

Our World Cup-winning heroes, led by Bobby Moore at the peak of his immaculate career and supplemented by the likes of Terry Cooper, Alan Mullery and Colin Bell, led 2–0 in that famous match. But Germany, admittedly helped by Alf Ramsey's decision to take off Bobby Charlton to protect him for later matches, fought back to win 3–2.

Doubts over doping by German teams stretch from the 1950s to the 1990s after research by Berlin's Humboldt University suggested the country's taxpayers funded the systematic drugs programme.

It is even alleged that three unnamed West German players who lost 4–2 to England in the World Cup Final at Wembley in 1966 were on the banned stimulant ephedrine.

The report says: "The hitherto unknown letter from FIFA official Dr Mihailo Andrejevic informs the president of the German athletics federation, Dr Max Danz, that in doping tests conducted by FIFA at the end of the 1966 World Cup, three players of the German team had 'slight traces' of ephedrine."

FIFA said last year, when the issue surfaced, that it had no knowledge of the letter. Ephedrine can act as a decongestant for head colds and last night the German federation denied they had ever been involved in drug cheating.

The report also implicated the 1954 West German team, which unexpectedly beat the Magical Magyars of Hungary 3–2 in the World Cup Final, known as the Miracle of Berne. It is alleged the players were not injected with Vitamin B – as was long suspected – but with Pervitin, an amphetamine-based drug developed by Nazi scientists to make soldiers fight longer and harder.

The drug – also called "panzer chocolate" – was still widely available from supplies manufactured during World War Two. All the players were given their doses with a shared syringe. Only a small number, including Alfred Pfaff, who went on to captain Eintracht Frankfurt's 1960 European Cup Finalists, declined the injections. Richard Herrmann, a winger, died of cirrhosis eight years later, aged 39.

The report, entitled Doping in Germany from 1950 to Today, also alleges "forbidden infusions" were given to another World Cup-winning squad – the 1974 side led by the great Franz Beckenbauer.

This sordid tale of deception – ranging from football across all Olympic sports – shows that the true horror of Cold War Germany's industrial-scale doping was not confined to the East.

The 800-page document reveals senior politicians, doctors and officials were involved in the fraud. The Interior Minister provided the money for research and administration of the illicit medication. The sorry revelations will not come as a total surprise in the world of athletics, given West Germany's obsession with matching the success of their rivals on the other side of The Wall.

A senior sports administrator is quoted as saying ahead of the 1972 Munich Olympics that "one thing matters above all else – medals". However, the relatively advanced nature of the doping, which encompassed early growth hormone drugs and EPO as well as stimulants and steroids, is more sinister than previously imagined.

Still, the scale of the operation is not comparable with the East Germans' programme. The study says Dr Joseph Keul, head of the West German Olympic team's doctors, who died in 2000, played a key role. In his lifetime he fought to get anabolic steroids removed from a banned drugs list.

The human cost of the programme is highlighted by Birgit Dressel, a leading heptathlete, who died of multiple organ failure in 1987, aged 26. An autopsy showed traces of 101 medicines in her body. The official report into her death concluded she died "due to unknown reasons" but German doping expert Werner Franke said anabolic doping was a cause.

The final part of the study, examining drug use since 1990, has been suppressed. But the report quotes a senior sports federation official in the early 1990s as saying: "Coaches always told me that, if you don't take anything, you will not become something. Anyone who became something was taking it (testosterone)."

The study was commissioned in 2008 by German Olympic Sports Confederation (DOSB) and Federal Institute of Sport Science.

On Monday DOSB president Thomas Bach, who is standing for the IOC presidency, said: "This is a good day for the fight against doping. A commission will now evaluate the report and give recommendations with regard to the tasks as well as about the future improvements of the fight against doping.

"I am confident we can reach our goals to have full knowledge about the past and learn the lessons for the future. This will strengthen our zero-tolerance policy."

For many, however, it will further reduce the credibility of sport.[83]

When this feature and the accusations were mentioned to a well-informed sports observer, he just laughed and quipped: "You mean the Germans took the right substances whilst our players were just high on alcohol and cannabis?" It was not a dig at the teams; more a cynicism about British morality at times and how our won players were hardly lilywhite in behaviour.

Is it likely that Germany knowingly cheated? No one, outside of those closely connected to the team will truly know, but the hard truth is that many took substances over the years to improve performances. The reality is that the German team was a very strong able team, with some superb players that were also part of the Bayern Munich team that would go to dominate the European Cup in the 70s.

Many resented the Germans as it was often felt that they were not the best team, but they would find a way to win. In 1970, England should have won the match regardless but a combination of factors contrived to lose the match. Bobby Charlton's substitution gave the Germans confidence to attack with greater freedom. The substitutions by England were defensive and it changed the momentum of the match. Finally, England's goalkeeper on the day, Peter Bonetti, had a poor day by his own standards. Whether the above is true or not, England lost their position in 1970 through their own decisions.

What is undoubtedly true is that the Germans are mentally focused and disciplined and strive to be the best that they can be. As controversial as their history may be, it does show a determination to conquer and be strong and it will be no different in sport.

In the 1975 European Cup Final, Leeds United played Bayern Munich. For the first 45 minutes, Leeds were the better team and looked on course to be champions. However, Bayern Muncih soaked up the pressure and scored two counter-attacking goals to win 2–0. Leeds were devastated. Many felt that Leeds had been robbed with a goal disallowed for an offside that was debatable. Many felt that Leeds were the better team, but this is so sad as a German team prevail and win. The Germans simply know how to stay calm in moments of pressure and how to win big matches.

Another, maybe more fair, article appeared in 2008 in *The Guardian* written by Scott Murray.

> *They're the third most successful country in international football, yet the Germans don't get much in the way of credit for their World Cup wins. In some respects, this is no wonder. For example, West Germany were the best side at Italia 90 by a long chalk, but then that tournament was pretty much the worst in World Cup history...Then there was the Miracle of Berne in 1954. West Germany have never been forgiven for ending*

the 36-match unbeaten run of Ferenc Puskas's imperious Hungary on the biggest stage of all. The last few years have seen some attempts at balancing out the long-held view that a vastly superior side were robbed by a gaggle of chancers: it's argued that Sepp Herberger's Germans were a tight-knit team armed with a tactical plan; Hungary, not that they knew it at the time, were already in decline, a collection of carefree individuals over-reliant on Puskas; the freewheeling Helmut Rahn was the equal of Nandor Hidegkuti, maybe even harder to mark.

Nice try, but nobody's really buying it. Hungary played a poor final, for sure, yet still scored twice, hit the woodwork three times, and had a goal disallowed for a ludicrous offside decision by a Welsh linesman with pieces of cheese on toast for retinas. Puskas was hopping around on one leg, his ankle having been reduced by Germany's Werner Liebrich in that 8–3 group debacle. And the entire Hungarian team were utterly spent: while the Germans sauntered to the Final thanks to an easy draw pitting them against Yugoslavia and Austria, Hungary had to beat the 1950 runners-up Brazil, engage in a 10-minute fist-and-bottle fight in the changing rooms afterwards, then contest extra-time in the semi-final against reigning world champions Uruguay, who had never previously lost a World Cup match. They were also kept up until 5am the night before the Final by the sweet soul sounds of a Swiss band parping away outside their hotel, the theme tune to Hancock's Half Hour on continuous loop. Whatever could go wrong for one of the greatest collection of players the world has ever seen, went wrong: no wonder the romantics are still apoplectic about it.

And then there's 1974.

Possibly because that World Cup was recorded in glorious Technicolor, rather than the grainy film of 20 years earlier, the Dutch team of 1974 is considered by many to be the greatest team to never win football's biggest prize. That year's West German vintage, meanwhile, are saddled with the reputation of party poopers, the roundheads who routed the cavaliers. It's a terrible distortion.

In a first-round group game against Sweden, Johan Cruyff turned a man on the left wing by sweeping the ball behind his own standing leg and racing off in the other direction. The move would define the entire tournament as Holland began to take the plaudits for their Total Football. They trounced Bulgaria 4–1, then went on to play some extravagant football in the semi-final group stage, routing Argentina 4–0 then seeing *off thuggish world champions Brazil 2–0 in an iconic battle, playing both South American giants off the park yet not being afraid to put the boot in when necessary: the team really could defend as well as they could attack. And they looked good; long-haired, decadent hipsters swanning around Germany for a month, love-beads a-clacking, as they romped with waitresses in hotel pools. (Which slightly ruined the tournament's austere aesthetic. It's always raining, somehow a bit monochrome even though it's in glorious colour, yet a bit steamy too. You get the feeling there were a **lot** of really good sex and drug parties going on somewhere. Although there's also an argument that Paul Breitner, Franz Beckenbauer and Gerd Muller were effortlessly cool in a way the Dutch were not, but I'm going way off piste here.)*

... It is, ultimately, Holland's performance in the Final that has sealed their legend, and West Germany's reputation as second-rate champions. The received wisdom goes like this. Holland go one up through a Johan Neeskens penalty before their opponents have even touched the ball. They dick around for 20 minutes or so, toying with the Germans, making Jim Baxter's antics at Wembley in 1967 appear more direct than Diego Maradona's second goal against England in 1986. The Germans draw level through a dodgy Breitner penalty after Bernd Hölzenbein dives over Wim Jansen's leg, then scramble a second before half-time through Muller. The second half is a slapstick farce, Sepp Maier being forced to make save after save as Holland lay siege to the German goal. And somehow it's not enough. Robbery.

All of this does indeed happen. Well, sort of. Jansen does bring Hölzenbein down, sticking his leg out with all the elegance of Noddy Holder circa The Grimleys. Muller's strike, meanwhile, was a master class in poaching, one of the most under-rated goals of all time (just look at that balance) and arguably the best to win any World Cup. And there is much more to consider.

... So West Germany deservedly won the World Cup, though Holland grabbed arguably the more precious prize, the title of People's Champions. But while it's a shame that Cruyff and Neeskens didn't get their hands on the World Cup – nobody's saying they weren't a great team – the alternative would have been far worse: no World Cup winner's medals to show for the careers of Beckenbauer, the ridiculously good Muller, Brietner, Vogts or Maier.

*It's also often forgotten that West Germany were the reigning European champions at the time, a 3–1 Gunther Netzer-inspired rout of England at Wembley their signature performance. They also went on to make the Euro 76 final, only to be undone by **that** Panenka penalty. Holland meanwhile petulantly refused to take a kick-off after conceding a goal at those 1976 Euro Finals, then lost to Scotland in the 1978 World Cup.[84]*

The great truth about Germany is that it possesses a determined sports ethic that means that they are very competitive and strong. They have been professional in their approach and they have deserved their success.

Captains

7 – MARTIN PETERS

Martin Peters is often a forgotten figure as England captain as he oversaw the elimination from the 1974 World Cup. It was one of England's worst moments as they has been crowned World Champions just seven years earlier and were still being viewed as the second best team in the world in 1970.

Martin Peters was the leading figure within the England set up between 1965 to 1973. He was regarded as one of the most naturally talented footballers that England had ever produced and had been a World Cup winner – and scored in the Final – in 66. He had been a steadfast figure during the great days under Ramsay and during the rebuilding process.

When one looks back at the photographs and film from 1973, it does not capture the natural aura and presence of the Martin Peters that crowds across England saw each week. In 1972 and 73 he was probably the best player in England. He was not an aggressive player, but he had vision and could change the course of a game in a single moment. He could play in the midfield, as a striker or on the wing. In October 1972, Peters' Tottenham team played at Old Trafford and won easily 4–1 with Peters scoring all four goals – he was the last man to score four goals against Manchester United.

Ramsay, after a game against Scotland in 1968, had described him as "ten years ahead of his time", but in 1972–73, he was at his peak as an authoritative player and he could have gone to be one of the great players on the 74 World Cup stage along with Cruyff, Neeskens, Muller, Beckenbeaur and Denya.

Peters was a relatively quietly spoken, modest man who lead through his behaviours and actions. He was a natural successor as captain to his old friend and colleague, Bobby Moore. The two were similar in many ways. Both had come through the ranks with West Ham. Both led through their actions. Both were naturally gifted players and carried the respect of their teammates. Both possessed a winning mentality.

It seems strange – but illustrative of the problem – that instead of Peters leading England to respect in 74, his international career came to an abrupt end with the 2–0 defeat to Scotland at Hampden Park just prior to the World Cup Finals at the age of just 30. He had already been replaced by England caretaker manager Joe Mercer as captain by Emlyn Hughes.

A year earlier he was Captain Marvel and in May 1974, it was all over. He captained England just four times during which time England had won once and drawn three times. He needed time to grow into the job. He had proven himself to be an exceptional leader at Tottenham and he could have been the same for England.

One should not shed too many tears. It may have been a disappointing end but Peters had a great career and will be always regarded as one of England's greatest.

Martin Peters had begun his career with West Ham in 1959, breaking into the first team on a regular basis in 1964. In 1965, he was a regular and part of West Ham's winning team of the European Cup Winners Cup. His England career debuted in 1966, but with West Ham he was always the junior of the Moore, Hurst, Peters trio. Moore and Hurst would see Peters in that way, but they were the more commanding figures at the club and Peters did sit in their shadows. A move away from West Ham was sensible for his own development and in March 1970, he joined Tottenham Hotspur where he really did flourish as his own man and then as captain. He played for Tottenham for five years and in that time won two League Cups, the UEFA cup against Wolves in 72 and played in an UEFA Cup Final against Feyenoord, which was lost 2–0. He made 189 appearances for Spurs, scoring 49 goals, in what was a successful period.

In March 1975, with his England career over and 31 years old, Peters transferred to Norwich City where he went on to play 206 matches scoring 46 goals. He helped establish Norwich City as a true First Division club. He was their player of the year two years in a row in 1976 and 1977 and played for them up to 1980.

Just maybe England forgot about their captain too quickly? In 1970 he had transferred at a record breaking £200,000 to Spurs. In 1975, he was transferred to Norwich for just £50,000.

One cannot say that a man who was part of the World Cup Winning team, who captained his country and won 67 caps did not fully realise his potential but there was more that could have come from Peters had the highest level. Ramsay recognised the value of the man and player and if things had been different against Poland, the chances are that Peters would have become recognised as one England's best captains as well as a player. But that is life – it can cruelly move on –and England needed to rebuild.

Chapter Eight

INDIA, CRICKET AND SPORT

M uch has been written about countries with the motivation to succeed. However, how would a country with an equally rich history and legacy as Britain possesses compare?

India is a simply intoxicating, fascinating country with as many contradictions as the British possess. India is one of the oldest civilisations in the world and is famed for its vastly contrasting attributes so well illustrated by its cricket, its extreme poverty, its religions, Bollywood and the Kama Sutra.

In just simple sporting terms, India has arguably had a genuine large problem in creating a real sporting dynasty. It is strong in cricket and in field hockey but otherwise has struggled. Sport is part of the culture in India but society is one of its barriers to success.

James Astill, in his book *The Great Tamasha* (2014) wrote about cricket:

"No other British Legacy, save perhaps the English language, has proved more popular or enduring than cricket. Nothing unites Indians, in all their legions and diversity, more than their love for it. No other form of entertainment – not even Bollywood or national politics – is so ubiquitous in India's media, and no Indian celebrity more revered than the country's best cricketeers. "God has a new House" – that is how the Times of India *splashed on the news that Sachin Tendulkar, the most adored Indian player, has been gifted a seat in parliament."* [85]

However, Astill cuts to the heart of the problem soon after:

"Yet the story of Indian cricket is not only about cohesion and success. It is also deeply pathetic. The poor children playing in India's streets and parks have almost no chance of emulating their heroes and representing India. They are unlikely to play the game in a proper fashion, with a good bat and a leather ball. That is because real cricket, as opposed to street games, is dominated by members of the privileged middle-class...in part, this reflects Indian cricket's 19th century origins... India's failure – over the ensuing 150 years – to spread more cricketing opportunity to its cricket-hungry people is nothing less than lamentable." [86]

However, the signs of change just may be in the air and once change does take place, India has the potential to be competitive in sports beyond cricket and hockey.

Cricket is almost like a religion in the country and yet overall few sports have prospered in India. It has one of poorest performance records in Olympic history and yet it is both hard and yet easy to explain the reasons. India is a country with so much potential that when it does eventually come together and find solutions to its problems then the continent will soar with the potential that exists. Many fall in love with India for the friendliness of its people, for its extremes, contradictions and as a country that does offer so much.

However, in sport, there is a genuine need to invest in the sporting infrastructure so that talent has the chance to be developed. There are many schools all across the country that do not possess any real facilities to encourage sport.

There is a school of thought that suggests that the traditional class structure is one of the core problems, as the wealthy are so used to being served by servants that they do not possess the motivation and for the poor, the facilities and structure do not exists. One can see from the example of the USA that many are motivated to break free from poverty so one of the challenges is to build a structure that allows for sport to be played in good facilities and for investment into coaching.

India has such a huge population, with a lot of untapped talent, which, if given the right support could change India's sporting opportunities at international level. The cricket 20/20 competition in India, the IPL, has been a major commercial success and has helped find a lot of great talent, which otherwise would have lost in the crowd. The IPL could mark a real change in the tide within India as it becomes one of the most glamorous events in the Cricket calendar. It has shown that India can host exciting sporting contests. It attracts stars from all the major countries including England, Australia and the West Indies and has the involvement of popular Bollywood faces. Every major sport requires proper budgets, advertising, endorsement from popular faces and most importantly television deals.

The IPL is a success story but cricket is their major sport. There is still a long way to go. It seems strange that a country of more than 1.2 billion people can only collect an average of less than one medal per Games. Beijing 2008 was India's most successful Olympics to date; it finished with one Gold and two Bronze medals. That is over 383 million people per medal, the highest ratio of all competing nations at Beijing. At London 2012, India left with two Silver and Four Bronze models.

It would be untrue to say that India does not produce good sportsmen and women. In cricket, there is a long heritage of world-class players such as Sachin Tendulkar, one of the sport's greatest ever players, Sunil Gavasker, Rahul Dravid and Kapil Dev to name just a few. The Indian men's field hockey team won six consecutive Olympic Golds in the mid-20th century (field hockey accounts for more than half of India's historical total of 20 Olympic medals).

There is no doubt that India has sporting talent, so why does it fail to translate this into Olympic success?

There have been some academic studies that suggest the total population of a country is irrelevant when it comes to Olympic medal tallies, but rather what counts is the part of a population that participates effectively in sports. Anirudh Krishna and Eric Haglund argue in a 2008 report in the Indian publication *Economic and Political Weekly* that; *"Olympians are drawn, not from the entire population of a country, but only from the share that is effectively participating. Low medal tallies can arise both because a country has very few people and because very few of its people effectively participate."*[87]

India's greatest social problem has been the vast divide that the country has between the wealthy and the poor. The major factors that limit effective participation include health, education, coaching and a lack of facilities.

The 2011 Indian Census tells us that the urban population in India is over 370 million people, the equivalent of the USA and Russia combined. This is a massive pool of talent and one with a strong economy. One does have to wonder why the government does not do more to invest in the sporting structure of the country. The stories of the USA, and Australia have shown just how important sporting success can be to the perception and image of a country. Investment in India is still a challenging process. India desires international investment and to achieve this goal then it is logical the government works to improve the overall sporting infrastructure as a wealth of great sports stars can only help to make the country attractive.

Of course, there will be those that point towards the success of the IPL and this is true, but still more does need to be done.

Madhuli Kulkarni, the founder of the ALTIUS Centre for Excellence in Delhi said in an interview with *Euronews:*

> *Parents here have the authority to take the decisions in their child's life. India was not a sports nation. Especially post-independence, Indian parents gave a lot of importance to academics and sport was considered as a "time pass" activity or just for recreational purpose. Sport was never a priority for a majority of parents and their kids. In fact we have a saying in Hindi – India's National language – "Kheloge kudoge to honge kharab, padhoge likhoge to banoge nawab," which means that your life will be a*

waste if you play but if you study or do well in academics you will be a king...although we have the best of the academic schools and universities, we do not have good sports facilities and good sports academics. We did not have well maintained playgrounds; equipment was not available and if it was, then it was not in good condition, no proper support staff, no athlete-friendly sports policies."

We are still in the developing phase. Young Indians are given opportunity but the facilities and opportunities are not enough, we still have to improve a lot. Things are definitely changing now and are changing for the better. Therefore you will see an improvement in the performance of our athletes in the London Olympic Games," [88]

India does have several reasons for optimism. The IPL being the main one as it has led to a perception change amongst the international community. India are also beginning to perform more effectively at an increasing number of sports.

It is encouraging but one has to ask how does one change the culture/society that does place academia ahead of sport. Surely the stories of other countries show just how important sport is in building belief and a strong psychology within society?

The view, in India, is that middle class families just do not consider sports as a career or life choice. One can understand why in a society with so much unemployment and poverty. Security and wealth must be the first priorities. This will only change as the government invests and builds the infrastructure and the media promote the success of all sports.

In India, even if children are interested in a sport, then first of all coaching is not available easily, secondly no proper grounds are available for practice and most importantly, children don't get proper exposure to competition. In India, a sport gets recognition only when a sportsperson wins a major tournament of his sport. But why wait for an athlete to win a tournament to give that sport some importance? Something has to be done so that athletes don't waste their talent sitting in front of a computer doing accounting.

The Indian government spends US$181 million a year on sports and youth affairs; China has recently put an estimated US$3 billion into each Olympic team. India has suffered from the same problem as Britain did for many years in that the administrators for India's sports bodies were often amateurs and not professionals in touch with the demands of top sport.

Kevin Fixler in the *Daily Beast* wrote:

In New Delhi, the capital city of the second-most populated nation in the world (behind only China), motorists appear to ignore all directive in an attempt to reach their own destinations. Regularly drivers straddle white stripes that distinguish the road's lanes, or ride the shoulder, where many pedestrians walk. It's not uncommon to see a moped cruise the pavement, and at roundabouts vehicles of all sizes and shapes, from the ubiquitous three-wheeled motorized rickshaws to bikes, buses, motorcycles and Mercedes, cumbersomely converge upon these commuter loops. The horns beep, howl, and bray from every direction not as a sound of caution, but as a method for announcing an individual's arrival, each forcing themselves toward separate agendas. As the noticeable haze of pollution settles in over the city each night, most simply go about their daily business.

No question, this system – a chaotic mess – works. There is certainly no lack of people getting from one point to another, but with each person figuratively going every which way. And it begins at the top with those who run the country. Despite also being the world's second-fastest growing economy (again, behind only China), many domestic critics point out that the country can never seem to get out of its own way, routinely referring to India as "the flailing state." Some of the government's own estimates have indicated approximately 450 million people – approaching a third of its entire population, larger than the whole of the United States – live on less than $1.25 a day. Between 50 and 100 million have risen above this widely accepted poverty line in the last 20 years, but India's economic and social problems remain vast due at least in part to the government's ineffectiveness."[89]

Another comment to consider is:

Let us consider an average Indian child. Think about the access to sports facilities that he has at the school age. The facilities probably will be there for one or two sports that are shared by so many other children. Many children do not have shared facilities as well. Even those who have access to facilities cannot use them properly due to insane education system in the country that makes every child slog. It gives very less time for children to look towards sports. Many schools even do not have a small ground forgetting any sports facilities. When the child is not even exposed to many sports, how can we even expect the child to aspire for excellence in any sport? But there are those who come from rich backgrounds and have access to many sports facilities. But what is the guarantee that these people enjoying the facilities have any interest in the particular sports? Even if they have interest, what is the competition that they are up to in

the country? Any talent will be identified when someone is a child. That
is where India lacks as compared to developed nations." [90]

Sport has traditionally been only for the wealthy. It is this that needs to change. The change has to start at the grass root level if sports are to become a source for income for the Indian population. In developed countries like the USA, there are grounds and sports complex for every sport everywhere. Children grow up playing with proper equipment and in the same environment. They don't have to adapt to any changes when they make transition to competitive level.

But India is changing. Inward investment is beginning to happen with new programmes to encourage children in schools across the country to be able to be developed and have the chance to play sports. As this investment grows, India has the potential to explode onto the International scene. If the progress can be maintained and even raised then India is a sports loving country with an audience that will adore its sports stars, which in turn will build a strong sporting culture that will build a sporting legacy that has not be the strongest to date.

Change is happening.

CAPTAINS

8 – Gareth Edwards

"He epitomises the values of fair play and courage which are central to rugby and in his off the field career as a broadcaster and businessman he remains a great ambassador for our game. Everyone who knows Gareth regards him as a true gentleman who is always approachable, courteous and welcoming despite his towering reputation as one of rugby's true greats." [91] (Gerald Davies)

Gareth Edwards is widely regarded as the greatest scrum-half and arguably the greatest all-round player in the history of rugby union. Edwards is one of the very few players that transcend both the game and nationality. He took the game of Scrum half to another level and scored tries that will forever live in the memory. The 1973 try for the Barbarians against New Zealand at Cardiff Arms Park is still regarded as the greatest try in history. His try for Wales versus Scotland at Murrayfield when he took the ball from his own five metre line will still rank as one of the greatest tries of the five nations. Edwards had all the skills. He was a potent attacking force; an exceptional pass that gave his fly-halves precious extra moments to play and exceptional balance as he moved around the pitch.

Barry John and Phil Bennett are revered as two of the game's greatest playmakers at fly-half. Would they have possessed as high a status without Edwards?

Edwards won 53 caps for Wales between 1967 and 1978, 13 as captain and represented the British and Irish Lions 10 times between 1968 and 1974. In 2003, in a poll of international rugby players conducted by Rugby World magazine, Edwards was declared the greatest player of all time. In 2007, former England captain Will Carling published his list of the '50 Greatest Rugby players' in The Telegraph, and ranked Edwards the greatest player ever, stating;

"He was a supreme athlete with supreme skills, the complete package. He played in the 1970s, but, if he played now, he would still be the best. He was outstanding at running, passing, kicking and reading the game. He sits astride the whole of rugby as the ultimate athlete on the pitch". [92]

Edwards is Wales's youngest ever captain, first taking the captaincy at the age of 20 in February 1968 against Scotland – a game which the Welsh side won 5–0.

They are few better or greater

Chapter Nine

2012 – THE AWAKENING OF BRITISH HOSPITALITY IN SPORT

There was a genuine change in 2012 in how the British public felt about their ability to host a major event. Leading up to 2012, almost literally to the day the London Olympics started, there was an unease amongst many that the games would be an embarrassment, that the weather would be poor – and it had been an appalling summer right up to the eve of the games – and that the British were just not that hospitable. However, 2012 proved the opposite to be true: Britain has become one of the greatest venues to watch sport.

One has to remember that during the 1970s and 80s sport had been plagued by a more aggressive approach to following sport. Hooliganism plagued football for many years and caused serious carnage and despair as Britain's teams played across Europe. Britain's teams may have been badly behaved, but they were targets for provocation and were the easy ones to blame. English football teams were banned from European competition for five years after the Heysel Stadium disaster in 1985 when 39 supporters died – 32 of them Italian.

In one sense, Heysel constituted the logical culmination of English disgrace in Europe. Tottenham supporters had twice been embroiled in ugly skirmishes in Rotterdam, in 1974 and 1983, while Manchester United's travelling band invited similar ignominy in St Etienne in 1977. Rioting by English hooligans in Basle in 1981, after a World Cup qualifier, was another stain impossible to ignore. But despite all the history and the evidence, Heysel still caused a shock wave. Hooliganism was a well-known problem but every time it was a surprise to the system.

In fairness, this was part of the backdrop but there had also been much discussion over the coldness of the British welcome and that the standard of hospitality was simply not world class.

As the event dawned, the sun emerged and the British emerged to be world class in their hospitality. The opening ceremony of the London Olympics set the tone – quirky, eccentric but fun – and suddenly a new confidence spread throughout London and the London Olympics became a carnival of sport. It shocked the world but most of all it shocked the British, but announced a new era where the British proved to be superb hosts and understood how to manage the best sporting events.

Three years later, the Ruby World Cup was hosted in England, and Wales and once again the event surpassed all expectations with record crowds attending matches as the British really embraced the event even though England were eliminated in the group stages. It made no difference.

2012 and 2015 openly displayed to all the love of sport that the British have. It showed the real passion of the supporter:

> An airplane taking off produces an ear-splitting 140 decibels of noise. So do the cheers in the Olympic velodrome. I know because I was there when the crowd cheered Victoria Pendleton's golden performance in the keirin the other day. The roar was thrilling, to the point of pain. If it had endured another minute, I am sure we'd all have gone deaf.

> Olympic officials confirmed that the noise levels in the velodrome went close to the 140-decibel level, making it the loudest Olympic venue, which shouldn't be surprising. The velodrome is small – it seats only 6,000 – and is enclosed. The ceiling is low. And the crowds, which included Paul McCartney on Saturday night, are screamers.

> The Dangerous Decibels Project, an American public health campaign whose goal is to reduce hearing loss induced by excessive noise, says 140 decibels is about equal to the fireworks and or the sound of a gunshot at close range. It is louder than jackhammer.

> The velodrome doesn't own the high-decibel market at the Olympics. Events at the beach volleyball arena in central London and the main Olympic arena are hitting 105 to 110 decibels when athletes perform spectacularly well, as Jess Ennis did Sunday, when she won the heptathlon. One reporter described it as "tsunami of noise," that builds in waves, making it impossible to speak to the person smack next to you.

> Decibels are the units that measure the power of noise and work on a logarithmic scale. That means an increase of 10 decibels in power is equivalent to increasing its power by a factor of ten. In other words, even a small numeric rise in the decibel level translates into significantly more noise.

> A few of us suffering from hearing loss note that the crowds are not the only source of noise at the Olympics. Many of the Olympic venues are designed to feel like cross between a rock concert and a dance hall. The music can be pounding and relentless. Some 2,500 songs were recorded for the various sports, each available at the touch of a button for the commentators. Layer on the booming commentators' voices and you have a noise-fest of, well, Olympic proportions.

At an Olympic press conference on Sunday, Paul Deighton, CEO of the London 2012 organizing committee, said; "There are some people who would prefer silence and complete focus on athletes."

In response, the music is being "toned down" a bit at some events, he said.

But most fans, especially the British ones, seem to love the noise. Been to an English soccer match lately? [93]

The accolades continued:

The Australian, Peter Wilson in the feature:

"British take gold as best Olympics Games hosts"

It is one thing for the British to thrash Australia in the medals table of the London Olympics. But now the Games are over, it is just as clear they have knocked Sydney off its pedestal as the best host of a modern Olympic Games. As awful as it is to admit, London 2012 was bigger, slicker, almost as friendly and more thoughtfully planned than Sydney in terms of the legacy it will leave the host city...It is, I'm afraid to say, bronze for Barcelona, silver for Sydney, and gold for London. [94]

The Age, Australia, Greg Baum: in "It's been a right bang-up job"

London, you didn't half do a decent job. These Olympics had Sydney's vibrancy, Athens's panache, Beijing's efficiency, and added British know-how and drollery. With apologies to Sydney, they might just represent a new PB for the Olympics. The Games were preceded by the usual fatalistic anticipation of a cock-up. It proved groundless. Moving masses of people around a mazy city was expected to be a nightmare but London made it look effortless. Security was plentiful but low key. The army, called in to meet a shortfall, proved to be Britain's finest ambassadors." [95]

China Daily " "Grand finale brings Games to an end"

"Despite concerns about the creaky transport system and a shortfall of private security guards, which forced the government to call in thousands of extra troops to help screen visitors, the Games have so far passed by fairly trouble-free. A furore over empty seats at several Olympic venues blew over, especially once the track and field showcase kicked in and drew capacity crowds for virtually every session. Even the weather improved as the Games wore on. Bright sunshine has graced the closing weekend of a festival that has helped to lift spirits in Britain." [96]

Corriere della Sera, Beppe Severgnini: in "Thank you London: a lesson for the pessimists";

> *This Olympics was a success for Great Britain...the capital had wanted to throw a party for the world. And when we're talking about parties, ceremonies and festivals, the English are unrivalled...The Olympics was a moveable feast, more Hemingway than Dickens. I have to say to my English friends, when they have recovered from the festivities (I can't say in what condition), it's only been two weeks from "Gosh we'll never make it!" to "Wow, we made it!". And this, if you like, is the news. Once, confronted by a difficult task, the English would be worried...today they are not hiding any more...Congratulations, and thank you for a fantastic party.* [97]

The Globe and Mail, Canada, Doug Saunders: in "Olympic elation envelops host nation"

> *On a patch of land scarred black by the industrial revolution, bombed flat by Hitler and denuded by decades of poverty and neglect, a country with little money and less self-confidence held the world's most expensive and difficult sporting event. And when it ended in a spectacle of pomp-free pop and quintessentially East London polyglot pageantry, there was a very surprising national sense of elation.* [98]

National Post, Canada, Bruce Arthur: in "Britain pulls off an Olympics to remember"

> *This was a brilliant Olympics, in almost every way: wonderful crowds, marvellous volunteers, logistical coherence, a galvanizing performance by the home side. There were some goof-ups, sure. London mayor Boris Johnson got stuck on a zip line, and compared women's beach volleyball players to glistening wet otters; the cops lost the keys to Wembley Stadium; early on, someone mixed up the North and South Korean flags. Buses occasionally went missing, and trains were occasionally delayed. But there is always a fraying, and the whole held together.* [99]

New Zealand Herald, David Leggat: in "Three cheers for a job well done"

> *"Hats off to the Lord Coe and his Locog planning chums. They can put their feet up knowing London did itself, and the Olympics, proud... What was out of whack was the hugely lopsided work of the BBC. They didn't just drop their cloak of impartiality; they biffed it over the bridge.*

Interviewers wore Team GB shirts and chatted to sixth or seventh-place finishers while races were still on. "We" was everywhere. It was cringeworthy, and unworthy of the organisation." [100]

In retrospect, it is hard to understand why there was such surprise or a lack of confidence. The English sporting summer has long been a highlight and the calendar events seem to have just intensified in their glory from The FA Cup Final to The Derby to Royal Ascot to the Test matches to Wimbledon, Henley Regatta, and The British Golf Open. Very few countries have the capacity to host such a calendar of events. The UK has the infrastructure – often an infrastructure that has been underrated – but also a deep passion for sport. It has just been shut away and forgotten, but 2012 released it out into the open and confidence flourished. The love was always there and it set the UK apart.

Many international players and coaches enjoy the atmospheres across the sporting arenas, as the crowds do possess a great knowledge and understanding of the sports. Attendances at professional sports events in the UK topped 70 million this year, up five percent on 2014. Football was the overall winner in the attendance stakes at 43.4 million, while three of the 10 best-attended showpieces were horse-racing events. Rugby union attendances, boosted by the 2.5 million fans at the Rugby World Cup, climbed to 7.5 million. This year's total was less than the 75 million at UK sports events in 2012. However, that year was boosted by 11 million visitors to the Olympic and Paralympic Games in London.

Excluding the Rugby World Cup, the 10 most popular individual sporting events of 2015 had a combined attendance of 2.5 million, with Wimbledon topping the list again. The tennis tournament attracted just under half a million spectators during the fortnight.

There is a school of thought that believes that the positive release of support will help Britain's sports stars as the emotion will feed their emotion and competitiveness. It can mark a change in the British psyche, which has been negative to one that is almost Americanesque in that it encourages winners to a level not seen for many years. So much of top-level sport is inner confidence and mind-set and a change in belief can only be advantageous on a number of levels.

This leads on to a number of fascinating but, at times, contradictory features and questions:

1. There is an argument that social media has had a positive impact on how players interact with fans. Players have been quick to learn how to engage effectively and this has made the players connect with their supporters. It has, in turn, made the fans feel more engaged, connected and able to have a voice.

2. The BBC also have played an important and valid role with *606* and radio Live as it has given the supporters a platform to express their passions and frustrations. It has created great entertainment and allowed a genuine freedom for expression for the supporter just as we ask the sportsman to express themselves on the field of play.

3. There has in recent years been a major debate about the fragmentation of British society, a growing fear of the erosion of social cohesion, a sense of the emptiness of national identity. Arguably 2012 showed this to be far from true with the collective spirit of the Olympic crowds. Little wonder that many have sought to capture the essence of those crowds and claim that it was "Britishness". 2012 had a lasting impact in a way many did not believe was possible. '

4. The Six Nations has become a real example for how supporters will sit together, cheer together, follow the match arm in arm and be friendly rivals.

Many attribute social fragmentation to the "multicultural" character of Britain. By this they mean that immigration, and the social diversity it has brought, has made more difficult the task of creating a common culture. Many yearn for a simpler age when being British was easier to define but the world has changed; Britain has changed and in many ways for the better. Old school "Patriots" create a mythical Britain with which all Britons are supposed to identify, a mythical nation from which the reality of conflict and struggle has been boxed away.

Britain today is an exciting society with so much potential. The Britain of immigration and diversity, a diversity celebrated in Danny Boyle's Olympic opening ceremony and that has resulted in the gold medals of Jessica Ennis, Mo Farah, Nicola Adams and countless others. We are a cosmopolitan society. It has been a long struggle to accept the change. Politically the debate rages on, but on the field of play, it is accepted. Most premier league teams are a team of nations and the fans still support their tribe.

Tribalism is important in sport. National pride is important but it is devoid of racism and small mindedness. It used to be argued that Britain possessed a "little islander" mentality. Today the supporter does not care where the players come from as long as they are prepared to play to the best of their ability for the shirt. The team is what matters not the origin of the player.

Professionalism has taken time but society has evolved a long way through the example of sport. The field of play has been one of the most positive influences in society over the last forty years.

CAPTAINS

9 – Gavin Hastings

Scotland and British Lions Rugby Captain

Gavin Hastings is arguably one of Scotland's best ever Rugby players. Hastings was a rugby player's player – full bloodied, competitive, skilled and with a wicked sense of humour. Hastings was well known for his antics as a player.

Hastings led the Lions to New Zealand in 1993. The series was lost 2–1 but is a series that should have been won. The first Test was lost to a last minute's penalty awarded by the referee for reasons that are hard to understand. The second Test was won by the Lions with the Third well won by the All Blacks. It was an impressive All Black team but the Lions were their match. The tour is remembered for the differences between Hastings and Will Carling, England's captain that had enjoyed Grand Slam success in 1991 and 1992. The Lions team was dominated by England players and many argued that Carling should have been captain. However, it is to Hastings credit, that he brought he team together – even with this in the background – to ensure that the team was competitive.

Hastings played for Watsonians, London Scottish, Cambridge University, Scotland and the Lions. He won 61 caps for Scotland, 20 of which as captain. Maybe his greatest moments were in Scotland's shirt with the 1990 Grand Slam and the 1991 World Cup campaign.

Some will recall Hastings missing a penalty in front of the posts in the semi-final of the Rugby World Cup 91, which let England off the hook. It was a poor miss but the great aspect of Hastings that no one thought that it would put Hastings off his game. He was mentally strong. He was robust and always ready to be competitive.

The Scotland team of 1990 and 1991 is one of its greatest ever with a number of great leaders with David Sole, Finlay Calder, Gavin Hastings, John Jeffrey and Scott Hastings (brother). They were true comrades in arms and Hastings has his place in history.

Former national coach Ian McGeechan said of him:

> Gavin is a big man in every sense of the word…his greatest asset was to engender confidence in those around him and to lead by example when the opposition had to be taken on. In New Zealand, they considered him simply the best full-back in the world.[101]

Richard Bath writes of Gavin Hastings that:

> *Caps do not make the man, but a quick look at Gavin Hastings' battle honours should be more than enough to establish his credentials as the finest player ever to wear the dark blue of Scotland.*
>
> *For the record though, here is an abridged version of one of the most impressive curriculum vitae in British rugby; Hastings captained the first Scottish schoolboys' side to win on English soil; he captained the victorious 1985 Cambridge University side; he won the Gallaher Shield with Auckland University during his sabbatical year; he was a central figure in Scotland's 1990 Grand Slam...he captained Scotland in one World Cup, and played in two others, including a semi-final; he captained his country and scored the winning try when Scotland registered their first win at the Parc des Princes... he played for the World XV in the New Zealand Centenary Celebrations; and he holds the British points-scoring record with 733 points in tests for Scotland and the Lions.*[102]

Chapter Ten

COMPETITIVE TO THE CORE

A Scottish politician once jokingly remarked to a concerned English Businessman as he was about to make a presentation in Edinburgh: "Do not worry about the Scots not liking you. Half the time they don't like each other. Historically we always fought each other. We may have improved but we are still ready to fight each other".

The British are a nation with tribal passion at heart. Sport is where one can see the British really express themselves and be free in spirit. In football, most especially, one's team is one's tribe. The Welsh, Scottish and Irish will invariably field teams full of passion, desire, commitment and courage – and with a determination to beat their historical nemesis, England. Once before a match between England and Scotland, a commentator joked that: "Bannockburn made it 1–0. Culloden made it 1–1. And every year the decider is played out".

Every year as the Six Nations is played, the intensity to defeat England is openly evident but so is the friendship, as supporters will walk arm in arm and drink together before and after the match, regardless of the result. The sport between the countries means much as it is about national pride and bragging rights between rivals. However there is real genuine affection too between the countries. It is the tribal passions and genuine competitive steel that comes with the passion that makes the UK stand apart from other countries.

It was Bill Shankly, the great Liverpool manager of the 60s and early 70s who stated:

> Some people believe football is a matter of life and death, I am very disappointed with that attitude. I can assure you it is much, much more important than that.[103]

Of course, it was tongue in cheek but Shankly understood more than most what football meant to the supporter standing on the terrace and he never took it lightly. England was a very different world in the 40s, 50s, 60s and 70s to what it is today. Football was about community and working class heroes. It was not the business that the large clubs are today. The connection between players and the supporters was deep and had importance. The captain represented both the team and the community at large. He was their symbol.

Leadership is so important to the British whether in sport, business or politics. Arguably we expect too much from leaders – beyond fair expectation – but the leader is key to success and a feeling of wellbeing. If the team is underperforming then the expectation is that the captain will be replaced.

In many countries, the leader and captain is not as important. The overall brand, or the team, is the lead, but the British need a more emotional connection to the leader in order to believe and trust. It is personal. There needs to be a connection between a leader and their followers.

The leader needs to be open, accessible and able to communicate and if this is effective, then the team will have a strong foundation. The British value the personal connection and the feeling of success is linked with the captain.

The British have a long list of captains that are still seen to stand above the teams that they led in the eyes of experts and supporters – Martin Johnson, Bobby Moore, Mike Brearley, Michael Vaughan, Finlay Calder, Graeme Souness, Will Carling, Billy Wright, Andrew Strauss, Lawrence Dalliaglio, Willie John McBride, Mervyn Davies, David Beckham, Sam Warburton and Gavin Hastings are just some of the names.

The captain is the commander on the field of play. Today one will often read that the captain's role is often over stated. It is a fair argument as coaches today are much more actively involved in the games. In cricket, the captain is the on-field strategist, decision maker and manager. In rugby, the captain is the man to ensure no one left their posts and all were committed to their task. In the crucial match between England and Wales, there are many that hold Chris Robshaw responsible for the defeat to Wales. In the last minute, with England trailing by three points, he made the decision not to kick a penalty but to go for a try and outright win. In fairness it was a difficult kick and at best only a 50–50 chance of converting but Robshaw was the man deemed responsible for not at least drawing the match.

When sport is so important to a society then the captain's role will naturally be elevated and the successful ones will be given a unique status. One should not underestimate the need for the tribe to follow their leader.

It may all sound old fashioned in such a world, which has become ever smaller and more accessible but sport should be tribal. It should be about rivalry and moments of brilliance that excite and inspire the watching supporters. Maybe the fact that Britain comes from a competitive tribal dynasty makes the game slightly different to the game in other countries, but sport should always be about competition between rivals.

One of the special features of sport in Britain is the relationship between supporters and the fans. The British supporter is knowledgeable about the games they follow. Arguably the bond between the supporter and the teams was at its height in the 1970s as sport began to take off.

The Seventies

Arguably the 1970s was the most competitive of eras. The film of the same era The Good, the Bad and the Ugly could have been the title of a sports report on the era. It was certainly an era when the supporters and players were aligned and lived their teams highs and lows together. The 1970s was one of the most intense sports loving eras but it was also one that was not always the most professional. It was a period of evolution.

Football in the 1970s.

Bill Shankly was a man that could delight with his masterful use of humour as he would make the most telling point that would register with the listener – just as when he commented:

> A lot of football success is in the mind. You must believe you are
> the best and then make sure that you are. In my time at Liverpool we
> always said we had the best two teams on Merseyside, Liverpool and
> Liverpool Reserves.(104)

The British let their emotions go with sport. It touches the heart and soul. In sport, the British live every triumph and failure as though they were playing the game they are watching. That is the beauty of sport – the emotion it conjures up within you. It can bring the greatest joy to the heart stopping moments to true despair. Some will say it is just a game. Very true, it is but that is hardly the point – it is passion, tribalism, patriotism, belief, and hope all rolled into one. Shankly's comment about sport meaning more than life or death reflected the passion and intensity that filled football stadiums each week in the 60s and 70s and which represented how the likes of Tommy Smith, Ron Harris, Frank McLintock, and Billy Bremner – the leading club captains in the 70s – approached the game. As exciting as it was for the fan, it was not a breeding ground for world-class talent able to compete with the likes of Cruyff, Neeskens, Beckenbauer and Muller.

The clubs and the international teams all boasted a large number of excellent footballers, playing within very competitive teams. Football was an escape from everyday hardship of the economic woes that plagued the country in 73. Football was important. Leeds were seen to be ready to take on the best of Europe with one of the best teams that had ever been built in club football. Tottenham Hotspur and Wolverhampton Wanderers had battled out the UEFA Cup Final in 1972. Little known Derby County had reached the semi-finals of the European Cup in 1972. Liverpool won the UEFA Cup in 1973. England's finest clubs could compete on equal terms with the best of Europe and the British game was proud of the achievement.

The club scene had become a formidable arena with a whole number of very competitive teams but there was a real battle between the technically skilful and the hard men that came to dominate the 1970s. George Best stood apart as an attacking player of skill, but he was one of a few that came into battle with the hard men of English football that the clubs and fans adored. English football became not just a match pitting team against team but between the flair players and hard, no nonsense tackling defenders that had become dominant both on and off the pitch. And here lies one of the crucial features of English football in the early 70s.

Tommy Smith and Ron Harris were both captains of their clubs: both were true, loyal servants to their clubs and both were adored by the fans on the terraces. Their approach to the game was full hearted and based on the old British premise of, "never give an inch and never shirk a tackle," and of course, many within their clubs followed their leadership and example. This meant that the English teams were united and combative in every game, but that the technically skilled players were pushed aside. No one could ever doubt the spirit that lived in every team and this spirit was admired across the world – but it would not win matches alone. English football became a "blood n' thunder" occasion that was exciting, fast and full of incident and drama. It was not an environment to nurture those of a different ilk.

This would last for a generation. Duncan McKenzie was often regarded as one of most talented players to emerge in the mid 70s but he never quite made the grade. Peter Marinello joined Arsenal in the early 70s with a great reputation but this too faded away. Glenn Hoddle emerged at Spurs in the late 70s and was widely admired and feted but never fully trusted by England. The naturally gifted were seen as a luxury to many teams. Keegan was feted as he had worked hard to make himself the best he could be. English football admired that trait but mistrusted the likes of Peter Osgood, Rodney Marsh and McKenzie who possessed technical skill. English football had arguably lost its balance. It had loved players such as Stanley Matthews and Tom Finney and in days gone by, had been able to find room for both the naturally gifted plus hard workers, but the balance had shifted towards the latter.

English football was dominated by toughness and it could be a very cynical game at times. It is hard to imagine a Johan Cruyff emerge in England as he did with Ajax in the 70s. Cruyff became the symbol of Total Football that caught the world game's imagination in the 74 World Cup and this illustrated the gap between the English game, mentality and that of other nations. England had become insular and was caught up in its own importance and the result was that the national team struggled to compete.

There were those that did see that the balance was all wrong. Brian Clough's famous argument with Don Revie on television after his sacking at Leeds highlighted the underlying problem. Clough had taken over from Revie at Leeds United and had tried to change the culture at Leeds United, which he saw as being cynical and not in the spirit of the game. His error was that he clearly had a burning anger at Leeds behaviour over many years and had tried to change the culture too quickly and he failed in spectacular fashion. But arguably Clough was right. Clough was more "suited" to be manager of England than Revie. Clough was the rising talent in tune with the 70s. If the FA had had the courage to appoint a man such as Clough who was in tune with the times, could history have been different?

Ramsay too could see the problem and understood that England possessed precious few players that technically stood above the club game and were world class. It is why he stayed so loyal and true to players in decline. Ramsay was no fool. He understood the world game better than anyone and knew what it took to compete but he could only work with the players that he had. If one look at the 73 team, it was filled by players that were technically skilled and could be nurtured. In those days, very few players went and played club football abroad but if they could – as happens today – then England could have had a very good team, as the players were good enough. The English game just did not nurture International players.

After 1973, the disappointments grew more common over the following decade as England struggled with their confidence, and were not united as a team in their approach to big games. The disappointments came with increased regularity – in Czechoslovakia 1975, in Italy 1977, and there were others. Even when we did qualify for the World Cup in 1982, there were some unsettling moments along the way – defeats in Switzerland and Norway in 1981 come to the mind. To many, it still remained a mystery as to why England struggled as badly as our club game flourished. However, the harsh truth is that if one takes away the home triumph in 1966, there is a long history where England has under-performed when it has mattered. England's club teams went from strength to strength but internationally England under achieved. .

Most football historians will talk of England's quite dramatic slide from being World Champions in 66; to possessing arguably their most complete side in 1970 to a period of failure and being in the wilderness until 1982. This is all factually true. England did underachieve for a decade but if the result had been different on that famous October night in 1973 against Poland and England had gone to the 1974 World Cup, how different would history have been?

Why the question? For England arguably possessed their most naturally talented squad ever in 1973 and if they had more time to gel as a squad and team, they could have competed against the very best in Germany 1974. Sport is so much about confidence but confidence never grew on the international stage, as the club game was so dominant. One has to remember that the English players never had much preparation time for matches. They would come together on a Sunday evening for a Wednesday match. The players would be playing against each other in full intensity on a Saturday and then were almost expected to be teammates three days later. Of course, it did not work but took a long period before this was recognised. At the same time, other nations understood the importance of rest and diet well before the English clubs. England may have had the players but the football environment that nurtured them was not one to nurture world-class players. The players that did emerge did so in spite of the system not because of the system.

Rugby in the 1970s.

When one mentions Rugby and the 1970s, then minds will turn immediately to the great Welsh team of the 1970s, which was one of the best teams ever to play the game. The Welsh team excited and inspired a generation of young rugby players with a game that was positive, bold and aggressive. They had playmakers that could break through the defences of the opposition with ease. Even forty years on, many of the names still carry great weight with the supporters of the game – Gareth Edwards, Barry John, Phil Bennett, Gerald Davies, J.P.R. Williams, Graham Price, Ray Gravell, J.J. Williams, Steve Fenwick, Bobby Windsor and Mervyn Davies.

The Welsh formed the backbone of the two great lions teams of the 1971 tour to New Zealand and the 1974 tour to South Africa. This was the height of the Lions as they tore apart the two great southern Hemisphere teams. In 1971, Barry John's name would be spoken in awe by schoolchildren across the country whilst Edwards was everyone's favourite scrum-half even in England, Scotland, and Ireland.

The highest compliment one can pay to the team is that the opposition recognised their ability. In later years, Will Carling would quip that he grew up, "thinking I was Welsh as those players were my heroes".

What made the Welsh team stand apart was not just their record, but also the way they played the game. They played an expansive game and with a back line that is as good as any in history. The team won Grand Slams in 1971, 76 and 78.

They won five Triple crowns in 1971, 1976–79. They won eight consecutive matches between 1970–72.

In a BBC Interview in 2003, Gareth Edwards explained the background to the team's *success:*

At that time, the schools system was good for producing young players with the skills that could then be developed at senior level. The club game in Wales was also very strong and there was good competition week in, week out. The games were not always classics, but you played under intense pressure so they were good preparation for international rugby. It was early days in the northern hemisphere in terms of coaching and preparation, but with a lot of natural ability, we thrived. Coaches Clive Rowlands and John Dawes understood our background and what made the boys tick. They didn't interfere too much and we played with a style, which suited our temperament.

We came from very close-knit communities and there were a lot of players from London Welsh, so a lot of the guys knew each other very closely. There was a great team spirit and success helps that, no question. There was a tremendous buzz and we all got caught up in it.

People say the present Welsh team is under pressure from losing so many games, but you also have that pressure when the expectation is so great.

It wasn't plain sailing but we were a happy squad and that was a distinct advantage. The main problem for opponents was that we had flair in every position. We had so many match-winners, they couldn't keep everybody quiet.

We had scoring power on the wings with J.J. Williams and Gerald Davies, and there was a lot of flair and experience through the spine of the team from J.P.R. at full-back through myself and Barry (John) or Phil at half-back, to Mervyn at number eight.

People remember the elusive running of Gerald and the guile of players like Phil Bennett, but we were very lucky to have exceptionally strong forwards and good ball winners like Geoff Wheel and Allan Martin.

Cardiff Arms Park was a real stronghold for us, but we didn't look forward to going to places like Twickenham or Murrayfield or Lansdowne Road.

We were a pretty difficult side to beat but there were one or two instances when we could have lost.

The match that typified our ability to soak up pressure was the 1978 match against Ireland in Dublin, when we were going for the "triple Triple Crown".

We rattled up a few early scores, which was unusual at Lansdowne Road, but then spent the next hour under the cosh as the Irish made a super comeback.

But the mental strength of the team was such that we took so much pressure and came back to score in the last couple of minutes to win 20–16.

From my position at scrum-half I could see the super-human effort of the forwards, as they started to turn possession over and get on the front foot.

In the cold light of day it seems matter of fact, but we were right up against it and ordinary sides would not have been able to come back from that.

We worked our way downfield and when the opportunity presented itself there was wonderful improvisation to get the ball along the line for J.J. to score.

In the dressing room afterwards the forwards couldn't move for an hour and we were all absolutely drained. We didn't even feel like going out that night.[105]

This Welsh team gave the Welsh public a real national identity and pride in being Welsh. In previous chapters, it has been written just how important the link between sport and the national identity can be and with the Celtic nations this link can be important in relieving the stress of day-to-day life. The argument has always been that England dominates the UK and that Scotland, Wales and N. Ireland have always been at Westminster's call. Interestingly, the English have not always seen the same picture and during the referendum on Scottish Independence in 2015, the English really wanted to keep the union together, not for the power but because of a special relationship that exists between all the nations. The English have a love for their Celtic partners.

Wales though has a poorer economic base than Scotland and could not really ever stand alone. No one really ever makes a serious argument for Welsh independence and during the years, the Welsh have felt downtrodden and a side show to others. The great rugby teams give Wales pride and an identity on a global basis and they love their heroes. Wales also a great heritage in their singing and its is no surprise that Tom Jones and Katherine Jenkins will be found singing at Welsh Rugby matches as rugby is the pride of Wales.

During the 1980s the Welsh team gradually declined and there was a real feeling of frustration and anger, as rugby was so important to their self-esteem and respect. They went through some torrid times losing World Cup matches to Western Samoa and Fiji before a resurgence under Warren Gatland and as success on the pitch returned so Welsh voices became increasingly positive.

In 2009, James Mortimer wrote a feature that compared Gatland's team to the great 1970s team:

> With two Six Nations Grand Slams in four years, the current Welsh team will go down in the annals of history – but still are short of the glory days of Gareth Edwards illustrious team.
>
> After winning Five Nations championships in 1965 and 1966, Welsh rugby took a backseat to the emergence of France as a world power who won back-to-back titles for the second time in the 1960s. However, in 1967, world rugby heralded the arrival of a young 19-year-old from Pontardawe, a small welsh town in the Swansea valley.
>
> Scrum-half Gareth Edwards, started his epic career by captaining his team one year later – yet in 1968 even he could not stop the French from recording their first ever Five Nations Grand Slam. The following year, the Welsh defeated England to win the championship and the Triple Crown (victory over all home unions) this being the genesis of the golden era of Welsh rugby.
>
> It was the beginning of legends that some label as the finest rugby team to walk the planet – as well as Edwards himself, no doubt the greatest No. 9 to ever play the game.
>
> In 1970 Wales shared the championship with France, but recorded a 6–6 draw against the mighty Springboks in Cardiff—at the time their best ever result against the Africans.
>
> 1971 was considered by some to be the finest year of Welsh rugby history, winning the Five Nations with a Grand Slam and using only 16 players in four games. The same year the renowned British and Irish Lions assembled with Welsh centre John Dawes captaining the side – and the Red Dragons contributing more players than any other team.
>
> With their recent form, confidence and belief had begun in the minds of the Welsh players, with Gerald Davies remarking, "we actually believed that we could defeat the might of the All Blacks" – whom themselves were in the midst a dominant age.

The Lions won that series 2–1, and to this day remains their only series win over the All Blacks. In 1972 the series was not completed due to "The Troubles" in Ireland. The subsequent year saw the Five Nations record its first and only five-way tie – although the Welsh destroyed the Wallabies 24–0 in Cardiff, their greatest victory against the Australians.

In 1975 the Welsh won the Five Nations, and then followed it up the next year with a Grand Slam triumph. Then in 1978 Wales repeated their heroics with another Grand Slam, at the same time becoming the first home union to record three consecutive Triple Crowns. Following their unprecedented success Phil Bennett and Gareth Edwards retired. Months later the Welsh controversially lost to the All Blacks 13–12, whom went to record their first touring Grand Slam.

1979 saw the Welsh record yet another Five Nations triumph with a Triple Crown, as their age came to an end. With the exception of a shared title with France in 1988—it would be fifteen long years before Wales again claimed a championship crown.

In this distinguished period of the seventies, Wales fielded legendary players such as Gareth Edwards, Gerald Davies, centre Ray Gravell, Welsh sprint champion John James Williams, and John Peter Rhys Williams— whom almost became Wales best tennis player before playing rugby.

The Red Dragons in this time won five championship titles, five Triple Crowns and three Grand Slams. They had an 80% winning record against all Five Nations teams over this time; with the exception of France— themselves a brilliant team over this period—but they still won six of ten games against the Tricolours in this time. They recorded 32 wins in this decade, for a 73% overall winning record.

We know the exploits and the players of the current Welsh team. Players such as Shane Williams, Stephen Jones, Martyn Williams and Gavin Henson form a world-class team.

We could judge the Welsh on the decade since 2000 – but a record of 47 wins and 53 losses does not make for greatness. In 1999 under Graham Henry the Welsh had a sparkling year, defeating England at Wembley to spoil their Five Nations party, beating France in Paris for the first time in 24 years, and recording their only ever victory over the Springboks in 93 years of attempts.

One solid comparison of the current and Welsh side of seventies – world rugby was very strong, as it was then, it is now. France, Ireland,

and England; despite their issues, can still beat any other Six Nations team, and the All Blacks and Springboks are as overwhelming now as they were then.

So this leads to see who is the stronger of the two Welsh teams. To be fair, this current Welsh side would need to win another Grand Slam or even World Cup in the next four years.

But to really call themselves the greatest, they need to do two things even Gareth Edwards and his lads could not do. Winning back-to-back Six Nations with Slams would go a long way.

But, of 11 games lost by the great 1970s side, six defeats were inflicted by the All Blacks – the same number of defeats inflicted by the Men in Black over Wales this millennium.

Overturn history, and beat the top two teams of the world – and then let the comparisons begin.[106]

The Welsh will continue to produce great rugby teams as it is such an important part of the culture and heritage but the 1970s team will stand as one of histories greatest ever.

Cricket in the 1970s

The England cricket team had some great highs and lows during the 1970s. The decade started well with Ray Illingworth's England team winning the 1970–71 Ashes series in Australia 2–0. It was a sign of times to come as Illingworth's victory was based on four aggressive fast bowlers led by Jon Snow who took 31 wickets.

The victory saw Illingworth feted as one of England's greatest captains but he lost his position after a 2–0 home defeat to the West Indies in 1973. England played some positive good cricket under Illingworth who has an excellent strategist and leader but he was perceived to be ageing.

The 1974 England team that went to Australia under Mike Denness was well and truly beaten 4–1 by a competitive, aggressive team led by Ian Chappell with Dennis Lillee, Jeff Thomson, Rod Marsh, and Greg Chappell following.

Denness had been a good captain of Kent but was not of international calibre. He was replaced by Tony Greig who was naturally combative. Greig was one of the few that had taken the fight to the Australians in the winter and he was a natural competitor. Over the next two years, English Cricket did see a rebuilding in spirit, belief and with a new team but only following some turbulent times as well as good.

It was always going to be an interesting period as Tony Greig was never an establishment man. He was a South African born player with a fierce competitiveness and openness that was not traditionally English. In 1974, he controversially ran out one of the West Indies leading batsman – Alvin Kallicharran – at the end of a day's play which led to almost a diplomatic incident. However, his belief and style was exactly what the England team needed at a time when their belief was a low.

In his first Test as captain, England showed some real spirit led both a feisty 96 from Grieg but also by the introduction of David Steele who went on to capture the hearts of the English public that summer. Steele did not look like a sportsman – far more an accountant – but he held off the force of Lillee and Thomson as England fought back. England were arguably in a wining position in the Third Test before vandals spoilt the pitch and the Fourth Test was a further well fought draw. England may have lost the series 1–0 but self-respect had been regained.

In 1976, England faced a torrid summer as the great West Indies of Clive Lloyd, Viv Richards and Andy Roberts easily beat England 3–0. It followed a famous comment by Greig at the start of the series that he would make the West Indies "grovel". It was never meant in racist terms but it did fuel the fires of the West Indies bowlers and they ruthlessly targeted Grieg. In one famous hour in the Third Test at Old Trafford, Brian Close and John Edrich faced one of the most brutal assaults of fast bowling ever seen.

The defeat marked a period of rebuilding that saw England bring in a number of new players to tour India including Mike Brearley (Vice Captain), Roger Tolchard, Derek Randall, John Lever and Graham Barlow. England won the series 3–1 playing some exceptional cricket that won over the Indian crowds. The tour to India arguably saw the very best of Greig and strangely there was a love affair that developed between Greig and the Indians – especially in Sri Lanka where he later became an Ambassador for Tourism.

England followed the tour with a fighting performance in the Centenary Test against Australia at the MCC where Derek Randall scored a thrilling 174. It showed that England had come a long way since their defeats just two years earlier.

The belief in England's followers was high again and many believed the new England team would win The Ashes due to take place the following summer in England. But suddenly the Cricket world was turned upside down with the Packer Revolution, which saw all the great Test teams lose a number of key players. Grieg was seen to be a leading light for Kerry Packer and was banned from playing from England following the 77 series and was dropped as captain. Mike Brearley led England to a 3–0 Ashes victory and went on to become viewed as one of England's greatest captains – but would he have even broken into the team without Greig's advocacy?

England went to enjoy a successful era under Brearley but one wonders what would have happened without the Packer Revolution? Grieg had effectively rebuilt the England team in one year, which was a substantial feat. He gave them belief and spirit again. His achievements have often been ignored or down played because he was seen to have betrayed the game with Packer but what was the truth of what Grieg contributed to the English game?

Grieg was anything but a conventional leader but he was a natural leader. Many did not know of his private struggle in life as always out on a brave face as he loved both the game and life and he lived both to the full. He was arguably England's first commercial captain and he was far more commercially orientated than most.

His love of the game may be encapsulated by a comment he made on Cricinfo in mid-2012: "*Give your hand to cricket and it will take you on the most fantastic journey, a lifetime journey both on and off the field*".[107]

The 1970s arguably saw England led by three exceptional leaders in Illingworth, Greig and Brearley. All three were so different. Illingworth the tough, steely, astute Yorkshireman; Greig the charismatic sports loving leader who understood the need to be positive, entertain and engage as a communicator with audiences. He was, in many ways, ahead of his time. On the 1976 India Tour, he used Derek Randall effectively to win over the Indian crowds with his fielding and eccentricities. Grieg too was loved by the Indians for his approach to the game. He was a natural for the Packer revolution. Maybe Packer saw a kindred spirit in Greig. Grieg was quickly alienated by the establishment who saw his alliance to Packer as close to betrayal and the English public still had genuine affection for the man that may have been South African, but had brought fight back into an England team that had been badly beaten by Australia in 74 and the West Indies in 76. Many – including Brearley – believed that Grieg could have been one of England's greatest leaders, but history will judge him differently as he did not have long enough at the helm.

Mike Brearley was different to both. Brearley was not really of international calibre in his technical abilities, but he was an exceptional strategist and motivator of men. Botham played his best games under Brearley who gave him the freedom and confidence to express himself. Bob Willis too prospered as did Gower, and Boycott. In the late 1980s England had a team that mixed the experience of Geoff Boycott, Bob Willis and Bob Taylor with the youthful brilliance of Gower, Botham and Gooch. His great moment came in 1981 when he inherited a team low on confidence and a player in Ian Botham that had endured a torrid time and allowed both to believe and play the game in a positive vein once again as England came from 1–0 down to win 3–1 against an Australian team that really should have won the series.

The 1981 Test match at Headingley will always go down as one of the greatest in history and it was a riveting match than was turned on its head on the fourth day as England went from certain defeat to an improbable victory. It was one of those very special moments and matches but what is forgotten is how the final day re-engaged the nation.

On the fourth day, as Ian Botham went out to bat, many supporters across the country had already switched off their radios and stopped following the match. It was assumed that Australia were on course for victory. However over the next few hours, Botham – with a licence from Brearley – went out to play with no expectations of success, but this freedom allowed him suddenly to bring pride back as he tore the Australian attack apart. As many supporters arose the next day they suddenly found that England had not only not lost, but were in a position to set Australia a small total to chase. It was likely that Australia would still win but stranger things have happened and sure enough as Bob Willis tore into the Australian batsmen and wickets fell, so work across the country would stop as people crowded around radios and televisions sets to watch the drama. Willis took eight wickets as England won the match and the Headingley ground celebrated a great sporting moment, but across the country the pubs filled up and suddenly cricket had re-engaged the public and over the next few months, cricket became the number one sport as the drama just continued to enthral.

In 2009, Michael Henderson wrote in The Telegraph

> But the three days I caught, the first three, brought only boredom and woe: boredom as John Dyson ground out a century so excruciating even the rack would have come as a merciful release; woe as Australia's bowlers made mincemeat of some lily-livered English batting.
>
> When people look back at the 1981 series, through the radiant filter of history, it is often overlooked just how awful England were in the first half of the summer. They lost a dreadful first Test at Trent Bridge, and collected a draw at Lord's, after which Ian Botham, who bagged a pair there, stood down as captain.
>
> So when they were dismissed for 174 at Leeds, 227 runs behind Australia, and immediately lost the wicket of Graham Gooch for a duck as they followed on, Headingley was a grim place to be.
>
> As we filed out through the drizzle that Saturday evening the scoreboard flashed up those famous odds, 500-1, set by Godfrey Evans. It made a good picture for the cover of Mike Brearley's subsequent book, Phoenix From The Ashes, but all that spectators could manage that day was derisive laughter. 'Here we go again,' people thought.

That unhappy situation supplied the context for what happened next, which will never be forgotten so long as cricket is played. Botham's impersonation of a blacksmith on a spree turned the match on its head, England claimed the most extraordinary victory in the game's history, and went on to win the series 3–1 amid scenes of unprecedented revelry

Can we ever hear or read too much about Headingley 81? Never! Monday, July 20, 1981 was the feast day of the greatest cricketer this country produced in the second half of the last century.

It was not Botham's finest innings – that came two Tests later, at Old Trafford – but it is the performance that made him immortal as the man who single-handedly beat the Aussies.

That is not the literal truth. Bob Willis played a fairly significant role, taking eight for 43 on that final afternoon, as he ran in, hypnotised, from the Kirkstall Lane End, with a point to prove (he was nearly dropped after Lord's) and Mr Dylan in his ear: "Beauty walks a razor's edge, some day I'll make it mine!"

But legends are not hammered into shape on the anvil of cold facts. Count them if you like – six first-innings wickets, a half-century in England's feeble total of 174, and then that 149 not out. No, legends are made by men who know no fear.

In the midsummer of his career Botham was as fearless a cricketer as any who ever lived. "Leonine" was the adjective Christopher Martin-Jenkins used to describe that brutal innings as a nation watched in amazement on BBC Two. Quite right. He roared that day, and the Aussies cowered.

The following day amazement became disbelief. Australia required only 130, and had laid 56 bricks along that road when their second wicket fell. Willis then enjoyed his own feast day, and when the players skipped from the field it was hard for anybody to take it all in. It still is.

That was the day the brokers stopped trading on the Stock Exchange so that the City could watch impossible events unfold 240 miles north.

It is a day that all who lived through it can remember, whether they were there or not. I recall spending the evening with friends (the Tuesday Night Club) at a pub in Manchester called the Punchbowl; I had never visited before, nor since. The place was transfixed as the Nine O'clock News enabled everybody to relive the drama of a day unparalleled.

Don Bradman was once the king of Headingley. The Don made 334 there in 1930, and another 304 four years later. But even kings must bend the knee. The ground belongs to Ian Botham because he changed a game, and a series, and, by altering the course of a tumultuous summer, became a national hero.

No England cricketer has known the glory that Botham knew in 1981. No England cricketer ever will. That is why Headingley matters.[108]

The 1981 series will always be known as Botham's Ashes but it was Brearley that helped to change the mind-set of the team to play a positive, never say die approach which connected the game back with a slightly bored audience. After 1981, few said cricket was dull and Botham had become a national hero.

The 1990s
Football

England football team in the 90s certainly had its highs and lows. In 1990, the team reached the semi-finals of the World Cup and only lost on penalties to the eventual champions. England felt proud and once again able to compete at the highest levels. However, under Graham Taylor's management the team declined and failed to qualify for the 1994 World Cup Finals. It was not just disappointing but England's play had declined and regressed.

Terry Venables took over in 1994 with the remit to prepare for Euro 96, which England hosted. The England team that played in the tournament once again raised spirits as Venables created a very fluid playing style with real attacking threats from Shearer, Sheringham, McManaman, Paul Gascoigne and Darren Anderton, coupled with defensive steel in Paul Ince, Tony Adams, Stuart Pearce, Gary Neville and David Seaman. This team played some of the best football by the England team since 1990 and had the potential to rival the team of 1970. England had beaten Holland 4–1 in the group stages in one of the best performances of any England team since the days of the 1966 team. England seemed to have the basis of a team that real world-class talent, flair and creativity that could challenge the best.

However, Venables was fighting a legal case and England's FA never felt that he was the right type of character to be their manager. Venables was one of the most talented coaches of his generation but he was perceived to be flawed in his business practices and therefore not the right man to lead England – even though the managers job had no connection to business. It was a lost opportunity.

Venables was succeeded by Glen Hoddle who after a mixed start to his tenure, did take the team on. They were unfortunate to go out of the 1998 World Cup on penalties after an excellent 2–2 draw against Argentina. It was the match that saw Michael Owen announce himself to the global footballing audience and saw David Beckham sent off for an innocuous foul.

England promised much but did not deliver. It was the same old story of so close and yet so far. Hoddle soon lost his job for non-footballing reasons and the promise of 96 had been lost.

Rugby 1990s.

The 1990s really was England's decade as the team won three Grand Slams in 1991, 92 and 95. In 1992 and 1995, the team did play some exceptional running rugby. However the decade started with the Scottish team of the ascendency.

The 1990 Grand Slam decider was one of Scotland's greatest matches and moments as it beat their old enemy and won the Grand Slam. It was match of genuine intensity but also illustrated just how important matches against England were. It was a match the displayed tribalism, passion and strength.

All those that watch the match recall how the England team ran on to the pitch to ready themselves for the match and Scotland, led by David Sole, walked slowly and intently on and this gesture raised the roof. As the anthem *Flower of Scotland* was sung everyone knew that this was never going to be anything but a battle for the first twenty minutes England looked shocked and lost as the Scots tore into tackles. England had their opportunities as they came back into the match with a superb Guscott try after a Carling break and then a series of five metre scrums on the Scottish line where England sought to impose themselves but Scotland stood tall, repelled the attacks and won the day.

Roddy Forsyth in 2010 wrote in *The Telegraph*:

> Brian (Moore) believes – understandably given the way the sky fell on England that afternoon – that almost supernatural forces propelled Tony Stanger across the line for the Scots' winning try.
>
> In his book, Beware of the Dog, which has rattled a few cages north of the border, Brian states that antipathy towards Margaret Thatcher, loathing of the poll tax and downright xenophobic anti-Englishness were behind Scotland's greatest ever victory on the rugby field.
>
> Well, it is certainly true that the Iron Lady was not held in the highest regard in Scotland, but the day she was demonised at a sporting event was when she turned up at Hampden Park for the Celtic v Dundee United Scottish Cup Final in 1985.
>
> She was greeted with a mass display of red cards in protest against health service cuts and then had to sit through a barrage of songs and

chants of such profanity – including one about her husband, Denis – that they cannot be hinted at here.

By contrast, Murrayfield, with its large numbers of supporters drawn from the Scottish public and private school system, was much more like Thatcher's natural constituency.

As for the poll tax, while substantial numbers protested by refusing to pay in Scotland, there was no civil disorder.

In fact, the worst violence, which left 5,000 injured and led to 339 arrests – happened in Trafalgar Square exactly two weeks after David Sole's side won the Grand Slam.

On the other hand, a certain frisson may have been created by the evident assumption on the part of several English players that they had only to turn up to collect the prize – hence their insistence on being photographed underneath the posts with the rugby WAGs an hour before kick-off, an event noted by the home support and players.

And, as my wife and I left Murrayfield that day, we came across a white woollen sweater trampled into the mud.

It bore the red rose crest, around which were the words "England 1990 Grand Slam Winners".

I have always regretted that we didn't take it home and stick it in the wash.

Still – and my dear friend Brian will be the first to say as much – it is never too late to cleanse the doors of perception.

The players though always viewed it as just another game of rugby. The players through Five and Six Nations history never carried the tribalism with them, as did the supporters. The players would come together on Lions tours and become the best of friends. They played and competed hard but they would enjoy time together away from the field.

The Scotsman in 2010 reported on a letter by David Sole, Scotland's captain, who criticised claims Scotland's 1990 Grand Slam victory over England was more than just a game.

In a letter in today's Scotsman, the man who captained Scotland to that historic 13–7 victory says it was not a question of "settling scores", of getting "one over" on the English or of putting political wrongs right.

It was, he said, just a great sporting moment.

Earlier this year, former England rugby hooker, Brian Moore, belittled Scotland's victory, claiming anti-English bigotry and hatred of the poll tax were behind the historic success.

In his autobiography Beware the Dog, Moore claimed the Scottish victory in the winner-takes-all Five Nations decider was fuelled not by superior skills and tactics, but by hatred over the imposition of the poll tax by Margaret Thatcher's government, as well as anti-English fervour.

Moore's view that the match was more than just the clash of two rival sides is echoed in Scotland of Sunday chief sports writer Tom English's new book The Grudge: Scotland vs England, 1990, in which Moore repeats his belief that Scotland saw the England side as "Thatcher's team".

The book also includes comments by the then England captain, Will Carling, who said that in the run up to the game he had been branded by the media as "Thatcher's captain".

However, Sole dismisses claims of a political or anti-English dimension in the Scottish team's phenomenal performance on the day.

He said there was already a bond of friendship between both teams that had been formed during a tough British Lions tour of Australia the year before.

"Friendships were forged that remain to this day but above all, a mutual respect grew amongst the squad of players – respect that carried over from 1989 to the Five Nations Championship of 1990," he said. "It was not a question of settling scores, of getting "one over" on the English or of putting political wrongs right. It was simply a game of rugby – the only difference was that there was a Grand Slam at stake.

It is a shame that the victory has been interpreted by some as something more than that, but if that is the belief that they hold, then that is their right, but to do so diminishes what the game represented for many others.

To continue to hold such xenophobic beliefs is not healthy for Scotland as a nation. We should continue to be fierce rivals of England, but in my view that rivalry should be no different to any other nation that we compete against. Let us be proud of our achievements – and I shall be extremely proud of the Grand Slam of 1990 – but let us view them for what they are – great moments in sport, no more, no less.

Over the years, alternative explanations have been given for the Scottish team's fervour on the pitch. They include tales of commemorative "England Grand Slam 1990" T-shirts and ties being on sale in Edinburgh before the game.

Others have even attributed the Scots' players' performance to irritation at seeing the wives and girlfriends of some English players taking photos of team members on the pitch an hour before kick-off – cementing in their minds the belief that England players felt they had only to turn up to claim the prize.[109]

England took time to recover from 1990 but won the 1991 Grand Slam and reached the World Cup Final in 1991. Carling's England was the first England team to be seen as professionals, as they conducted themselves as professionals even though still, in theory, amateur. Moreover this England team connected to the public like no other since the great Welsh team of the 70s and Rugby's stock at speed. When one looks back it is hard to believe that it was just 13 years between the 1990 game and the 2003 Rugby World Cup win. It seemed like two decades and more. The England team on the early 90s made headway as they were organised and structured, under Geoff Cook. The Woodward team though took everything to another level. Martin Johnson made his England and Lions debut in 1993 and captained the Lions successfully in 1997, but the start of the success of 2003 lay with the work of Carling, Guscott, Brian Moore, Rory Underwood, Dean Richards, Peter Winterbottom, Mike Teague and Mickey Skinner who engaged and enthralled the nation.

In the quarter-final of the 1991 Rugby World Cup, England played France in Paris in one of the most brutal, tense matches ever to be played. From the first minute of the match the game stood on the edge of exploding into violence. With the scores tied at 10–10 with twenty minutes to go, the French had a scrum five metres from the England line. This, all believed, would be the moment which would define the match. It was to be but maybe not as many believed. The French Number 8 picked the ball from the scrum and started his run for the line, only for Skinner to not just tackle him, but pick him up into the air and drive him back five metres. At that moment every English heart leapt in relief and confidence and the French wilted. England went on to win 19–10 in one of the toughest of matches and Skinner became a cult hero with his own videos on hard tackles.

In the semi-final, England played their old foes Scotland at Murrayfield and after another tough match prevailed 9–6. It was a close game with arguably Scotland's finest ever team and really decided by two moments – a Rob Andrew drop goal and missed penalty by Gavin Hastings in front of the English posts.

In the Final, Australia won and in fairness were the best team of the tournament. Many felt that England played the wrong tactics on the day but Australia were an exceptionally talented team. However, England had reached the Final and now they and the public believed that they belonged at the highest levels of the game maybe for the first time in their history.

It was this generation that inspired the players that came through a few years later to be the key players for Woodward – Dallaglio who broke through in England's 1993 World Cup win in the seven's format and then into the England squad in 1994. Wilkinson broke into the England team on the "Tour of Hell" in 1998. Richard Hill debuted in 1997, as did Will Greenwood. Matt Dawson in 1995. It was a seven-year journey for Woodward, Johnson and Wilkinson to Rugby World Cup glory.

The Noughties

There were a number of great sporting moments that saw the British public and sports connect during the noughties and the leading of these were – 2003 Rugby World Cup, 2005 Ashes and the three Olympic games of Sydney in 2000, Athens in 2004 and Beijing in 2008 which also marked a new level of sporting excellence by British Athletes

2005 Ashes

Australia had dominated the Ashes from 1989 to 2005 when England, under Michael Vaughan, took them at their own game. So often England had played a conservative game but the 2005 England played a very positive game that surprised the Australians and led to one of the best sporting contests seen in Ashes history. The English public had become so accustomed to defeat that when the first Test match was lost the general consensus was one of déjà vu but a subtle change had already taken place. On the first morning of the Lord's Test (first), England had bowled with more aggression and intent than any of the Aussies had seen from an England team and they knew that the England team was going to play a hard brand of cricket.

Vaughan always appeared to be a relaxed character which belied his Yorkshire steel and highly competitive character. However he did believe that players needed to be relaxed in order to play their cricket. He was almost a cross between Ray Illingworth and David Gower in style and the players responded playing some superb and sporting cricket. The second Test was a classic with England winning by just two runs on the final morning. It was a very close win that could easily have been lost, but it marked a change in fortunes. England were ready to fight fire with fire.

The Guardian in 2013 carried a report on the match:

> *I was taught as a kid always respect the opposition first and celebrate after, which I did. I went over to Brett Lee and shook his hand and there's that picture, where I whisper in his ear: "It's 1–1, son."*

So quipped Andrew Flintoff earlier this month during an entertaining chat with his fellow 2005 Ashes seamers on BBC Radio 5 Live. Or at least we presume he was joking. The lack of laughter from his mates suggested otherwise: either they've heard Freddie tell this anecdote too many times to elicit any kind of response, or it's true. Flintoff told another story: "Contrary to popular belief, before I did that, Steve [Harmison] went to Brett first."

"Yeah, I went there first but the camera didn't pick up on it."

"Steve's never been camera savvy." Cue hilarity then.

Flintoff's commiseration for Lee, if indeed it was that, was the snapshot that seemed to sum up the very essence of sportsmanship – the hand of consolation offered by one champion of his sport, victorious at the last, and taken by another, struck down after an almighty epic tussle. The truth of that rare private moment is something only the protagonists will ever know but it is all the more poignant because the unrelenting human drama of the three and a bit previous days – a plot packed full of twists and turns, mixing scenes of spectacular action with others of suspense, contemplation and psychological intrigue – had revealed so much publicly about a tremendously varied cast of heroic and flawed characters.

The moment England wrapped up that famous two-run victory had been the most dramatic ending to a match that was itself the high point of the greatest series the game's most riveting rivalry has produced. The Greatest Test DVD was on sale when they collided again at Old Trafford only four days later. Four weeks later the Greatest Test Series DVD became a bestseller. The labels were no exaggeration. Never before had there been such a close margin in an Ashes Test – three-run wins had previously been recorded at Old Trafford 1902 and Melbourne 1982–83. Perhaps only Australia v West Indies at The Gabba in December 1960, the first tied Test match at the start of a titanic series, carried with it comparable resonance to Edgbaston 2005.

Here was a game that alone merits a newspaper website dedicating to it a 20 great moments series. Every ball carried with it enormous significance, a microcosm of the seven weeks that gripped the two nations. The bare figures are remarkable enough. 1,176 runs were scored from 1,632 deliveries at a ferocious 4.32 an over. There were 40 wickets in that time, at an unsettling one every 41 balls.[110]

England went on to win the series 2–1 and the English public rejoiced. They had endured 16 years of disappointments and defeat to their traditional foe and at last they could feel proud again. They had not just won but won in style.

The English players celebrated their win "old school" and fair to say, that the next days as they visited the Prime Minister at No.10 and Trafalgar Square to wave to the massive crowds gathered, some of the players were the worse for wear. No one cared. Everyone just giggled and laughed for England had won The Ashes. The BBC reported on the day that supporters and the players came together to celebrate: **"England's cricketers were given a rapturous reception in Trafalgar Square at the end of the Ashes victory parade to celebrate their win over Australia."**

Captain Michael Vaughan thanked the "fantastic" thronging crowd and admitted: "This is beyond a dream."

The team later enjoyed a Downing Street reception and went to Lord's to hand over the Ashes urn for safe-keeping.

England beat Australia in a series for the first time since 1987 after drawing the final Test at The Oval on Monday.

England's women's team were also part of the parade, following their own Ashes triumph in August.

"It's been a long night," said Vaughan, who clasped the replica Ashes urn throughout the celebrations. "We've celebrated in true English fashion and this is incredible.

"This is fantastic, thank you for the support, not just today, but all through the season.

"The team have been magnificent, the management have been magnificent and these people (the fans) have been even better.

"We believed at the beginning of the summer we could win. We went 1–0 down, there were challenges set upon us and the guys responded fantastically well."

Opener Marcus Trescothick conceded it would take time for their achievements to sink in and admitted the sight of England's 2003 Rugby World Cup winners celebrating in London acted as an incentive.

"I remember in Sri Lanka watching the Rugby World Cup Final with Michael Vaughan and Ashley Giles," Trescothick revealed.

"It was great and, when we saw their street celebrations, we felt we wanted a piece of that. That has helped drive us."

The tens of thousands gathered in Trafalgar Square cheered highlights of the exhilarating summer series and interviews with each member of the victorious squad before a rendition of Jerusalem *rounded the presentation off.*

The ceremony followed a 90-minute open-topped parade from Mansion House during which the two buses crawled through thousands of flag-waving fans as crowds built up in a sun-drenched Trafalgar Square.

Vaughan and player of the series Andrew Flintoff soaked up the atmosphere at the front of the bus with their young daughters as office workers leant out of windows along the route to catch a glimpse of the team.

Australian-raised wicketkeeper Geraint Jones held up a giant inflatable Dalek emblazoned with the words "Aussies exterminated".

And Kevin Pietersen, man of the match in the final Test at The Oval, repeatedly sprayed those on the street below with champagne.

"These are amazing scenes and it's fantastic what is happening to English cricket," Pietersen told BBC Sport. "I'm taking it all in and this is great for the game of cricket."

After a heavy night of celebrating, Flintoff admitted to BBC Sport: "Getting up this morning was a bit of a chore but I'm enjoying it.

"The people of London have turned out for us and it shows how much cricket and the Ashes mean to them. It's fantastic."

Reflecting on the momentous victory and the reaction of the public, Vaughan told BBC Sport: "This has been an awesome series – not just the standard of play but the spirit in which the game has been played.

"The most amazing moment today was seeing the sheer volumes of people greeting us, but it was also good to meet the Prime Minister.

"He didn't give us any wine to start with but he eventually had to crack some open from his fridge! I know Freddie Flintoff wasn't too happy initially."

England battled back after losing the first Test to win the series 2–1 after a tense draw at The Oval.

Following the celebrations in Trafalgar Square the squad were guests of honour at a 10 Downing Street garden reception before heading to Lord's, where they presented the Ashes urn to the MCC for safe-keeping.[111]

(13 September 2005)

2003 Rugby World Cup

So much has been written about England's triumph in 2003 that is difficult to find new words to write, but once again it gave the nation real pride and joy and once again sports and the public connected as one.

In 2014, Allyn Freeman wrote a piece entitled *That fabulous day* which described the team's Victory parade in London:

> What no one in England could imagine was the spontaneous outpouring of joy that culminated in a parade through London that attracted 750,000 cheering people, the largest attended sporting celebration in its history. The central London crowd surpassed the record set in 1966 when England won the soccer World Cup.
>
> Fans arrived early to find a curbside place to view the arrival of the team, outfitted in grey jackets and red ties. Two double-decker buses – named "Sweet Chariot" – transported the entourage through the London Streets, festooned with the England flag.
>
> The players, by now recognizable names, carried the William Webb Ellis trophy aloft and waved it to the throng of people that clapped in appreciation. At Lilywhites, the famous sports emporium in Piccadilly, the bottom floor, always reserved for soccer, carried England rugby world cup merchandise, and, seemingly, half of the shirts honoured drop-kick hero Jonny Wilkinson. After the parade, the team visited Buckingham Palace where they were feted by Queen Elizabeth, who posed with them and her corgis. The fabulous day ended with a stop at 10 Downing Street and an official tribute by Prime Minister Tony Blair. Interviewed the day afterward, Wilkinson delighted the nation by saying that the Queen "reminded me of my Mum."[112]

There was even a motion in Parliament tabled by David Davis that commented:

> That this House congratulates the England rugby team and squad on their magnificent victory over Australia to win the Rugby World Cup; further congratulates Clive Woodward, the RFU, and all the supporting staff including those at the training base for their role in this tremendous achievement; commends the success of all the British rugby teams during the tournament; notes the undoubted impact this will have on British rugby as a whole; recognises in particular the positive encouragement the result will give to young people who want to play rugby; and welcomes the positive health and social benefits increased participation will bring.

The *Scotsman* printed a feature on 9 Dec 2003 entitled "After so many years of hurt, England gets to celebrate a sporting victory"

> THERE was no mistaking the joy, excitement and sheer national pride emanating en masse from 750,000 supporters who turned up to watch England's rugby heroes in London yesterday.
>
> It was clear from the reluctant smiles on the faces of the capital's famously irascible taxi drivers – faced with their worst nightmare as a city centre full of potentially laden Christmas shoppers ground to a standstill – that something wonderful was being celebrated.
>
> But amid the sea of red and white, the heady flag-waving, the deafening cheers, whistles and klaxons, there was definitely something else going on – and it wasn't just sighs of relief from the Scots and the Welsh as they realised that, finally, this was the last day for a while they would be forced to endure English rugby players on telly every hour.
>
> This wasn't just a victory parade. This was payback time – the flipside of a nation's pent-up frustration at decades of sporting under-achievements.
>
> It was palpable all along the two-mile route, from the hordes gathered at Marble Arch, to the 20-deep throngs along Oxford Street and down Regent Street, right up to those who had gathered at dawn in Trafalgar Square. Parents had allowed their children off school for the historic occasion, this business of beating everyone else in the world at something.
>
> Many of those who had come to cheer on a freezing December Monday had not even seen the game, let alone understood it. They were not about to become converts either. But it didn't matter. They were jubilant because, for the next four years, they could say that, at rugby at least, England are the best in the world. A sobering thought, to some.
>
> "It's brilliant, fantastic," shouted Sandra Hurst, 28, as she struggled to be heard over the whistles and horns around us.
>
> "No, I'm not really a fan, but I wanted to be here. It's awesome that we actually won something. It doesn't happen that often."
>
> As if to echo the sentiment, a voice then bellowed out from the loudspeaker: "How many Australians are here?" before being drowned out by three-quarters of a million boos.
>
> Even those atop the victory buses, the champions themselves, appeared slightly stunned by their effect on the country.
>
> A few of the 31-strong squad videoed the crowds for posterity, or spoke excitedly into their mobile phones, describing the scene to friends and relatives.

They knew they had won. They were there when it happened. They even had the Webb Ellis Trophy to prove it and had brought it along, in case anyone was in any doubt.[113]

GB and The Olympics

The noughties was a period that saw Great Britain really begin to compete on a far broader scale than in previous times. In 1980, GB's main Gold medals were from Athletics in the form of Allan Wells, Steve Ovett, Seb Coe and Daley Thompson. In 1988, GB won five Gold medals from Rowing (Steve Redgrave/Andy Holmes), Swimming (Adrian Moorhouse), shooting, sailing and Hockey. Four or five gold medals was the average. 1992, saw five gold, three silver and twelve bronze. This equalled the number of golds won at the previous three Summer Games but was the lowest total medals achieved since the Montreal Games in 1976. 1996 saw 184 men and 116 women, take part in 175 events in 22 sport with just one gold medal being won. It was simply not good enough – not for a country that loved sport so much.

Sydney marked a change in fortunes and there is little doubt that this is the first games that saw the impact of lottery funding was having on athletes. British competitors winning a total of 28 medals, 11 of which were gold.

In 2004, GB won 30m medals with nine being Gold and in 2008, Great Britain's medal performance at the 2008 Summer Olympics was its best in a century with 19 gold medals being won; only its performance at the 1908 Summer Olympics, which Britain hosted in London, resulted in more gold medals being awarded. The total medal count, 47, was also the third highest Great Britain has ever achieved, with only the 1908 and the 2012 Games resulting in more medals. Great Britain finished fourth overall in the medal tables

In 2012, in London, Great Britain left the Summer Olympic Games with a total of 65 medals (29 gold, 17 silver, and 19 bronze), finishing third in the medal table rankings, and fourth in the total number of medal rankings. At least one medal was awarded to Team GB in seventeen sports, eleven of them contained at least one gold. British athletes dominated the medal standings in cycling, wherein they won a total of 12 Olympic medals, including eight golds, seven from the 10 track cycling events alone, and in equestrianism, wherein they won five medals including three golds from six events. Great Britain also topped the medal table in triathlon, boxing and rowing. Twelve British athletes won more than a single Olympic medal in London.

In just over 16 years, GB had gone from one gold win to 29 and third in the table. Atlanta may have been the low point but the average for many decades have been on the low single figures. Britain today was a world-class sporting power for the first time since the pre war years.

Maybe the real illustration of how the British embraced sport again was that it was not just the Olympics that was a success story for the sport loving nation but the Paralympics. A Telegraph feature (9 Sept 2012) reported that:

Lord Coe praised the "extraordinary summer of sport", which has made household names of homegrown Paralympians such as swimmer Ellie Simmonds, wheelchair racer David Weir and sprinter Jonnie Peacock.

And he said the Paralympics coverage had helped raise awareness of disability in sport, providing a lasting legacy.

Reflecting on the Games, Lord Coe said: "We set a goal to create awareness, I really think we have done that in helping converting some of those extraordinary talents into household names.

"I really genuinely think we have had a seismic effect in shifting public attitudes. I don't think people will ever see sport the same way again, I don't think they will ever see disability in the same way again. One of the most powerful observations was made to me, by one of our volunteers, who talked about having lifted some of the clouds of limitation." [114]

International Olympic Committee president Jacques Rogge predicted there is "no doubt that the citizens of London and Great Britain will benefit from the Games for a long time to come".[114]

Rogge said:

"A year ago, the London 2012 Olympic Games wrote a thrilling chapter in the annals of Olympic legacy. London's commitment to delivering a strong Games legacy was clear, and plans for sustainable legacies were explicitly detailed in the city's initial bid to host the Games.

These happy and glorious Games are now on their way to leaving a fantastic legacy that will benefit the population of London and beyond, whether it be the regeneration of a massive industrial wasteland in east London, the upgraded public infrastructures and transport, the employment and business opportunities, or the creation of the next generation of sporting champions by inspiring and enabling young people everywhere to become more involved in physical activity. [115]

The Huffingdon Post July 2013

The London 2012 Games have definitively served as a catalyst for development and improvements, both tangible and intangible, which would otherwise have taken decades to achieve. [116]

Captains

10 – Martin Johnson

World Cup Winning Captain for England – Rugby World Cup 2003

Martin Johnson holds a legendary position in the English game as the man that led England to glory in 2003. He did not always look a particularly athletic figure but he was physically commanding and had the strength of character that allowed the players around him to play with freedom. Playing with Johnson, one knew that they were playing with one of the biggest in the playground and this gave confidence. No one was going to intimidate Johnson.

Fair to say that England did possess a team, in 2002 and 2003, of great players which included the likes of the great Jonny Wilkinson, Richard Hill, Neil Back, Will Greenwood and Jason Robinson but Johnson gave them an inner strength.

Consider two moments in England's great year of 2003.

In the Six Nations, England played the decisive game for the Grand Slam against Ireland. As England lined up for the anthems, they took the Irish position. The English claimed it was by accident. Others claim that it was premeditated. It was, in truth, probably accidental but once England were in the wrong position, Johnson was not going to move his team. The story circulates that some Irish steward had asked the England team to leave their dressing room five minutes early to go onto the pitch. England were unimpressed and declined. It was the same steward who approached Johnson to tell him to move when the players had lined up for the anthems. He must have been a brave man for Johnson just scowled at him. The Irish team became bemused and lined up even further down the pitch and the Irish President had to leave the red carpet and walk on the grass to meet the Irish team. England – maybe accidently – had won a psychological advantage but it was Johnson's clear aggression and intent that all noticed. England went onto win the match with ease.

Later in the year, England played New Zealand in New Zealand. England were the pretenders to the world crown and New Zealand were confident of winning in their own backyard.

Late in a closely fought match, England were winning by two points and were camped on their own five metre line as the All Blacks went for the win. England defended in every way they could and had both Lawrence Dallagio and Neil Back sin binned for ten minutes. England were down to thirteen men and the situation looked desperate but still they held out. It wasn't just the fact that England had won in New Zealand that mattered; it was the fact that New Zealand could not break them down when it mattered most.

Afterwards, in the press conference, Johnson was asked about those key moments. His first response was to joke that it clearly showed how little both Dallaglio and Back pushed in the scrum as they were not missed. He was then asked what he had said to inspire his men. He laughed and commented; "You guys do love your Churchillian speeches. I think I just said, "get down and push".

The point though was that no one thought for one second that Johnson would think of defeat and would just play the moment. He was famed for understanding that you played in the moment of the game and that you just accepted and handled all that is thrown at you.

Johnson maybe have been a Rugby World Cup winning captain but his greatest attribute was that his sheer strength of character allowed others to play

Chapter Eleven

SPORT IS FOR THE BRAVE

It has been a long journey to the present day. Britain undoubtedly is once again a deserved world force again in sport. Britain's performance in many of the Individual sports are at the highest levels with a range of world leading athletes that include the likes of Andy Murray (Tennis), Jason Kenny (Cycling), Greg Rutherford (Long Jump) Jessica Ennis (Athletics), Laura Trott (Cycling), Rory McIlroy (Golf), Danny Willets (Golf), Justin Rose (Golf), and Helen Glover and Heather Stanning (Rowing).

Athletes in sports today are disciplined and regimented in terms of training, rest, diet and behaviours. British sport has come a long way since the mid 90s. Britain has always possessed the talent; the barrier has been a mix of education and knowledge, infrastructure, investment, and professional ethic. One could make an argument that not only has the talent always been there, the British have been competitive in a greater breadth of sports than most other countries. However the players have been left to their own abilities to find lasting success. These barriers have gradually been eroded and the future does look promising, as finally all understand what is needed in order to create a lasting sporting dynasty of real depth.

However team sport has arguably still some way to go as often talent appears to be stifled and the international teams often do not play to their potential as they do not seem to play with real freedom and bravery.

The 2014, World Cup in Brazil was disappointing for England's footballers. In the 2015 Rugby World Cup, one of the debates that has been raging is whether England lost the match against Wales even before a ball was kicked as England played a conservative approach with the selection of Sam Burgess to counter the threat of Jamie Roberts (Wales). George Ford, who had been the fly-half throughout the Six Nations, was dropped and England had played some excellent running rugby – especially against France – that had proved to be incisive and effective. Ford had led that play. When the pressure moment came, England's management withdrew to what was viewed as being a safe option – except of course it was not a safe course. Burgess was vastly inexperienced and England had lost any real attacking threat that Ford could have brought as could maybe a braver choice of Henry Slade of even Owen Farrell at first centre. Farrell would go onto combat Roberts effectively in the 2016 Grand Slam campaign. Worse it sent a message to Wales that England were concerned. Lancaster was a good man but this was a poor decision that gave the Welsh team belief that England were the more nervous team.

Of course it is conjecture but England's thinking was certainly not sound. They, at best, selected an inexperienced first centre for that most important match in four years and dropped their fly-half of the last year. Was the England back line really set up to play brave rugby or safe rugby?

It is the word brave that is key. Sport is about bravery. Sometimes, the spectators and everyday fans have more understanding and insight than the management teams seem to have. Too often England's managers have rejected the calls of the public and played a conservative game that has gone to little success. The supporters love the players than can change a game in a moment of genius and so often these players are seen as being high risk in the most important games. Ford is a good example in the match against Wales, but he is not the only one. International management should be about providing a framework to allow talent to express themselves but too often the talent has been left helpless and restricted by a pre-occupation with systems. Sport is about a moment in time, a piece of skill that can make that 1% difference in a match.

Maradona was almost a one-man team at times on Argentina's successful World Cup campaign in 1986. His goals against England and Belgium were certainly moments of absolute brilliance that turned the matches and made Argentina World Champions. The Brazil team of 1970 and Holland's of 1974 will always hold special places in history as they played a bold, imaginative game with great flair that excited audiences beyond their own countries.

Unfair?

Maybe. The view expressed after Stuart Lancaster's removal as England coach in 2015 was that England were too innocent, too restricted. Will Carling spoke of how the England players were treated like school children and could not think for themselves. Eddie Jones, on his arrival, felt that England had forgotten about to carry some menace in their play and wanted his team to be more combative. Jones worked to free the same players than been eliminated in the World Cup and they won a poor Six Nations – but at least they won. Was Jones the real difference in just three months as coach or was it that the players had been given more freedom?

History is littered by such examples. Glenn Hoddle was one of the most talented players of his generation and yet he was mistrusted by the England managers. Bobby Robson talked of building his England team around Hoddle before he took the job but it rarely happened. Much has been written about Glenn Hoddle. He seemed to play a different game to other England players with his subtle touches and long range of passing. Even in a Tottenham midfield that included World Cup winning players such as Ossie Ardiles and Ricky Villa, Hoddle stood up and was a leader. In the early 80s, Spurs played some of the best football since the 60s as they genuinely challenged for the league title – inspired by the midfield axis of Hoddle and Ardiles. Hoddle made the game look easy and appeared to have so much time on the ball. Many managers admired the players but struggled to build teams around him. It was the Spurs manager, Keith Burkinshaw, that really brought the best of the player as both a player and a midfield general.

It can be argued that Tottenham's relegation after the 1976–77 season helped Hoddle emerge as a player as he became the "Star" player" as Spurs won promotion after one season. Hoddle's skill and vision made Spurs stand a step above.

He made his England debut in November 1979 and scored a goal in a 2–0 win that had expert commentators purring in delight. He followed this up with four goals in his first 10 Internationals but he struggled ever to become a regular in the England midfield until after the 1982 World Cup. He played only 53 times for England over nine years and only achieved regular selection under Bobby Robson for the 86 World Cup and 88 European Championships. Ron Greenwood's (England Coach from 1977–82) preference was for the solidity of Wilkins, Coppell, Robson and Rix in midfield for the 1982 Finals and England came home undefeated but they did not win either of the second stage matches against West Germany (0–0) and Spain (0–0). Trevor Brooking was Greenwood's creative midfield player but he was injured for the majority of the 82 Finals. One has to wonder if Hoddle's creativity could have unlocked the German or Spanish defences in those crucial stages. He played only a substitute in the opening stage group matches against Kuwait and Czechoslovakia.

In fairness, Hoddle never was able to assert himself on the international stage as he could with Spurs. The Spurs team was built around him and he flourished. With England, he just another player and the England managers could not just build a team around one player as the needed more in their armoury.

Even when he was a regular, he rarely dominated matches at international level. His most striking performances were when he was a young player breaking through and in the latter years, it was almost as he felt hindered from playing with the freedom he needed. Against Argentine in 86, he is best remembered for being one of the players Maradona ran past for his wonder goal and his last appearance was for a broken team against the Soviet Union in the 1988 European Championships.

Hoddle became England manager in succession to Terry Venables in 1996 and could have become a great international manager. He evolved and built a very good team that played in the one of the best matches of the 1998 World Cup in France against Argentine – the match that made Michael Owen's name as an international striker as he ran at the Argentinian defence to score a wonderful solo goal. The game ended 2–2 and England lost on penalties but the team had played most of the second half with 10 men after David Beckham's sending off.

Hoddle sadly lost the job after some controversial personal comments came to light but he was a man that really did understand the game at the highest level. Bar those comments, he could have had a better career as a manager than as a player, which is a thought provoking observation for one of England's finest creative midfielders.

Football has never been a rocket science and has always required successful teams to possess to require real craft mixed, the balance of attacking prowess and steel in defence and the confidence to really play the game. The 1966 team needed the presence of Jack Charlton and Nobby Stiles to give the freedom to their world-class trio of Charlton, Moore and Peters to play their games. The 1996 team needed the craft of Anderton and McManaman with the steel of Adams and Ince. The 1966, 1996 and 1990 teams all started their tournaments nervously but built confidence through a balance that really threatened the opposition.

History has never been any different. All the great teams – bar 1966 and 1970 – possessed great wing play combined with the steely defence. Consider Stanley Matthews with Tom Finney in the 40s and early 50s. Barnes and Waddle. Barnes and Coppell. Anderton and McManaman.

Historically England's attacking prowess lay in a combination of a strong physical centre-forward combined with wingers that would attack the full-backs and send in cross after cross to threaten the opposition's goal. Ramsay built a system – the wingless wonders – that worked for a period of time until superior teams developed strategies to reduce the threat. In 1977, Greenwood reintroduced an attack minded 4-4-2 with wingers in Peter Barnes and Steve Coppell to great effect. During the late 60s and early 70s, the system had become too important and the result was that the hard men dominated and the skilful players literally were kicked out of the game. At international level a team needs the unpredictable to unlock defences. England had become too predictable and their play lacked inspiration and flair. Greenwood's team possessed a balance that has the physical presence of a strong centre-forward – Bob Latchford – served by two wingers and supported with the subtle runs and skill of Trevor Brooking ad Kevin Keegan who were the fulcrum of the team. Suddenly England looked balanced and possessed more variety to their play.

If one analyses what are arguably England's two best teams since 1970 in 1990 and 96, one can see the skill and balance to both attack and defend. In 1996, under

Terry Venables, England had again the strong physical presence of a traditional English centre-forward in Alan Shearer supported alongside him by the subtle approach play of Terry Sheringham and supported by Steve McManaman and Darren Anderton – both with the ability to unlock a defensive system with a moment of skill – supported by Paul Gascoigne. In defence, England were resolute with David Seaman (Goalkeeper), Tony Adams, Stuart Pearce, Gary Neville, Gareth Southgate and Paul Ince in a holding position. Arguably this was England's most exciting and balanced team since the great days as World Champions and England played some superb football.

The 1990 team, under Bobby Robson, also possessed a similar structure with the able Gary Lineker supported by Peter Beardsley and supported by two more excellent wingers in John Barnes and Chris Waddle, Paul Gascoigne played some of his best football as the attacking threat from midfield and David Platt came into the team to score some very important goals with late runs into the box. Again, this line up possessed both balance and the unpredictable skill that could unlock the very best defences. In the rearguard, stood a defence that included Shilton, Terry Butcher, Stuart Pearce, and Paul Parker.

It is easy to see why both these England teams had their golden moments when the team came together as a genuinely competitive force. It also serves to highlight the lack of creativity and flair that existed within the systems that so dominated the thinking in the 70s, 80s and early 90s. England simply defeated themselves by employing tactics and strategies that had become out-dated. The world game had moved on and England had fallen behind.

England still dreamed of the success of Ramsay's exceptional team of 66 which was built not just round a system as is so often stated but five or six exceptional players in Gordon Banks, Bobby Moore, Bobby Charlton, Martin Peters, Jimmy Greaves and Geoff Hurst. Ramsay's system arguably went on to set the example for every club team in the early 70s and made the game regress but for the 1966 team the system freed these four players to be able to be themselves.

The 1996 team had a set of genuinely unique players in Banks, Moore, Charlton and Peters. Peters was, as Ramsay famously later said, a player ten years ahead of his time. He would have graced the 1974 World Cup, where his style and thinking was more widespread. Moore is arguably England's greatest ever defender and leader. He was just a natural on the international stage and could read play so astutely. Banks was simply world class – agile, strong and athletic. Charlton though was the heartbeat of the team as he could unleash an attack from his own half and could shoot with ease from 35 yards out. He spread fear into the opposition in a way no other England midfield player ever has and of course his threat kept the opposition with a defensive mind-set.

The 66 "system" allowed Charlton and Peters to attack from midfield and they supplemented the strikers to create four goal threats. Everyone recalls Geoff Hurst's hat trick in the Final but Peters almost scored the winning goal (he scored England's second) bar for a German goal in the final minute and Charlton's goals were crucial in the run to the final. Following 66, management became too pre-occupied with systems rather than a structure that allowed world-class players to develop and express themselves.

One can argue that the reason that the story of Manchester United's "Class of 92" came so well known as it was a rare example of great talent being nurtured. Sir Alex Ferguson understood what young talent needed and the class of 92 included David Beckham, Paul Scholes, Gary Neville, Phil Neville, Ryan Giggs and Nicky Butt. All became International players and the core of the most successful team in England (and European Champions) in the late 90s. In 1992, they won the FA Youth Cup and were carefully developed by Ferguson.

It is a great story but it should not be unique. There should have been one such story at least every five years since 1966 through to today. That would have been the fitting legacy of the 66 triumph, but it simply has not happened. Not even the great Liverpool teams of the late 70s, and 80s nurtured talent through the youth system. They acquired their best players from Dalglish to Souness, John Barnes, Peter Beardsley, Ian Rush, Alan Hansen, Mark Lawrensen and Kevin Keegan. They bought players from the lower leagues and developed them which was excellent in itself but still different. The great Leeds team of the 70s left no legacy in its players. The Derby teams which won two championships in the early 70s left no legacy either. Maybe the two clubs who did develop players through was the Arsenal club and Nottingham Forest team of Brian Clough from the late 70s to the early nineties.

Maybe the example of Leicester and Tottenham Hotspur in 1015/16 will see a change. The future always lies in the development of talent and youth.

England's two great rugby teams have been the 1991-95 team and the 2001–03 team. Both teams were well organized but had players who could express themselves on the international stage. The management of Geoff Cooke – with Roger Uttley and then Dick Best – wanted to play great rugby and they allowed Carling, Guscott and Underwood freedom from a firm platform that a strong scrum and tactical fly-half (Rob Andrew) allowed. The 2003 team had an equally strong scrum, two exceptional flankers in Neil Back and Richard Hill who were a constant threat and a talented back line. Woodward created the structure and the education for the players to play great rugby. Jonny Wilkinson was a constant threat with the boot whilst Jason Robinson, Will Greenwood and Ben Cohen were a threat with the ball in hand. Johnson and Dallaglio were two heavyweights that could intimidate an opposition almost on their own.

Maybe the real difference between the 1991 team and the 2003 team lay in how they responded to setbacks. After the defeat in the 1990 Grand Slam decider, England reverted back to a forward led, conservative game plan. They retreated from the   exciting expansive game they played in 1990 up to the Scotland game. Did they learn the real lessons from 1990 or did they just change tactics? The 2003 team also failed at the final hurdle in Grand Slams and more often the 1991 team but they learnt and just worked harder to improve and rightly they stand as the benchmark for all England teams.

Arguably England's best cricket teams since the Compton era were those of Michael Vaughan and Andrew Strauss. Both were astute tactically but allowed their players to play positive, aggressive cricket. The great Australian teams of the 90s and early 2000s with the likes of Shane Warne, Adam Gilchrist, Glenn McGrath, Ricky Ponting, and the Waugh brothers played with real boldness and intent. They played some of the best cricket by any side of many years and were rightly the number one side in the world for a long period. They were a great example of how international sport should be played – with a firm structure that allows great players to be themselves.

The best British sides have always played in a positive vein – Brearley's England, Grieg's on the tour to India, Illingworth's 1970 team, Vaughan and Strauss's are the best examples. It freed players such as Gower, Botham, Randall, John Snow, Andrew Flintoff, Alaistair Cook, Kevin Pieterson, Marcus Trescothick and Geoff Boycott to do what they do best.

The lottery funding that has come into sport has allowed for the athletes to be able to have better coaching and training. It is easier to be to express oneself in an individual sport, as there is no risk to anyone else. It is no coincidence to see how British sport has risen once again to the top of the International field, as the best talent has been able to compete.

It is now just time for the teams to be to be free mentally so that too can be increasingly competitive. A feature on Channel 4 news entitled *How lottery funding makes a difference to Team GB* in August 2012 stated:

> *Back in 1996 Britain won a solitary gold in the Atlanta Olympics, courtesy of the ever-reliable Steve Redgrave and his rowing partner Matthew Pinsent.*

Two years earlier, however, the launch of the National Lottery had given John Major's Conservative government the chance to invest in Olympic sports.

Sixteen years on from Atlanta, and the lottery has helped to deliver an Olympic Games and fund one of Britain's most successful ever medal-winning performances.

More than £264m has been shared between 27 Olympic sports from 2009 to 2013 to help British athletes perform to their potential at London 2012.

Rowing and cycling, two of Britain's most successful Olympics sports of recent Games, are among the best funded, with athletics a close third. Sailing and canoeing have also been well supported.

At the other end of the funding league are shooting, wrestling and weightlifting, with only tennis and football not receiving any funding whatsoever.

The current backing enjoyed by Jessica Ennis and other track and field competitors is leagues ahead of the support that athletes received prior to the Atlanta Games.

No social life

Clova Court is one of Ennis's predecessors as Britain's number one heptathlete. Without receiving lottery funding she qualified for the European Championships, World Championships and Commonwealth Games in the early 1990s, competing against champions like the USA's Jackie Joyner-Kersee, Germany's Sabine Braun and her better-known compatriot Denise Lewis.

To support herself she worked from 6.30am as a manager in a petrol station in her native West Midlands, squeezing in up to five hours of training into her lunch break and after work.

Court said that heptathlon is a particularly tough sport to fund and admits to having no social life during this time. "There are so many different pairs of shoes and pieces of equipment for heptathlon," she explains. "It's really gruelling, yet it is difficult to get anyone to consider funding."

As well as being fortunate to have a husband as a coach and an understanding boss who accommodated her training schedule, Court was sponsored by the petrol station where she worked.

Funding guarantee

In 2012 funding for Olympic sports is split almost 50/50 between the exchequer and the lottery. This funding is guaranteed for the lifetime of the current parliament but from 2015 the government's share will reduce.

A bigger share of lottery money beyond 2015 will provide some of the shortfall, with UK Sport getting as much as two thirds of funding from the lottery.

As well as funding prospects for the Rio Olympics in 2016, UK Sport will fund the development of talent for future games, a UK Sport spokesperson said.

"These are people on the talent path for Rio," he added. "There are people we find now who will win medals in Rio who you will have never heard of." [117]

A feature on the BBC entitled "Olympic success: How much does a gold medal cost?" in August 2012 noted that:

How much does an Olympic gold medal cost? With a minimum six grams of gold and a large chunk of silver, the pithy answer is about £450.

But as Britain basks in the glory of what is shaping up to be the most triumphant Olympics for Team GB in more than 100 years, it is worth reflecting for a moment on the reasons behind the success.

Talent, punishing training regimes, pride in a home games and fervent support have of course played a key part in so many record-breaking performances.

But, in the end, as cynical and unpalatable as it may sound, the main reason behind the team's overall success is cold, hard cash.

In the Atlanta Games in 1996, the British team won a grand total of one gold medal, and 15 in all.

The following year, National Lottery funding was injected directly into elite Olympic sports for the first time.

The return was instant. In the Sydney Games of 2000, the British team won 11 golds – the first time Britain won more than 10 golds since the Antwerp Games in 1920 – and 28 medals in total.

Athens in 2004 saw a similar return, the last games before the Olympic Committee awarded the 2012 games to London.

Investment in Olympic sports in the UK immediately rocketed in preparation for the country's first games since 1948, and again the return was both immediate and spectacular – the British team won 19 golds and 47 medals in total in Beijing in 2008.

"When Great Britain went to Beijing, the team benefited from £235m investment in training programmes in the years running up to the Olympics – that's a fourfold increase on what was spent [in the run up to Athens]," says Prof David Forrest, a sports economist at the University of Salford.

"We spent an extra £165m and got 17 more medals, so that's about £10m a medal."

This massive increase in investment in elite sports was funded in large part by the National Lottery.

"Lottery funding in the 90s has a lot to do with [Great Britain's recent success]," says Stefan Szymanski, professor of sports management at the University of Michigan.

"That devotion of financial resources, particularly on building up elite teams, has had a big effect on Britain."

In fact, the Lottery accounts for about 60% of funding for GB's Olympic teams' preparation for the London Games. Almost 40% comes directly from the UK exchequer – in other words, directly from our pockets via taxes.

This equates to about 80p a year per UK taxpayer. About £7m also comes from money raised by Team 2012, mainly through corporate sponsors.

Just how big an impact all this money has had becomes even clearer when you look at individual sports.

In Beijing, the most successful sports were those that received the most funding. Between them, athletics, cycling, rowing, sailing and swimming accounted for half of all Olympic team funding. They also accounted for 36 of the 47 medals won.

The same pattern can be seen in the current Olympics – almost half of all funding went to these five sports and, so far, together they have won 27 out the 40 medals won.

Of course, there is a chicken and egg element here, as funding is rewarded on the basis of success.

Once the pattern in established, however, it is hard to break, as the more successful sports get more money, allowing them to become even more successful.

In fact, there are some sports that are in effect closed to all but the wealthiest nations.

"That really cost us...the money is the difference between silver and gold" - Kevan Gosper, Australian member of the International Olympic Committee

"We have identified four sports where there is virtually no chance that anyone from a poor country can win a medal - equestrian, sailing, cycling and swimming," says Prof Forrest.

He points to a study suggesting there is one swimming pool for every six million people in Ethiopia.

Wrestling, judo, weightlifting and gymnastics, he says, tend to be the best sports for developing nations.

For the majority of other disciplines, money is key.

According to Prof Szymanski, 15% of all Olympic medals ever awarded have been won by the US, with European countries accounting for 60%.

"These are two very rich and relatively highly populated regions. The combination of these two is probably what goes to producing Olympic medals over the long term," he says. [118]

There is no doubt that much has changed over the last twenty years. Maybe as we look back at history, it will be argued that 1997 marked a change as Blair's government did bring a new approach and attitude towards sport and the arts. It was Blair's government that encouraged all the arts and a focus on creativity. However change had begun earlier under John Major. Major began the process to bring politics and sport closer together and the introduction of the lottery marked the sea change. Blair's government took it on and marked a new thinking and a new generation that wanted to free itself of the past. Too long had Britain been restrained by the thinking of the past, of beliefs that had almost become institutionalised but were wrong. Sport, culture and politics are all entwined in the modern world. The politicians may not like it but sport is as influential if not more influential in the modern media world. Change is never fast; it is an evolution but it is happening.

Just as sports was in need of change in the 90s, so politics today is need of change in 2016. There is a general cynicism and disillusionment over politics. In 1997, Blair's governments seemed to announce the change that so many desired and many believed that the 1997 elected government would create lasting change. It was, after all, an impressive leadership team, led not just by Blair but with Brown, Straw Campbell and Mandelson – people that really believed in a new Britain and a new set of values. In politics it was an exciting time; a time that was lost with the debate and fall out of the Iraq war in 2003 and the banking crisis of 2008–09. However, the greatest legacy of the Labour Government of 1997–2010 just may be their work in sports and the arts. Cool Britannia seemed a move by politics to court celebrities, but in time it freed a belief in the worlds that stand beyond politics and the results are there to be seen. At last there are real links between sport, government and funding. There is still work to be done but just maybe good days in international sport for British sport will become more regular.

Change is the air. The Premiership season of 2015–16 maybe illustrates this more than anything else, as the two dominant teams have been the unfancied teams with good English players in the lead. The future looks promising with the likes of Harry Kane, Demi Alli, Eric Dier, James Vardy, Danny Rose, John Stone and Ross Barkley. Add in cricketers such as Joe Root, Ben Stokes, Johnny Bairstow, Jos Butler and Rugby's Anthony Watson, Richie and Johnny Gray, George Ford, Maro Itjo and Owen Farrell, and the future looks bright. Rory McIlroy too, as well as many young Olympic hopefuls who are going to Rio with belief that the games will change their lives. They may fall short, but they represent a new generation and new hope.

One suspect that the Victorians, who really invented modern sport, would be looking on approvingly. It may have been a difficult journey. There is no doubt that at times the British approach has hindered itself but 120 years on, and there is real belief in the future once again.

THE CAPTAINS

11 – Lawrence Dallaglio

The 2003 England team was fortunate to possess two natural, highly competitive leaders in Martin Johnson and Lawrence Dallaglio. Neither would give an inch and both believed they would win. To watch matches between Leicester and Wasps during the years 2001–04, one would see two of England's greats captains lead their teams from the front as they would both boldly and physically try to lead their teams to victory. There would be no quarter given. Both were world–class players and leaders and it was to England's fortune.

Maybe more importantly both would inspire those around them. Dallaglio led his club side, Wasps, with a belief and conviction that allowed the team to punch above its weight and achieve a golden era for the club.

Dallaglio was a member of the inaugural World Cup Sevens winning squad with England in 1993. He made his debut for England in November 1995 as a substitute against the Springboks and toured South Africa as a member of the 1997 British and Irish Lions squad. He was given the England captaincy in the autumn of 1997 by new coach Clive Woodward. Dallaglio had the same quality as Johnson. Neither would be intimidated by the opposition and the opposition would never feel comfortable coming up against either.

Dallaglio was a key member of the 2003 England Grand Slam and World Cup-winning side, being the only player to play in every minute of England's World Cup campaign. With the World Cup win, he became one of the two players – the other being England scrum-half Matt Dawson – to have won the World Cup in both the 15- and seven-a-side competitions.

Dallaglio will always be best remembered for the 2003 triumph but maybe the untold story was the 2007 campaign in France when England, against all the odds, reached the World Cup Final. Dallaglio was near to the end of his international career coming on as a replacement in the last twenty minutes. However he was the natural leader within the group – as he would be in any group – alongside Jonny Wilkinson and Phil Vickery. It was rumoured that after the poor initial matches, it was this group that took control of the players and ensured that England turned round their performances.

The turnaround was remarkable. In the group stages, England had lost 36–0 to South Africa without offering any real attacking threat. In the Final the score was

15–6 and England could – maybe should – have scored a try when Matthew Tait broke for the line. England crossed the line but Mark Cueto was perceived to have had a foot in touch. If England had scored, could they have won? The truth is that it was a triumph for England to have reached the Final. England had in 2005, and 2006, under Andy Robinson, played some very poor rugby. Brian Ashton had been brought in, but never had enough time to turn performances. But the alliance in leadership between Ashton (a very creative and innovative coach) and the senior players gave England the chance to do the impossible and they came so very close.

APPENDIX

1 THE HISTORICAL HOME OF SPORT

Britain has often been described as the historical inventor and home of many sports but do you know how many sports have been originated by the British?

Many will initially answer with the responses of football, rugby, golf and cricket, but there are far more and some of the below may surprise:

- **Cricket** – It is believed that cricket was first played as far back as the Tudor period although the game grew to become the national sports in the 1700s. The first international matches began in 1844 with the first Test match in 1877.

- **Football** – The Victorians are really the founders of modern football as they organised the game via the public schools in the 1800s. Before then, football was more of an anarchic "mob game", with more than 30 laws being passed to ban it in England between 1324 and 1667. The game was in decline before the Victorian Public Schools rekindled the passion for the game.

- **Rugby Union** – The game first created when William Webb Ellis picked up the ball at Rugby School. The first set of written rules were created in 1845, and the formation of the *Rugby Football Union* was in 1871. William Webb Ellis is seen as the founder of rugby but credit should really go to the first clubs that generated interest and play. Maybe the most important were Blackheath in London, Dublin University and Edinburgh AFC. Blackheath FC was founded in 1858 and is the oldest open rugby club in the world since becoming open in 1862. It is also the third oldest rugby club in continuous existence in the world, after *Dublin University Football Club* and *Edinburgh Academical Football Club*. The Blackheath club also helped organise the *world's first rugby international* between *England* and *Scotland* in *Edinburgh* on 27 March 1871

- **Badminton** – Badminton is thought to have had its roots in "battledore and shuttlecock", a game played by British soldiers in India during the 18th century. Eventually, the soldiers took badminton back to England, where its rules were standardised for the first time.

- **Baseball** – Baseball is one of America's leading national sports but its roots lie in 16th and 17th Century Britain. There's even a reference to it in Jane Austen's *Northhanger Abbey*, when the heroine Catherine Morland is described as preferring "cricket, base ball, riding on horseback and running about the country to books."

- **Snooker** – Snooker is another product of Empire, thought to have been developed from the game of billiards by British soldiers stationed in India in the 19th century. It's said that the name comes from British army slang for a first-year cadet.

- **Tennis** – In fairness, France will dispute that Tennis was founded in Britain and it is true that many historians believe that tennis's origins go as far back as 12th-century France. Many historians believe that game originated in the monasteries of Northern France. During the 16th century, an indoor variation of the sport, which involved hitting a ball off a wall became very popular in England. However, Lawn Tennis – the basis of Wimbledon – was invented on a croquet lawn in Birmingham in the 1860s. The World's first Tennis club was founded in Leamington Spa in 1874

- **Darts** – Another game with origins that go back to the 1400s. In 1530, Anne Boleyn even gave Henry VIII a set of darts as a gift.

- **Table Tennis** – Table Tennis has long been a favourite pastime in Britain. It was born as a Victorian parlour game, with participants playing it over a dinner table. The first official World Championships were held in London in 1926, and it became an Olympic sport in 1988

- **Netball** – The first ever version of netball was created in 1892 when a PE teacher who had seen basketball in action decided to adapt and change the rules for her female students making it more acceptable and appealing to a feminine audience. However this early version of netball was very different to modern day rules and regulations, having the court split into thirds with only three players on each team.

- In 1893 a PE teacher called Martina Bergman-Osterberg introduced a version of "women's basketball" to her female students, she adjusted the rules of the game and over several years substantial revision were made. Netball moved outdoors onto grass courts, the playing court was divided into three zones, and the baskets placed on *netball posts* instead of on the side of walls removing the backboard. The first ever rules were published in with 250 copies made.

- **Golf** – The modern game is often claimed to have been born in Scotland in the 15th century. The oldest golf course in the world is Musselburgh Links in East Lothian, where Mary, Queen of Scots is rumoured to have played a game in 1567

- **Bowls** – Bowls is one of Britain's oldest sports, with a bowling green in Southampton dating back to at least 1299. Sir Francis Drake is memorably said to have played bowls in Plymouth before defeating the Spanish Armada in 1588.

- **Curling** – Curling is thought to have first been played in medieval Scotland. Kilsyth Curling Club, which was established in 1716, claims to be the oldest bowls club in the world.

- **Squash** – Games involving hitting balls against walls have been popular in many countries throughout history, but squash is said to have been invented at Harrow School in the 19th century. It was probably partially based on "rackets", which was developed by bored prisoners in Fleet Street Prison.

- **Rounders** – Primary school favourite rounders, a close relation of cricket and baseball, is thought to have been played in England and Ireland for hundreds of years.

For any country to found and develop so many sports, it is reasonable to assume that there has also been a deep love of sports. However the heart of the following text is whether sport was just ever a recreation to the British or did it hold a more important place in culture and society as with other countries such as the USA, Australia, Germany and Brazil?

2 SOURCING REFERENCES
Sourcing

1.   Barbara Cartland Quote – http://www.finestquotes.com/author_quotes-author-Barbara%20 Cartland-page-0.htm

2.   John Carlin *Playing the Enemy* – Nelson Mandela and the Game that made a nation. Page 3.

3.   John Carlin *Playing the Enemy*. Page 4.

4.   David Benedictus – *Radio Times*, (8–15 July 1978).

5.   BBC report James Standley, 22 September 2005 – British sport – structurally unsound?

6.   *The Guardian,* 2013, Tim Adams British sport: we are the champions (21 July).

7.   *The Guardian,* 2013, Tim Adams British sport: we are the champions (21 July).

8.   http://www.historyandpolicy.org/policy-papers/papers/on-your-marks-formulating-sports-policy-and-britains-olympic-legacy

9.   BBC Report – Sir Dennis Follows – http://news.bbc.co.uk/onthisday/hi/dates/stories/march/25/ newsid_2531000/2531175.stm

10.   Active Sport Survey, 2015.

11.   Active Sport Survey, 2015.

12.   *The Telegraph,* 23 June 2015, "UK triathlons set investors' pulses racing" by Prof Gregg Whyte OBE.

13.   Paul Rees, *The Guardian,* April 2012 – The Welsh Wizard who retired too soon.

14.   Paul Rees, *The Guardian,* April 2012 – The Welsh Wizard who retired too soon.

15.   *Metro,* 12 April 2016.

16. The Forbes List of Highest Paid Athletes.

17. Topend Sports.

18. Keith Suter, *The Importance of Sport in Society* (Global Direction) http://www.globaldirections. com/Articles/Business/EconomicImpactOfSport.pdf

19. http://quotationsbook.com/quote/3003

20. http://thinkexist.com/quotation/i_think_its_the_mark_of_a_great_player_to_be/295337.html

21. *Improving Leisure-Time Physical Activity in the Local Arena towards social equity, inter-sectoral collaboration and participation.* (2011).

22. Thomas M. Hunt, *American Sport Policy and the Cultural Cold War: The Lyndon B. Johnson Presidential Years* (2006). http://library.la84.org/SportsLibrary/JSH/JSH2006/JSH3303/jsh3303b. pdf

23. Thomas M. Hunt, *American Sport Policy and the Cultural Cold War: The Lyndon B. Johnson Presidential Years* (2006).

24. BBC News report 2001.

25. http://www.presentationmagazine.com/winston-churchill-speech-we-shall-fight-them-on-the-beaches-8003.htm

26. Paul Rees, *The Guardian*, April 2012 - The Welsh Wizard who retired too soon.

27. Roy Peskett – *The Best of Cricket.*

28. Paul Rees, *The Guardian*, April 2012 - The Welsh Wizard who retired too soon

29. *The Guardian* - Jonny Wilkinson: 'the most famous, most talented, most grounded'. 23 May 2014 – interviews by Donald McRae.

30. http://izquotes.com/quote/60601

31. http://thinkexist.com/quotation/don-t_ask_what_the_world_needs-ask_what_makes_ you/346829.html

32. http://www.sports-quotes.com/cricket/captaincy.html

33. https://en.wikipedia.org/wiki/Phil_Bennett

34. Martin Williamson, *Shell-shocked and bloodied* (1974) http://www.espncricinfo.com/magazine/ content/story/788525.html

35. Martin Williamson, *Shell-shocked and bloodied* (1974) http://www.espncricinfo.com/magazine/ content/story/788525.html

36. https://en.wikipedia.org/wiki/Douglas_Jardine

37. https://en.wikipedia.org/wiki/Douglas_Jardine

38. https://en.wikipedia.org/wiki/Douglas_Jardine

39. Neville Cardus, *Everybodys weekly* – Cricket all the year (1952).

40. *The Telegraph,* 24 April 1997 – http://www.telegraph.co.uk/news/obituaries/sport-obituaries/5173457/Denis-Compton.html

41. http://www.telegraph.co.uk/news/obituaries/sport-obituaries/5173457/Denis-Compton.html

42. Swanton, E.W., *Denis Compton A Cricket Sketch,* Playfair Books Ltd. (1949).

43. Chris Sheppardson, *If Only*, DB Publishing (2014)

44. Chris Sheppardson, *If Only*, DB Publishing (2014)

45. Chris Sheppardson, *If Only*, DB Publishing (2014)

46. Chris Sheppardson, *If Only*, DB Publishing (2014)

47. http://knowledge.wharton.upenn.edu/article/david-beckham-and-the-selling-of-european-football/

48. Associated Press. (2009).

49. http://www.dailymail.co.uk/sport/football/article-2451723/Graham-Taylor-Do-I-Not-Like-That-documentary-remembered-Rob-Shepherd-recalls-bust-England-manager.html#ixzz48dBU6nEU

50. Emma John, *Following On*. Page 8.

51. Emma John, *Following On*. Page 9.

52. http://thinkexist.com/quotation/i-ve_missed_more_than-shots_in_my_career-i-ve/216033.html

53. John Carlin, *Playing the Enemy*. Page 3.

54. John Carlin, *Playing the Enemy*. Page 3.

55. Mark Naison, *Why Sports History is American History* - http://www.gilderlehrman.org/history-by-era/reform-movements/essays/why-sports-history-american-history

56. The School Sport Survey. (2011).

57. The School Sport Survey. (2011).

58. *Daily Mail*. (April 2016).

59. http://www.theatlantic.com/magazine/archive/2013/10/the-case-against-high-school-sports/309447/

60. *The Huffingdon Post* – http://www.huffingtonpost.com/kai-sato/high-school-sports_b_3997391.html

61. http://www.myscorecard.com/blog/?p=1973

62. https://www.realbuzz.com/articles/top-20-greatest-sports-quotes/

63. Jeff Powell, Daily Mail. (1993).

64. Harry Rednapp, Harry. (2013).

65. Jeff Powell, *Daily Mail*. (2012).

66. The Australian Sporting Obsession. (1987)

67. *Sports* (1973).

68. Jack Kramer, *Sports*. (1973).

69. http://www.sportskeeda.com/cricket/the-six-most-feared-batsmen-ever

70. **http://www.smh.com.au/sport/cricket/keith-miller-was-my-sporting-idol-a-war-hero-a-sharp-thinker-and-the-best-captain-australia-never-had-20111025-1mi2s.html**

71. Martin Williamson, *Shell-shocked and Bloodied*. (1974). http://www.espncricinfo.com/magazine/content/story/788525.html

72. Roy Preskett, *The Best of Cricket*.

73. http://people.hws.edu/mitchell/oz/papers/ParkerOz.html

74. Brian Mossop, *Blood, Sweat and Tears*. (1989).

75. David Benedictus, *Radio Times*. (8–15 July 1978).

76. David Goldblatt, *Telegraph*. (31 May 2014).

77. David Goldblatt, *Telegraph*. (31 May 2014).

78.   Jeff Powell *Daily Mail.* (2 July 2012).

79.   Jonathan Stevenson - BBC (12 May 2010).

80.   Adam Powley, *The Mirror.* (2014 10 Jun).

81.   http://www.sundayoliseh.tv/why-the-germans-are-so-successful/

82.   Mike Costello. BBC report. (23 April 2013).

83.   *Daily Mail* (5 August 2013).

84.   *The Guardian,* (19 September 2008).

85.   James Astill, in his book *The Great Tamasha.* (2014).

86.   James Astill, in his book *The Great Tamasha.* (2014).

87.   Anirudh Krishna and Eric Haglund, (2008) report in the Indian publication *Economic and Political Weekly.* http://www.euronews.com/2012/07/19/why-does-india-perform-so-poorly-at-the-olympics/

88.   Madhuli Kulkarni, *Euronews* (19 July 2012) – http://www.euronews.com/2012/07/19/why-does-india-perform-so-poorly-at-the-olympics/

89.   *The Daily Beast.* (2 June 2014).

90.   *The Daily Beast.* (2 June 2014).

91.   Gerald Davies, *The Telegraph.* (12 June 2015).

92.   *The Telegraph.* (13th August 2007).

93.   (http://www.theglobeandmail.com/sports/olympics/crowd-noise-in-london-reaches-olympic-levels/article4463898/)

94.   *The Australian.* **Peter Wilson in the feature** "British take gold as best Olympics Games hosts (13 August 2012).

95.   *The Age*, **Australia, Greg Baum**: in "**It's been a right bang-up job**" (13 August 2012).

96.   **China Daily.** "Grand finale brings Games to an end" (13 August 2012). http://www.chinadaily.com.cn/2012olympics/2012-08/13/content_15668773.htm

97.   **Beppe Severgnini,** *Corriere della Sera***.** "Thank you London: a lesson for the pessimists" (13 August) – Telegraph http://www.telegraph.co.uk/sport/olympics/news/9471860/London-2012-wins-gold-medal-for-best-Olympics-ever.html

98.   *The Globe and Mail*, **Canada, Doug Saunders**: in "Olympic elation envelops host nation" (12 August 2012). http://www.theglobeandmail.com/sports/olympics/olympic-elation-envelops-host-nation/article4478146/

99.   **Bruce Arthur,** *National Post,* **Canada**, in "Britain pulls off an Olympics to remember" (12 August 2012). **http://news.nationalpost.com/sports/olympics/britain-pulls-off-an-olympics-to-remember**

100. **David Leggat,** *New Zealand Herald,* in "Three cheers for a job well done" – (13 August) – the Telegraph - http://www.telegraph.co.uk/sport/olympics/news/9471860/London-2012-wins-gold-medal-for-best-Olympics-ever.html

101. http://www.redirectify.com/people/gavin-hastings.html

102. http://www.wow.com/wiki/Gavin_Hastings

103. http://liverpoolfc.com/news/latest-news/bill-shankly-in-quotes

104. http://liverpoolfc.com/news/latest-news/bill-shankly-in-quotes

105. BBC – 19th August 2003

106. http://www.theroar.com.au/2009/01/28/which-welsh-team-is-better-the-70s-magicians-or-gatlands-lads/

107. http://www.smh.com.au/sport/cricket/the-2012-mcc-spirit-of-cricket-cowdrey-lecture-20121229-2c0f4.html

108. *The Telegraph*. (7 August 2009).

109. English WAGs helped inspire Scotland to 1990 Grand Slam victory over England. (5 February 2010).

110. Mike Adamson, *The Guardian* (24 June 2013).

111. BBC. (13 September 2005).

112. Allyn Freeman, *Rugby Today*. "That fabulous day" (2014).

113. *The Scotman*. "After so many years of hurt, England gets to celebrate a sporting victory". (9 December 2003).

114. The Telegraph. (9 September 2012).

115. https://www.gov.uk/government/uploads/system/uploads/attachment_data/file/224148/2901179_OlympicLegacy_acc.pdf

116. The Huffingdon Post. London 2012 Olympics Gave Economy £9.9bn Boost. (19 July 2013).

117. Channel 4. How lottery funding makes a difference to Team GB. (8 August 2012). http://www.channel4.com/news/how-lottery-funding-makes-a-difference-to-team-gb

118. BBC. Olympic success: How much does a gold medal cost? (7 August 2012). http://www.bbc.co.uk/news/business-19144983

3 Research and Referencing

In the modern era, there have been many excellent sources of information and material and would like to pay special note to:

- BBC archive and website
- Wikipedia
- The Telegraph archive
- The Guardian archive
- The Daily Mail archive
- The Independent archive
- The Metro and Standard
- *Harry* by Harry Rednapp
- *Playing the Enemy* – John Carlin Atlantic Books, 2008
- *Following on* Emma John, John Wisden & Co 2016
- *Winter Colours* by Donald McRae 1998 Simon and Schuster
- *The Beautiful Game* by Garry Jenkins –1998 – Simon and Schuster
- *The Great Tamasha* by James Astill 2014 - Bloomesbury
- *The Wounded Tiger* by Peter Osborne 2014 – Simon and Schuster
- *The History of Golf* by Hamlyn Publish 1986

- *The Best of Cricket* by Roy Peskett – 1985 – Newnes Books
- *If Only* by Chris Sheppardson 2015
- *THE IMPORTANCE OF SPORT IN SOCIETY* by Keith Suter (Global Direction)
- Active Sport Survey 2015
- "Improving Leisure-Time Physical Activity in the Local Arena towards social equity, inter-sectoral collaboration and participation". (2011)
- American Sport Policy and the Cultural Cold War: The Lyndon B. Johnson Presidential Years *Thomas M. Hunt*   2006
- Denis Compton A Cricket Sketch by Swanton, E.W. Playfair Books Ltd., 1949.

ND - #0203 - 270225 - C0 - 234/156/10 - PB - 9781780915371 - Gloss Lamination